Projections of Education Statistics to 2022

Forty-first Edition

FEBRUARY 2014

William J. Hussar
National Center for Education Statistics

Tabitha M. Bailey
IHS Global Insight

NCES 2014-051

U.S. DEPARTMENT OF EDUCATION

U.S. Department of Education
Arne Duncan
Secretary

Institute of Education Sciences
John Q. Easton
Director

National Center for Education Statistics
John Q. Easton
Acting Commissioner

The National Center for Education Statistics (NCES) is the primary federal entity for collecting, analyzing, and reporting data related to education in the United States and other nations. It fulfills a congressional mandate to collect, collate, analyze, and report full and complete statistics on the condition of education in the United States; conduct and publish reports and specialized analyses of the meaning and significance of such statistics; assist state and local education agencies in improving their statistical systems; and review and report on education activities in foreign countries.

NCES activities are designed to address high-priority education data needs; provide consistent, reliable, complete, and accurate indicators of education status and trends; and report timely, useful, and high-quality data to the U.S. Department of Education, the Congress, the states, other education policymakers, practitioners, data users, and the general public. Unless specifically noted, all information contained herein is in the public domain.

We strive to make our products available in a variety of formats and in language that is appropriate to a variety of audiences. You, as our customer, are the best judge of our success in communicating information effectively. If you have any comments or suggestions about this or any other NCES product or report, we would like to hear from you. Please direct your comments to

> NCES, IES, U.S. Department of Education
> 1990 K Street NW
> Washington, DC 20006-5651

February 2014

The NCES Home Page address is http://nces.ed.gov.
The NCES Publications and Products address is http://nces.ed.gov/pubsearch.

This report was prepared in part under Contract No. ED-08-DO-0087 with IHS Global Insight. Mention of trade names, commercial products, or organizations does not imply endorsement by the U.S. Government.

Suggested Citation
Hussar, W.J., and Bailey, T.M. (2013). *Projections of Education Statistics to 2022* (NCES 2014-051). U.S. Department of Education, National Center for Education Statistics. Washington, DC: U.S. Government Printing Office.

For ordering information on this report contact:

> Bernan
> 1-800-865-3457
> www.Bernan.com

Content Contact
William J. Hussar
(202) 502-7359
william.hussar@ed.gov

ISBN: 978-1-60175-910-8

Foreword

Projections of Education Statistics to 2022 is the 41st report in a series begun in 1964. It includes statistics on elementary and secondary schools and postsecondary degree-granting institutions. This report provides revisions of projections shown in *Projections of Education Statistics to 2021* and projections of enrollment, graduates, teachers, and expenditures to the year 2022.

In addition to projections at the national level, the report includes projections of public elementary and secondary school enrollment and public high school graduates to the year 2022 at the state level. The projections in this report were produced by the National Center for Education Statistics (NCES) to provide researchers, policy analysts, and others with state-level projections developed using a consistent methodology. They are not intended to supplant detailed projections prepared for individual states.

Assumptions regarding the population and the economy are the key factors underlying the projections of education statistics. NCES projections do not reflect changes in national, state, or local education policies that may affect education statistics.

Appendix A of this report outlines the projection methodology and describes the models and assumptions used to develop the national and state projections. The enrollment models use enrollment data and population estimates and projections from NCES and the U.S. Census Bureau. The models are based on the mathematical projection of past data patterns into the future. The models also use projections of economic variables from IHS Global Insight, an economic forecasting service.

The projections presented in this report are based on the 2010 census and assumptions for the fertility rate, internal migration, net immigration, and mortality rate from the Census Bureau. For further information, see appendix A.

John Q. Easton, Acting Commissioner
National Center for Education Statistics

This page intentionally left blank.

Contents

List of Tables

Text Tables

Appendix B. Supplementary Tables

List of Figures

About This Report

PROJECTIONS

This edition of *Projections of Education Statistics* provides projections for key education statistics, including enrollment, graduates, teachers, and expenditures in elementary and secondary public and private schools, as well as enrollment and degrees conferred at postsecondary degree-granting institutions. Included are national data on enrollment and graduates for the past 15 years and projections to the year 2022. Also included are state-level data on enrollment in public elementary and secondary schools and public high schools from 2004, with projections to 2022. This report is organized by the level of schooling with sections 1, 2, 3, and 4 covering aspects of elementary and secondary education and sections 5 and 6 covering aspects of postsecondary education.

There are a number of limitations in projecting some statistics. First, state-level data on enrollment and graduates in private elementary and secondary schools and on enrollment and degrees conferred in postsecondary degree-granting institutions are not included. Neither the actual numbers nor the projections of public and private elementary and secondary school enrollment include homeschooled students.

Similar methodologies were used to obtain a uniform set of projections for each of the 50 states and the District of Columbia. These projections are further adjusted to agree with the national projections of public elementary and secondary school enrollment and public high school graduates contained in this report.

The summary of projections provides highlights of the national and state data, while the reference tables and figures present more detail. All calculations within *Projections of Education Statistics* are based on unrounded estimates. Therefore, the reader may find that a calculation, such as a difference or percentage change, cited in the text or figure may not be identical to the calculation obtained by using the rounded values shown in the accompanying tables.

Appendix A describes the methodology and assumptions used to develop the projections; appendix B presents supplementary tables; appendix C describes data sources; appendix D is a list of the references; appendix E presents a list of abbreviations; and appendix F is a glossary of terms.

LIMITATIONS OF PROJECTIONS

Projections of a time series usually differ from the final reported data due to errors from many sources, such as the properties of the projection methodologies, which depend on the validity of many assumptions.

The mean absolute percentage error is one way to express the forecast accuracy of past projections. This measure expresses the average of the absolute values of errors in percentage terms, where errors are the differences between past projections and actual data. For example, based on past editions of *Projections of Education Statistics*, the mean absolute percentage errors of public school enrollment in grades prekindergarten through 12 for lead times of 1, 2, 5, and 10 years were 0.3, 0.6, 1.3, and 2.5 percent, respectively. In contrast, mean absolute percentage errors of private school enrollment in grades prekindergarten through 8 for lead times of 1, 2, 5, and 10 years were 2.6, 5.8, 10.0, and 17.9 percent, respectively. For more information on mean absolute percentage errors, see table A-2 in appendix A.

This page intentionally left blank.

Section 1
Elementary and
Secondary Enrollment

INTRODUCTION

Total public and private elementary and secondary school enrollment was 55 million in fall 2011, representing a 5 percent increase since fall 1997 (table 1). Between fall 2011, the last year of actual public school data, and fall 2022, a further increase of 6 percent is expected. Public school enrollment is projected to be higher in 2022 than in 2011 while private school enrollment is projected to be lower. Public school enrollments are projected to be to be higher in 2022 than in 2011 for Blacks, Hispanics, Asians/Pacific Islanders, and students of two or more races, and enrollment is projected to be lower for Whites and American Indians/Alaska Natives, (table 3). Public school enrollments are projected to be higher in 2022 than in 2011 for the Northeast, Midwest, South, and West (table 6).

Factors affecting the projections

The grade progression rate method was used to project school enrollments. This method assumes that future trends in factors affecting enrollments will be consistent with past patterns. It implicitly includes the net effect of factors such as dropouts, deaths, nonpromotion, transfers to and from public schools, and, at the state level, migration. See appendixes A.0 and A.1 for more details.

Factors that were not considered

The projections do not assume changes in policies or attitudes that may affect enrollment levels. For example, they do not account for changing state and local policies on prekindergarten (preK) and kindergarten programs. Continued expansion of these programs could lead to higher enrollments at the elementary school level. Projections exclude the number of students who are homeschooled.

Students of two or more races

This is the second edition of *Projections of Education Statistics* to include actual and projected numbers for enrollment in public elementary and secondary school for students of two or more races. Collection of enrollment data for this racial/ethnic group began in 2008. The actual values from 2008 through 2011 and all the projected values for enrollments of the other racial/ethnic groups are lower than they would have been if this racial/ethnic category had not been added.

Accuracy of Projections

An analysis of projection errors from the past 29 editions of *Projections of Education Statistics* indicates that the mean absolute percentage errors (MAPEs) for lead times of 1, 2, 5, and 10 years out for projections of public school enrollment in grades preK–12 were 0.3, 0.6, 1.5, and 2.5 percent, respectively. For the 1-year-out prediction, this means that the methodology used by the National Center for Education Statistics (NCES) has produced projections that have, on average, deviated from actual observed values by 0.3 percent. For projections of public school enrollment in grades preK–8, the MAPEs for lead times of 1, 2, 5, and 10 years out were 0.3, 0.6, 1.5, and 3.1 percent, respectively, while the MAPEs for projections of public school enrollment in grades 9–12 were 0.4, 0.7, 1.2, and 2.5 percent, respectively, for the same lead times. An analysis of projection errors from the past 11 editions of *Projections of Education Statistics* indicates that the mean absolute percentage errors (MAPEs) for lead times of 1, 2, 5, and 10 years out for projections of private school enrollment in grades preK–12 were 2.2, 5.5, 8.3, and 15.2 percent, respectively. For projections of private school enrollment in grades preK–8, the MAPEs for lead times of 1, 2, 5, and 10 years out were 2.6, 5.8, 10.0, and 17.9 percent, respectively, while the MAPEs for projections of private school enrollment in grades 9–12 were 2.7, 4.2, 3.0, and 6.6 percent, respectively, for the same lead times. For more information, see table A-2 in appendix A.

NATIONAL

Total elementary and secondary enrollment

▲ increased 5 percent between 1997 and 2011; and

▲ is projected to increase 6 percent between 2011 and 2022.

Enrollment in prekindergarten through grade 8

▲ was 2 percent higher in 2011 than in 1997; and

▲ is projected to increase 8 percent between 2011 and 2022.

Enrollment in grades 9–12

▲ increased 13 percent between 1997 and 2011; and

▲ is projected to increase 1 percent between 2011 and 2022.

For more information:
Tables 1 and 2

Figure 1. Actual and projected numbers for enrollment in elementary and secondary schools, by grade level: Fall 1997 through fall 2022

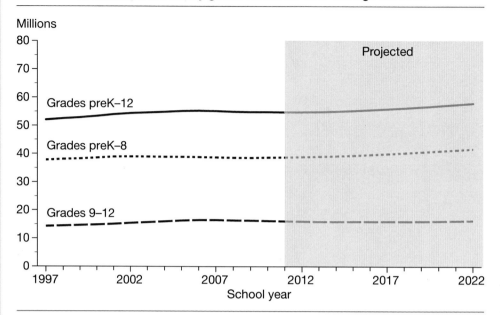

NOTE: PreK = prekindergarten. Enrollment numbers for prekindergarten through 12th grade and prekindergarten through 8th grade include private nursery and prekindergarten enrollment in schools that offer kindergarten or higher grades. Since the biennial Private School Universe Survey (PSS) is collected in the fall of odd-numbered years, private school numbers for alternate years are estimated based on data from the PSS. Some data have been revised from previously published figures. Mean absolute percentage errors of selected education statistics can be found in table A-2, appendix A. SOURCE: U.S. Department of Education, National Center for Education Statistics, Common Core of Data (CCD), "State Nonfiscal Survey of Public Elementary/Secondary Education," 1997–98 through 2011–12; Private School Universe Survey (PSS), selected years 1997–98 through 2011–12; and National Elementary and Secondary Enrollment Model, 1972–2011. (This figure was prepared February 2013.)

Figure 2. Actual and projected numbers for enrollment in elementary and secondary schools, by control of school: Fall 1997 through fall 2022

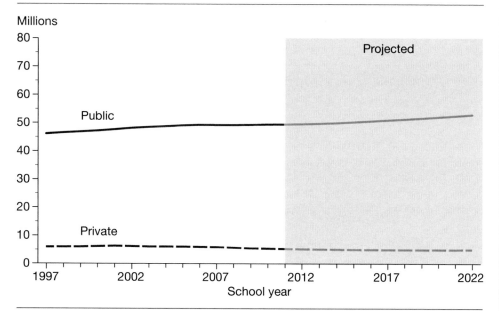

NOTE: Private school numbers include private nursery and prekindergarten enrollment in schools that offer kindergarten or higher grades. Since the biennial Private School Universe Survey (PSS) is collected in the fall of odd-numbered years, private school numbers for alternate years are estimated based on data from the PSS. Some data have been revised from previously published figures. Mean absolute percentage errors of selected education statistics can be found in table A-2, appendix A.
SOURCE: U.S. Department of Education, National Center for Education Statistics, Common Core of Data (CCD), "State Nonfiscal Survey of Public Elementary/Secondary Education," 1997–98 through 2011–12; Private School Universe Survey (PSS), selected years 1997–98 through 2011–12; and National Elementary and Secondary Enrollment Model, 1972–2011. (This figure was prepared February 2013.)

Enrollment by control of school

Enrollment in public elementary and secondary schools

▲ increased 7 percent between 1997 and 2011; and

▲ is projected to increase 7 percent between 2011 and 2022.

Enrollment in private elementary and secondary schools

▼ decreased 11 percent between 1997 and 2011; and

▼ is projected to be 5 percent lower in 2022 than in 2011.

For more information:
Table 1

Figure 3. Actual and projected numbers for enrollment in public elementary and secondary schools, by race/ethnicity: Fall 1997 through fall 2022

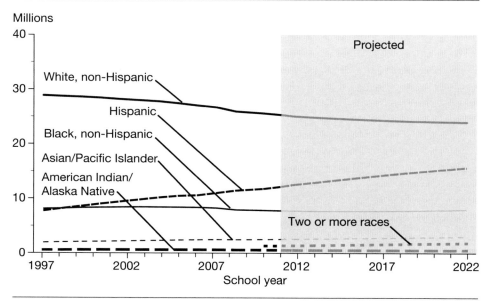

NOTE: The historical racial/ethnic time-series were constructed using racial/ethnic enrollment data at the state level for individual grades. In some instances, enrollment data by race/ethnicity had to be imputed. Further, in some instances, the racial/ethnic enrollment data for individual grades had to be adjusted to the state total for that grade. For additional information see the Elementary and Secondary Enrollment section A.1 in appendix A. Race categories exclude persons of Hispanic ethnicity. Mean absolute percentage errors of selected education statistics can be found in table A-2, appendix A. Some data have been revised from previously published figures.
SOURCE: U.S. Department of Education, National Center for Education Statistics, Common Core of Data (CCD), "State Nonfiscal Survey of Public Elementary/Secondary Education," 1997–98 through 2011–12; and National Public Elementary and Secondary Enrollment by Race/Ethnicity Model, 1994–2011. (This figure was prepared February 2013.)

Enrollment by race/ethnicity

Enrollment in public elementary and secondary schools is projected to

▼ decrease 6 percent between 2011 and 2022 for students who are White;

▲ be 2 percent higher in 2022 than in 2011 for students who are Black;

▲ increase 33 percent between 2011 and 2022 for students who are Hispanic;

▲ increase 20 percent between 2011 and 2022 for students who are Asian/Pacific Islander;

▼ decrease 5 percent between 2011 and 2022 for students who are American Indian/Alaska Native; and

▲ increase 44 percent between 2011 and 2022 for students who are two or more races. (The line for this racial/ethnic group in figure 3 begins in 2010 because that is the first year when data for that group is available for all 50 states and the District of Columbia.)

For more information:
Tables 3, 4, and 5

STATE AND REGIONAL (PUBLIC SCHOOL DATA)

Enrollment by state

The expected 7 percent national increase in public school enrollment between 2011 and 2022 plays out differently among the states.

▲ Enrollments are projected to be higher in 2022 than in 2011 for 39 states, with projected enrollments

- 5 percent or more higher in 25 states; and
- less than 5 percent higher in 14 states.

▼ Enrollments are projected to be lower in 2022 than in 2011 for 11 states and the District of Columbia, with projected enrollments

- 5 percent or more lower in 2 states and the District of Columbia; and
- less than 5 percent lower in 9 states.

For more information:
Tables 6 through 11

Figure 4. Projected percentage change in enrollment in public elementary and secondary schools, by state: Fall 2011 through fall 2022

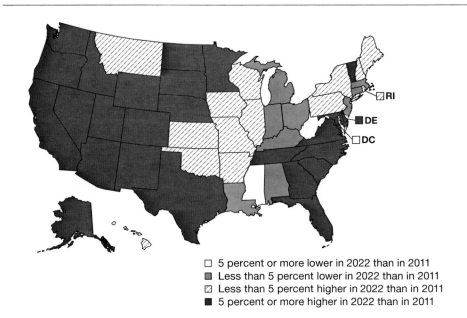

□ 5 percent or more lower in 2022 than in 2011
▨ Less than 5 percent lower in 2022 than in 2011
▨ Less than 5 percent higher in 2022 than in 2011
■ 5 percent or more higher in 2022 than in 2011

NOTE: Calculations are based on unrounded numbers. Mean absolute percentage errors of enrollment in public elementary and secondary schools by state and region can be found in table A-7, appendix A.
SOURCE: U.S. Department of Education, National Center for Education Statistics, Common Core of Data (CCD), "State Nonfiscal Survey of Public Elementary/Secondary Education," 2011–12; and State Public Elementary and Secondary Enrollment Model, 1980–2011. (This figure was prepared February 2013.)

Enrollment by region

Public elementary and secondary enrollment is projected to

▲ be less than 1 percent higher in 2022 than in 2011 in the Northeast;

▲ increase 1 percent between 2011 and 2022 in the Midwest;

▲ increase 9 percent between 2011 and 2022 in the South; and

▲ increase 12 percent between 2011 and 2022 in the West.

Figure 5. Actual and projected numbers for enrollment in public elementary and secondary schools, by region: Fall 2004, fall 2011, and fall 2022

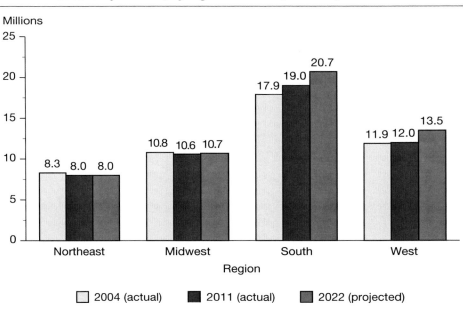

□ 2004 (actual) ■ 2011 (actual) ■ 2022 (projected)

NOTE: Calculations are based on unrounded numbers. See the glossary for a list of the states in each region. Mean absolute percentage errors of enrollment in public elementary and secondary schools by state and region can be found in table A-7, appendix A. Some data have been revised from previously published figures.
SOURCE: U.S. Department of Education, National Center for Education Statistics, Common Core of Data (CCD), "State Nonfiscal Survey of Public Elementary/Secondary Education," 2004–05 and 2011–12; and State Public Elementary and Secondary Enrollment Model, 1980–2011. (This figure was prepared February 2013.)

For more information:
Tables 6 through 11

Section 2
High School Graduates

INTRODUCTION

The number of high school graduates increased nationally by 27 percent between 1997–98 and 2009–10, the last year of actual data for public schools (table 12). The number of high school graduates is projected to be 2 percent lower in 2022–23 than in 2009–10. The number of public high school graduates is projected to be higher in 2022–23 than in 2009–10 while the number of private high school graduates is projected to be lower. The numbers of high school graduates are projected to be higher in 2022–23 than in 2009–10 in the South and West and lower in the Northeast and Midwest (table 14).

Factors affecting the projections

The projections of high school graduates are related to projections of 12th-graders and the historical relationship between the number of 12th-graders and the number of high school graduates. The methodology implicitly includes the net effect of factors such as dropouts, transfers to and from public schools, and, at the state level, migration. For more details, see appendixes A.0 and A.2.

About high school graduates

A high school graduate is defined as an individual who has received formal recognition from school authorities, by the granting of a diploma, for completing a prescribed course of study. This definition does not include other high school completers or high school equivalency recipients. Projections of graduates could be affected by changes in policies influencing graduation requirements.

High school graduates of two or more races

In the 2008–09 school year, five states reported high school graduate counts for graduates of two or more races and in the 2009–10 school year, 14 states reported such counts. These high school graduate counts were proportioned across the other racial/ethnic categories. When more complete sets of data for high school graduates of two or more races are compiled, separate projections for that category will be presented.

Accuracy of Projections

For National Center for Education Statistics (NCES) projections of public high school graduates produced over the last 22 years, the mean absolute percentage errors (MAPEs) for lead times of 1, 2, 5, and 10 years out were 1.0, 1.1, 1.7, and 4.6, respectively. For the 1-year-out prediction, this means that one would expect the projection to be within 1.0 percent of the actual value, on average. For NCES projections of private high school graduates produced over the last 11 years, the MAPEs for lead times of 1, 2, 5, and 10 years out were 0.7, 1.2, 4.1, and 4.9 percent, respectively. For more information, see table A-2 in appendix A.

The total number of high school graduates

▲ increased 27 percent between 1997–98 and 2009–10, a period of 12 years; and

▼ is projected to decrease 2 percent between 2009–10 and 2022–23.

The number of public high school graduates

▲ increased 28 percent between 1997–98 and 2009–10; and

▲ is projected to be 1 percent higher in 2022–23 than in 2009–10.

The number of private high school graduates

▲ increased 18 percent between 1997–98 and 2009–10; and

▼ is projected to decrease 29 percent between 2009–10 and 2022–23.

For more information:
Table 12

Figure 6. Actual and projected numbers for high school graduates, by control of school: School years 1997–98 through 2022–23

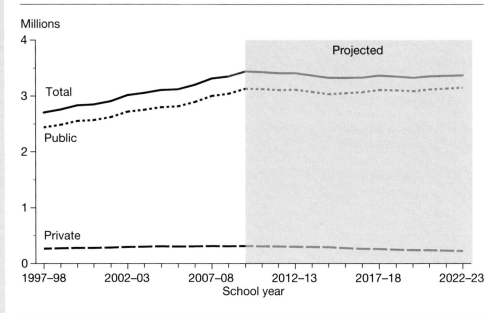

NOTE: The number of high school graduates in private schools in 2010–11 is an actual number. Since the biennial Private School Universe Survey (PSS) is collected in the fall of odd-numbered years and the numbers collected for high school graduates are for the preceding year, private school numbers for odd years are estimated based on data from the PSS. Some data have been revised from previously published figures. Mean absolute percentage errors of selected education statistics can be found in table A-2, appendix A.
SOURCE: U.S. Department of Education, National Center for Education Statistics, Common Core of Data (CCD), "State Nonfiscal Survey of Public Elementary/Secondary Education," 1998–99 through 2010–11; Private School Universe Survey (PSS), selected years, 1999–2000 through 2011–12; and National High School Graduates Model, 1972–73 through 2010–11. (This figure was prepared February 2013.)

Figure 7. Actual and projected numbers for public high school graduates, by race/ethnicity: School years 1997–98 through 2022–23

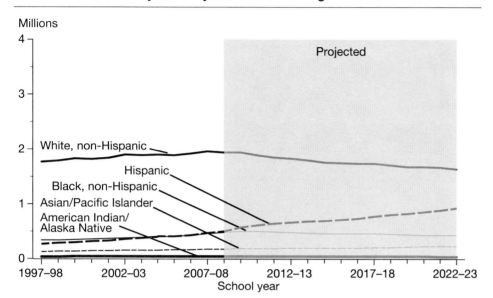

NOTE: The historical racial/ethnic time series were constructed using racial/ethnic high school graduate data at the state level. In some instances, high school graduate data by race/ethnicity had to be imputed. Further, in some instances, the racial/ethnic data had to be adjusted in order for them to sum to the state total for high school graduates. For additional information, see the High School Graduates section A.2 in appendix A. Race categories exclude persons of Hispanic ethnicity. Some data have been revised from previously published figures. Mean absolute percentage errors of selected education statistics can be found in table A-2, appendix A.
SOURCE: U.S. Department of Education, National Center for Education Statistics, Common Core of Data (CCD), "State Nonfiscal Survey of Public Elementary/Secondary Education," 1998–99 through 2009–10; and National Public High School Graduates by Race/Ethnicity Model, 1995–96 through 2008–09. (This figure was prepared February 2013.)

High school graduates by race/ethnicity

The number of public high school graduates is projected to

▼ decrease 16 percent between 2009–10 and 2022–23 for students who are White;

▼ decrease 14 percent between 2009–10 and 2022–23 for students who are Black;

▲ increase 64 percent between 2009–10 and 2022–23 for students who are Hispanic;

▲ increase 23 percent between 2009–10 and 2022–23 for students who are Asian/Pacific Islander; and

▼ decrease 29 percent between 2009–10 and 2022–23 for students who are American Indian/Alaska Native.

For more information:
Table 13

High school graduates by state

The number of public high school graduates is projected to higher in 2022–23 than in 2009–10. This plays out differently among the states.

▲ High school graduates are projected to be higher in 2022–23 than in 2009–10 for 26 states, with projected high school graduates

- 5 percent or more higher in 16 states; and

- less than 5 percent higher in 10 states.

▼ High school graduates are projected to be lower in 2022–23 than in 2009–10 for 24 states and the District of Columbia, with projected high school graduates

- 5 percent or more lower in 16 states and the District of Columbia; and

- less than 5 percent lower in 8 states.

For more information:
Tables 14 and 15

High school graduates by region

The number of public high school graduates is projected to

▼ decrease 10 percent between 2009–10 and 2022–23 in the Northeast;

▼ decrease 8 percent between 2009–10 and 2022–23 in the Midwest;

▲ increase 9 percent between 2009–10 and 2022–23 in the South; and

▲ be 5 percent higher in 2022–23 than in 2009–10 in the West.

For more information:
Tables 14 and 15

Figure 8. Projected percentage change in the number of public high school graduates, by state: School years 2009–10 through 2022–23

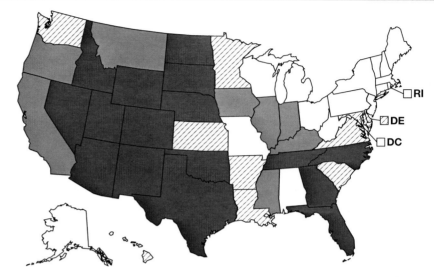

☐ 5 percent or more lower in 2022–23 than in 2009–10
◼ (gray) Less than 5 percent lower in 2022–23 than in 2009–10
▨ Less than 5 percent higher in 2022–23 than in 2009–10
■ 5 percent or more higher in 2022–23 than in 2009–10

NOTE: Calculations are based on unrounded numbers. Mean absolute percentage errors of public high school graduates by state and region can be found in table A-10, appendix A.
SOURCE: U.S. Department of Education, National Center for Education Statistics, Common Core of Data (CCD), "State Nonfiscal Survey of Public Elementary/Secondary Education," 2010–11; and State Public High School Graduates Model, 1980–81 through 2009–10. (This figure was prepared February 2013.)

Figure 9. Actual and projected numbers for public high school graduates, by region: School years 2004–05, 2009–10, and 2022–23

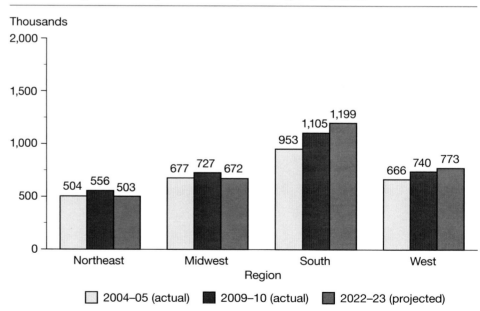

Thousands

Northeast: 504, 556, 503
Midwest: 677, 727, 672
South: 953, 1,105, 1,199
West: 666, 740, 773

☐ 2004–05 (actual) ■ 2009–10 (actual) ◼ 2022–23 (projected)

NOTE: See the glossary for a list of states in each region. Mean absolute percentage errors of public high school graduates by state and region can be found in table A-10, appendix A. Calculations are based on unrounded numbers. Some data have been revised from previously published figures.
SOURCE: U.S. Department of Education, National Center for Education Statistics, Common Core of Data (CCD), "State Nonfiscal Survey of Public Elementary/Secondary Education," 2005–06 and 2010–11; and State Public High School Graduates Model, 1980–81 through 2009–10. (This figure was prepared February 2013.)

Section 3
Elementary and Secondary Teachers

INTRODUCTION

Between fall 2011, the last year of actual public school data, and fall 2022, the number of teachers in elementary and secondary schools is projected to rise (table 16). The increase is projected to occur in public schools. The number of teachers in private schools in 2022 is projected to be similar to the number in 2011. Public and private schools are projected to experience a decline in pupil/teacher ratios (table 17). The annual number of new teacher hires is projected to be higher in 2022 than in 2011 in both public and private schools.

Factors affecting the projections
The projections of the number of elementary and secondary teachers are related to projected levels of enrollments and education revenue receipts from state sources per capita. For more details, see appendixes A. 0 and A.3.

Factors that were not considered
The projections do not take into account possible changes in the number of teachers due to the effects of government policies.

About pupil/teacher ratios
The overall elementary and secondary pupil/teacher ratio and pupil/teacher ratios for public and private schools were computed based on elementary and secondary enrollment and the number of classroom teachers by control of school.

About new teacher hires
A teacher is considered to be a new teacher hire for a certain control of school (public or private) for a given year if the teacher teaches in that control that year but had not taught in that control in the previous year. A teacher who moves from teaching in one control of school to the other control is considered a new teacher hire, but a teacher who moves from one school to another school in the same control is not considered a new teacher hire.

Accuracy of Projections

An analysis of projection errors from the past 22 editions of *Projections of Education Statistics* indicates that the mean absolute percentage errors (MAPEs) for projections of classroom teachers in public elementary and secondary schools were 0.8 percent for 1 years out, 1.6 percent for 2 years out, 3.0 percent for 5 years out, and 5.2 percent for 10 years out. For the 1-year-out prediction, this means that one would expect the projection to be within 0.8 percent of the actual value, on average. For more information on the MAPEs of different National Center for Education Statistics (NCES) projection series, see table A-2 in appendix A.

TEACHERS IN ELEMENTARY AND SECONDARY SCHOOLS

Number of teachers

The total number of elementary and secondary teachers

▲ increased 12 percent between 1997 and 2011, a period of 14 years; and

▲ is projected to increase 12 percent between 2011 and 2022, a period of 11 years.

The number of teachers in public elementary and secondary schools

▲ increased 13 percent between 1997 and 2011; and

▲ is projected to increase 13 percent between 2011 and 2022.

The number of teachers in private elementary and secondary schools

▲ increased 8 percent between 1997 and 2011; and

■ is projected to be about the same number in 2011 and 2022.

For more information:
Table 16

Figure 10. Actual and projected numbers for elementary and secondary teachers, by control of school: Fall 1997 through fall 2022

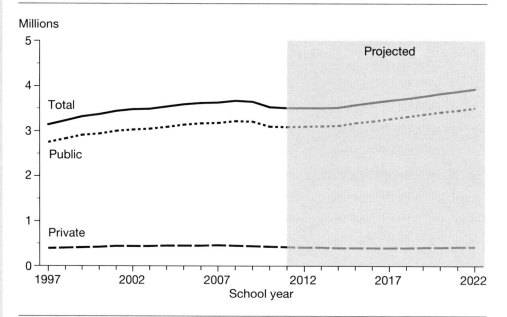

NOTE: Since the biennial Private School Universe Survey (PSS) is collected in the fall of odd-numbered years, private school numbers for alternate years are estimated based on data from the PSS. The number of teachers reported in full-time equivalents. Some data have been revised from previously published figures. Mean absolute percentage errors of selected education statistics can be found in table A-2, appendix A.
SOURCE: U.S. Department of Education, National Center for Education Statistics, Common Core of Data (CCD), "State Nonfiscal Survey of Public Elementary/Secondary Education," 1997–98 through 2011–12; Private School Universe Survey (PSS), selected years, 1997–98 through 2011–12; Elementary and Secondary Teacher Model, 1973–2011. (This figure was prepared April 2013.)

Figure 11. Actual and projected numbers for the pupil/teacher ratios in elementary and secondary schools, by control of school: Fall 1997 through fall 2022

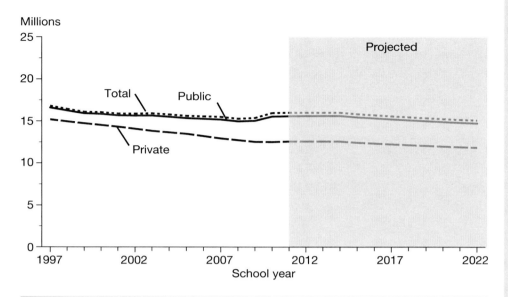

NOTE: Since the biennial Private School Universe Survey (PSS) is collected in the fall of odd-numbered years, private school numbers for alternate years are estimated based on data from the PSS. The pupil/teacher ratios were derived from tables 1 and 16. Teachers are reported in full-time equivalents. Some data have been revised from previously published figures. Mean absolute percentage errors of selected education statistics can be found in table A-2, appendix A.
SOURCE: U.S. Department of Education, National Center for Education Statistics, Common Core of Data (CCD), "State Nonfiscal Survey of Public Elementary/Secondary Education," 1997–98 through 2011–12; Private School Universe Survey (PSS), selected years, 1997–98 through 2011–12; National Elementary and Secondary Enrollment Model, 1972–2011; and Elementary and Secondary Teacher Model, 1973–2011. (This figure was prepared April 2013.)

Figure 12. Actual and projected numbers for elementary and secondary new teacher hires, by control of school: Fall 1999, fall 2011, and fall 2022

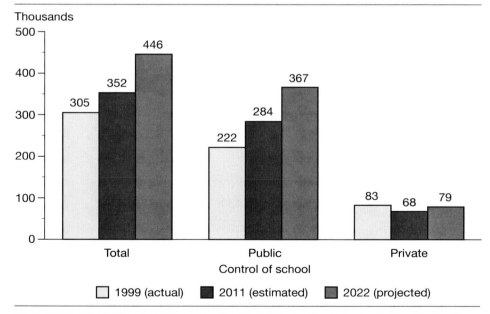

NOTE: Public and private new teacher hire numbers for 2011 are estimated using the New Teacher Hires Model. For more information about the New Teacher Hires Model, see appendix A.3. Calculations are based on unrounded numbers. Some data have been revised from previously published figures. Teachers are reported in full-time equivalents.
SOURCE: U.S. Department of Education, National Center for Education Statistics, Common Core of Data (CCD), "State Nonfiscal Survey of Public Elementary/Secondary Education," 1999–2000; Private School Universe Survey (PSS), 1999–2000; Schools and Staffing Survey (SASS), "Public School Teacher Data File," 1999–2000 and "Private School Teacher Data File," 1999–2000; Elementary and Secondary Teacher Model, 1973–2011; and New Teacher Hires Model, 1988–2007. (This figure was prepared April 2013.)

Pupil/teacher ratios

The pupil/teacher ratio in elementary and secondary schools

▼ decreased from 16.6 to 15.5 between 1997 and 2011; and

▼ is projected to decrease to 14.7 in 2022.

The pupil/teacher ratio in public elementary and secondary schools

▼ decreased from 16.8 to 16.0 between 1997 and 2011; and

▼ is projected to decrease to 15.1 in 2022.

The pupil/teacher ratio in private elementary and secondary schools

▼ decreased from 15.2 to 12.5 between 1997 and 2011; and

▼ is projected to decrease to 11.9 in 2022.

For more information:
Table 17

New teacher hires

The number of new teacher hires in public schools

▲ was 28 percent higher in 2011 than in 1999 (284,000 versus 222,000); and

▲ is projected to increase 29 percent between 2011 and 2022, to 367,000.

The number of new teacher hires in private schools

▼ was 18 percent lower in 2011 than in 1999 (68,000 versus 83,000); and

▲ is projected to increase 16 percent between 2011 and 2022, to 79,000.

For more information:
Table 16

This page intentionally left blank.

Section 4
Expenditures for Public Elementary and Secondary Education

INTRODUCTION

Current expenditures for public elementary and secondary education are projected to increase 27 percent in constant dollars between school years 2009–10, the last year of actual data, and 2022–23 (table 18).

Factors affecting the projections

The projections of current expenditures are related to projections of economic growth as measured by disposable income per capita and assistance by state governments to local governments. For more details, see appendixes A.0 and A.4.

Factors that were not considered

Many factors that may affect future school expenditures were not considered in the production of these projections. Such factors include policy initiatives as well as potential changes in the age distribution of elementary and secondary teachers as older teachers retire and are replaced by younger teachers, or as older teachers put off retirement for various reasons.

About constant dollars and current dollars

Throughout this section, projections of current expenditures are presented in constant 2011–12 dollars. The reference tables, later in this report, present these data both in constant 2011–12 dollars and in current dollars. The projections were developed in constant dollars and then placed in current dollars using projections for the Consumer Price Index (CPI) (table B-6 in appendix B). Projections of current expenditures in current dollars are not shown after 2014–15 due to the uncertain behavior of inflation over time.

Accuracy of Projections

An analysis of projection errors from similar models used in the past 22 editions of *Projections of Education Statistics* that contained expenditure projections indicates that mean absolute percentage errors (MAPEs) for total current expenditures in constant dollars were to 1.3 percent for 1 year out, 2.1 percent for 2 years out, 2.6 percent for 5 years out, and 3.9 percent for 10 years out. For the 1-year-out prediction, this means that one would expect the projection to be within 1.3 percent of the actual value, on average. MAPEs for current expenditures per pupil in fall enrollment in constant dollars were 1.3 percent for 1 year out, 2.0 percent for 2 years out, 2.9 percent for 5 years out, and 4.9 percent for 10 years out. See appendix A for further discussion of the accuracy of recent projections of current expenditures, and see table A-2 in appendix A for the mean absolute percentage errors (MAPEs) of these projections.

CURRENT EXPENDITURES

Current expenditures

Current expenditures in constant 2011–12 dollars

▲ increased 37 percent from 1997–98 to 2009–10, a period of 12 years; and

▲ are projected to increase 27 percent, to $699 billion, from 2009–10 to 2022–23, a period of 13 years.

For more information:
Tables 18 and 19

Figure 13. Actual and projected current expenditures for public elementary and secondary schools (in constant 2011–12 dollars): School years 1997–98 through 2022–23

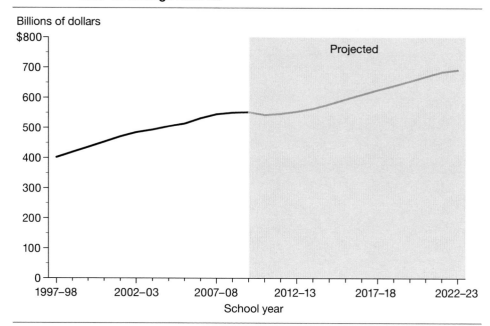

NOTE: Numbers were placed in constant dollars using the Consumer Price Index (CPI) for all urban consumers, Bureau of Labor Statistics, U.S. Department of Labor. For more detail about CPI, see table B-6 in appendix B. Some data have been revised from previously published figures. Mean absolute percentage errors of selected education statistics can be found in table A-2, appendix A.
SOURCE: U.S. Department of Education, National Center for Education Statistics, Common Core of Data (CCD), "National Public Education Financial Survey," 1997–98 through 2009–10; Public Elementary and Secondary School Current Expenditures Model, 1969–70 through 2009–10. (This figure was prepared February 2013.)

Figure 14. Actual and projected current expenditures per pupil in fall enrollment in public elementary and secondary schools (in constant 2011–12 dollars): School years 1997–98 through 2022–23

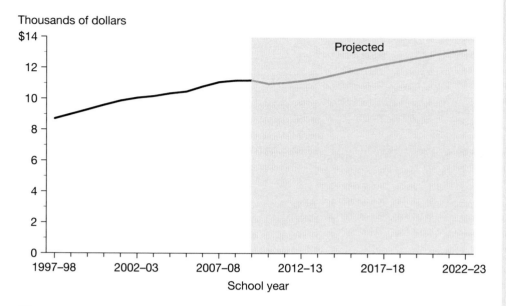

Thousands of dollars

NOTE: Numbers were placed in constant dollars using the Consumer Price Index (CPI) for all urban consumers, Bureau of Labor Statistics, U.S. Department of Labor. For more detail about CPI, see table B-6 in appendix B. Some data have been revised from previously published figures. Mean absolute percentage errors of selected education statistics can be found in table A-2, appendix A. Fall enrollment pertains only to students for whom finance data were collected. This enrollment count differs slightly from enrollment counts reported on some tables.
SOURCE: U.S. Department of Education, National Center for Education Statistics, Common Core of Data (CCD), "State Nonfiscal Survey of Public Elementary/Secondary Education," 1997–98 through 2011–12; "National Public Education Financial Survey," 1997–98 through 2009–10; National Elementary and Secondary Enrollment Model, 1972–2011; and Elementary and Secondary School Current Expenditures Model, 1969–70 through 2009–10. (This figure was prepared February 2013.)

Current expenditures per pupil

Current expenditures per pupil in fall enrollment in constant 2011–12 dollars

▲ increased 28 percent from 1997–98 to 2009–10; and

▲ are projected to increase 18 percent, to $13,200, from 2009–10 to 2022–23.

For more information:
Tables 18 and 19

This page intentionally left blank.

Section 5
Enrollment in Postsecondary Degree-Granting Institutions

INTRODUCTION

Total enrollment in postsecondary degree-granting institutions is expected to increase 14 percent between fall 2011, the last year of actual data, and fall 2022 (table 20). Degree-granting institutions are postsecondary institutions that provide study beyond secondary school and offer programs terminating in an associate's, baccalaureate, or higher degree and participate in federal financial aid programs. Differential growth is expected by student characteristics such as age, sex, and attendance status (part-time or full-time). Enrollment is expected to increase in both public and private postsecondary degree-granting institutions.

Factors affecting the projections

The projections of enrollment levels are related to projections of college-age populations, disposable income, and unemployment rates. For more details, see appendixes A.0 and A.5. An important factor in the enrollment projections is the expected increase in the population of 25- to 29-year-olds (table B-4 in appendix B).

Factors that were not considered

The enrollment projections do not take into account such factors as the cost of a college education, the economic value of an education, and the impact of distance learning due to technological changes. These factors may produce changes in enrollment levels. The racial/ethnic backgrounds of nonresident aliens are not known.

Figure 15. Actual and projected population numbers for 18- to 24-year-olds and 25- to 29-year-olds: 1997 through 2022

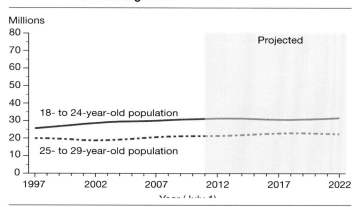

NOTE: Some data have been revised from previously published figures. Projections are from the U.S. Census Bureau's 2012 National Population Projections, ratio-adjusted to line up with the most recent historical estimate. SOURCE: U.S. Department of Commerce, Census Bureau, Population Estimates, retrieved December 19, 2012, from http://www.census.gov/popest/data/index.html; and 2012 National Population Projections, retrieved December 12, 2012, from http://www.census.gov/population/projections/data/national/2012/downloadablefiles.html. (This figure was prepared March 2013.)

Accuracy of Projections

For projections of total enrollment in postsecondary degree-granting institutions, an analysis of projection errors based on the past 15 editions of *Projections of Education Statistics* indicates that the mean absolute percentage errors (MAPEs) for lead times of 1, 2, 5, and 10 years out were 1.6, 2.5, 5.8, and 13.1 percent, respectively. For the 1-year-out prediction, this means that one would expect the projection to be within 1.6 percent of the actual value, on average. For more information, see table A-2 in appendix A.

TOTAL ENROLLMENT

Total enrollment in postsecondary degree-granting institutions

▲ increased 45 percent from 1997 to 2011, a period of 14 years; and

▲ is projected to increase 14 percent, to 24 million, from 2011 to 2022, a period of 11 years.

For more information:
Table 20

Figure 16. Actual and projected numbers for total enrollment in all postsecondary degree-granting institutions: Fall 1997 through fall 2022

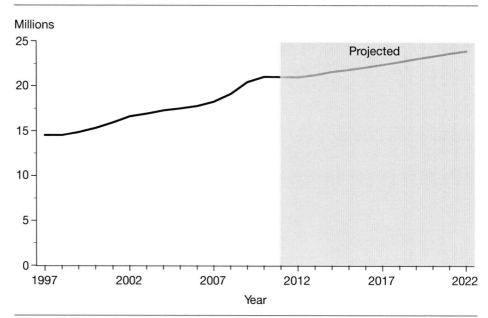

NOTE: Some data have been revised from previously published figures. Mean absolute percentage errors of selected education statistics can be found in table A-2, appendix A.
SOURCE: U.S. Department of Education, National Center for Education Statistics, Integrated Postsecondary Education Data System (IPEDS) "Fall Enrollment Survey" (IPEDS-EF:97–99); IPEDS Spring 2001 through Spring 2012, Enrollment component; and Enrollment in Degree-Granting Institutions Model, 1980–2011. (This figure was prepared February 2013.)

ENROLLMENT BY SELECTED CHARACTERISTICS AND CONTROL OF INSTITUTION

Figure 17. Actual and projected numbers for total enrollment in all postsecondary degree-granting institutions, by age group: Fall 1997, fall 2011, and fall 2022

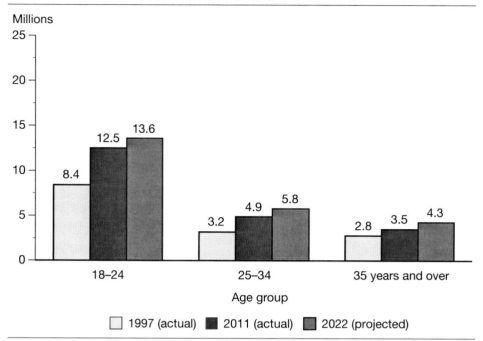

NOTE: Some data have been revised from previously published figures. Data by age are based on the distribution by age from the Census Bureau. Mean absolute percentage errors of selected education statistics can be found in table A-2, appendix A. Calculations are based on unrounded numbers.
SOURCE: U.S. Department of Education, National Center for Education Statistics, Integrated Postsecondary Education Data System (IPEDS) "Fall Enrollment Survey" (IPEDS-EF:97); IPEDS Spring 2012, Enrollment component; Enrollment in Degree-Granting Institutions Model, 1980–2011; and U.S. Department of Commerce, Census Bureau, Current Population Reports, "Social and Economic Characteristics of Students," various years. (This figure was prepared February 2013.)

Figure 18. Actual and projected numbers for enrollment in all postsecondary degree-granting institutions, by sex: Fall 1997 through fall 2022

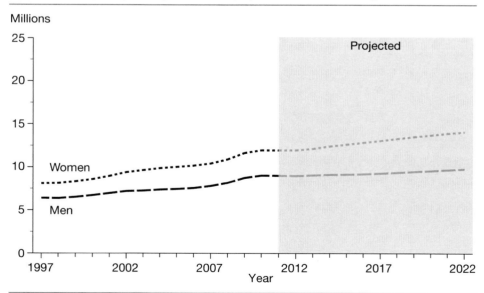

NOTE: Some data have been revised from previously published figures. Mean absolute percentage errors of selected education statistics can be found in table A-2, appendix A.
SOURCE: U.S. Department of Education, National Center for Education Statistics, Integrated Postsecondary Education Data System (IPEDS) "Fall Enrollment Survey" (IPEDS-EF:97–99); IPEDS Spring 2001 through Spring 2012, Enrollment component; and Enrollment in Degree-Granting Institutions Model, 1980–2011. (This figure was prepared February 2013.)

Enrollment by age of student

Enrollment in postsecondary degree-granting institutions of students who are 18 to 24 years old

▲ increased 49 percent between 1997 and 2011; and

▲ is projected to increase 9 percent between 2011 and 2022.

Enrollment in postsecondary degree-granting institutions of students who are 25 to 34 years old

▲ increased 51 percent between 1997 and 2011; and

▲ is projected to increase 20 percent between 2011 and 2022.

Enrollment in postsecondary degree-granting institutions of students who are 35 years old and over

▲ increased 26 percent between 1997 and 2011; and

▲ is projected to increase 23 percent between 2011 and 2022.

For more information:
Table 21

Enrollment by sex of student

Enrollment of men in postsecondary degree-granting institutions

▲ increased 41 percent between 1997 and 2011; and

▲ is projected to increase 9 percent between 2011 and 2022.

Enrollment of women in postsecondary degree-granting institutions

▲ increased 48 percent between 1997 and 2011; and

▲ is projected to increase 18 percent between 2011 and 2022.

For more information:
Tables 20–22

Enrollment by attendance status

Enrollment in postsecondary degree-granting institutions of full-time students

▲ increased 54 percent between 1997 and 2011; and

▲ is projected to increase 12 percent between 2011 and 2022.

Enrollment in postsecondary degree-granting institutions of part-time students

▲ increased 32 percent between 1997 and 2011; and

▲ is projected to increase 16 percent between 2011 and 2022.

For more information:
Tables 20–22

Figure 19. Actual and projected numbers for enrollment in all postsecondary degree-granting institutions, by attendance status: Fall 1997 through fall 2022

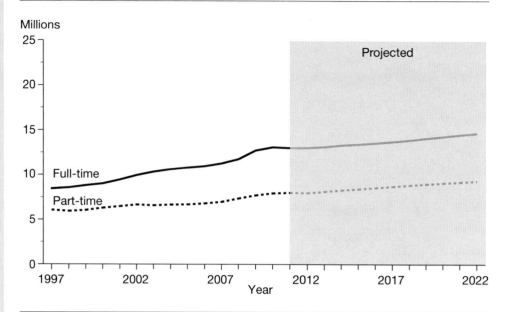

NOTE: Some data have been revised from previously published figures. Mean absolute percentage errors of selected education statistics can be found in table A-2, appendix A.
SOURCE: U.S. Department of Education, National Center for Education Statistics, Integrated Postsecondary Education Data System (IPEDS) "Fall Enrollment Survey" (IPEDS-EF:97–99); IPEDS Spring 2001 through Spring 2012, Enrollment component; and Enrollment in Degree-Granting Institutions Model, 1980–2011. (This figure was prepared February 2013.)

Enrollment by level of student

Enrollment in postsecondary degree-granting institutions of undergraduate students

▲ increased 45 percent between 1997 and 2011; and

▲ is projected to increase 13 percent between 2011 and 2022.

Enrollment in postsecondary degree-granting institutions of postbaccalaureate students

▲ increased 43 percent between 1997 and 2011; and

▲ is projected to increase 19 percent between 2011 and 2022.

For more information:
Tables 27–28

Figure 20. Actual and projected numbers for enrollment in all postsecondary degree-granting institutions, by level of degree: Fall 1997 through fall 2022

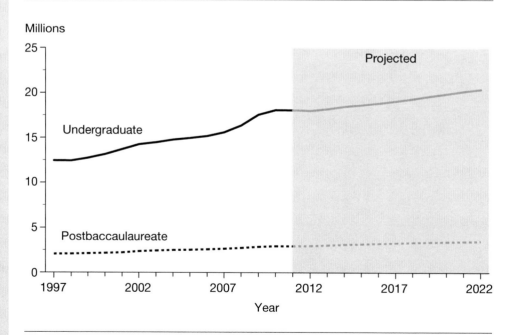

NOTE: Some data have been revised from previously published figures. Mean absolute percentage errors of selected education statistics can be found in table A-2, appendix A.
SOURCE: U.S. Department of Education, National Center for Education Statistics, Integrated Postsecondary Education Data System (IPEDS) "Fall Enrollment Survey" (IPEDS-EF:97–99); IPEDS Spring 2001 through Spring 2012, Enrollment component; and Enrollment in Degree-Granting Institutions Model, 1980–2011. (This figure was prepared February 2013.)

Figure 21. Actual and projected numbers for enrollment of U.S. residents in all postsecondary degree-granting institutions, by race/ethnicity: Fall 1997 through fall 2022

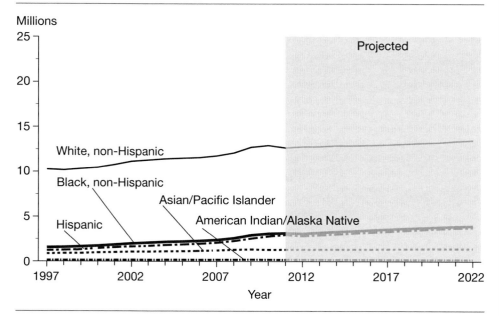

NOTE: Race categories exclude persons of Hispanic ethnicity. Because of underreporting and nonreporting of racial/ethnic data and nonresident aliens, some estimates are slightly lower than corresponding data in other published tables. Enrollment data in the "race/ethnicity unknown" (all years) and "two or more races" (2008 through 2011 only) categories of the IPEDS "Enrollment component" have been prorated to the other racial/ethnic categories at the institutional level. Mean absolute percentage errors of selected education statistics can be found in table A-2, appendix A. Some data have been revised from previously published figures. SOURCE: U.S. Department of Education, National Center for Education Statistics, Integrated Postsecondary Education Data System (IPEDS) "Fall Enrollment Survey" (IPEDS-EF:97–99); IPEDS Spring 2001 through Spring 2012, Enrollment component; and Enrollment in Degree-Granting Institutions by Race/Ethnicity Model, 1980–2011. (This figure was prepared February 2013.)

Enrollment by race/ethnicity

Enrollment of U.S. residents is projected to

▲ increase 7 percent for students who are White between 2011 and 2022;

▲ increase 26 percent for students who are Black between 2011 and 2022;

▲ increase 27 percent for students who are Hispanic between 2011 and 2022;

▲ increase 7 percent for students who are Asian/Pacific Islander between 2011 and 2022; and

■ is projected to be about the same number in 2011 and 2022 for students who are American Indian/Alaska Native.

For more information:
Table 29

Figure 22. Actual and projected numbers for enrollment in all postsecondary degree-granting institutions, by control of institution: Fall 1997 through fall 2022

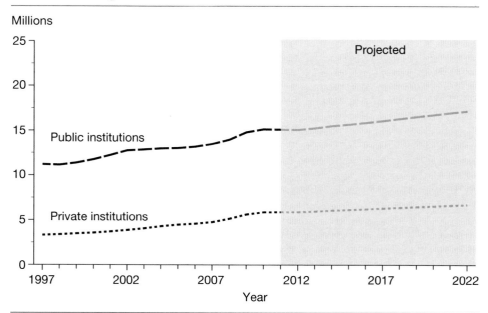

NOTE: Some data have been revised from previously published figures. Mean absolute percentage errors of selected education statistics can be found in table A-2, appendix A. SOURCE: U.S. Department of Education, National Center for Education Statistics, Integrated Postsecondary Education Data System (IPEDS) "Fall Enrollment Survey" (IPEDS-EF:97–99); IPEDS Spring 2001 through Spring 2012, Enrollment component; Enrollment in Degree-Granting Institutions Model, 1980–2011. (This figure was prepared February 2013.)

Enrollment in public and private institutions

Enrollment in public postsecondary degree-granting institutions

▲ increased 35 percent between 1997 and 2011; and

▲ is projected to increase 14 percent between 2011 and 2022.

Enrollment in private postsecondary degree-granting institutions

▲ increased 78 percent between 1997 and 2011; and

▲ is projected to increase 14 percent between 2011 and 2022.

For more information:
Table 20

FIRST-TIME FRESHMEN ENROLLMENT

First-time freshmen fall enrollment

Total first-time freshmen fall enrollment in all postsecondary degree-granting institutions

▲ increased 39 percent from 1997 to 2011; and

▲ is projected to increase 16 percent between 2011 and 2022.

First-time freshmen fall enrollment of men in all postsecondary degree-granting institutions

▲ increased 39 percent from 1997 to 2011; and

▲ is projected to increase 11 percent between 2011 and 2022.

Total first-time freshmen fall enrollment of women in all postsecondary degree-granting institutions

▲ increased 40 percent from 1997 to 2011; and

▲ is projected to increase 20 percent between 2011 and 2022.

For more information:
Table 30

Figure 23. Actual and projected numbers for total first-time freshmen fall enrollment in all postsecondary degree-granting institutions, by sex: Fall 1997 through fall 2022

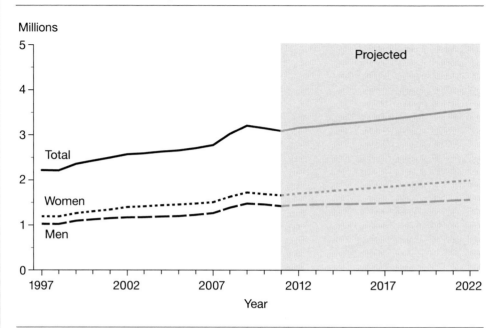

NOTE: Some data have been revised from previously published figures. Mean absolute percentage errors of selected education statistics can be found in table A-2, appendix A.
SOURCE: U.S. Department of Education, National Center for Education Statistics, Integrated Postsecondary Education Data System (IPEDS) "Fall Enrollment Survey" (IPEDS-EF:97–99); IPEDS Spring 2001 through Spring 2012, Enrollment component; Enrollment in Degree-Granting Institutions Model, 1980–2011; and First-Time Freshmen Model, 1975–2011. (This figure was prepared February 2013.)

Section 6
Postsecondary Degrees Conferred

INTRODUCTION

Continuing growth in enrollment in postsecondary degree-granting institutions has been reflected by increases in the numbers of associate's, bachelor's, master's and doctor's degrees conferred (tables 20, 32, 33, 34, and 35). Increases in the number of degrees conferred are expected to continue between academic year 2010–11, the last year of actual data, and academic year 2022–23.

Factors affecting the projections

The projections of the number of degrees conferred are related to projections of the college-age populations developed by the Census Bureau and college enrollments from this report. For more details, see appendixes A.0 and A.6.

Factors that were not considered

Some factors that may affect future numbers of degrees, such as choice of degree and labor force requirements, were not included in the projection models.

Changes in degree classifications

The National Center for Education Statistics (NCES) no longer uses the first-professional degree classification. Most degrees formerly classified as first-professional—such as M.D., D.D.S., and law degrees—are now classified as doctor's degrees. However, master's of divinity degrees are now classified as master's degrees. This is the second edition of *Projections of Education Statistics* to use these new classifications. With this change, the actual numbers of master's and doctor's and degrees conferred are higher than the actual numbers in *Projections of Education Statistics to 2020* and earlier editions of this report. The revisions of actual numbers are reflected in the projections.

Accuracy of Projections

No mean absolute percentage errors (MAPEs) were calculated for degrees conferred as the current model used for producing their projections has been used for only four other editions of *Projections of Education Statistics* for associates and bachelor's degrees and, due to the changes in classifications described above, only one other edition for master's and doctor's degrees. For more information on the MAPEs of different NCES projection series, see table A-2 in appendix A.

DEGREES, BY LEVEL OF DEGREE AND SEX OF RECIPIENT

Associate's degrees

The total number of associate's degrees

▲ increased 69 percent between 1997–98 and 2010–11; and

▲ is projected to increase 49 percent between 2010–11 and 2022–23.

The number of associate's degrees awarded to men

▲ increased 66 percent between 1997–98 and 2010–11; and

▲ is projected to increase 60 percent between 2010–11 and 2022–23.

The number of associate's degrees awarded to women

▲ increased 70 percent between 1997–98 and 2010–11; and

▲ is projected to increase 43 percent between 2010–11 and 2022–23.

For more information:
Table 32

Figure 24. Actual and projected numbers for associate's degrees conferred by postsecondary degree-granting institutions, by sex of recipient: Academic years 1997–98 through 2022–23

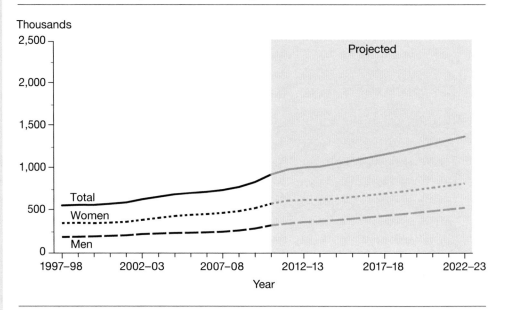

NOTE: Some data have been revised from previously published figures. Mean absolute percentage errors of selected education statistics can be found in table A-2, appendix A. SOURCE: U.S. Department of Education, National Center for Education Statistics, Integrated Postsecondary Education Data System (IPEDS), "Completions Survey" (IPEDS-C:98–99); IPEDS Fall 2000 through Fall 2011 Completions component; and Degrees Conferred Model, 1980–81 through 2010–11. (This figure was prepared March 2013.)

Bachelor's degrees

The total number of bachelor's degrees

▲ increased 45 percent between 1997–98 and 2010–11; and

▲ is projected to increase 17 percent between 2010–11 and 2022–23.

The number of bachelor's degrees awarded to men

▲ increased 41 percent between 1997–98 and 2010–11; and

▲ is projected to increase 11 percent between 2010–11 and 2022–23.

The number of bachelor's degrees awarded to women

▲ increased 48 percent between 1997–98 and 2010–11; and

▲ is projected to increase 22 percent between 2010–11 and 2022–23.

For more information:
Table 33

Figure 25. Actual and projected numbers for bachelor's degrees conferred by postsecondary degree-granting institutions, by sex of recipient: Academic years 1997–98 through 2022–23

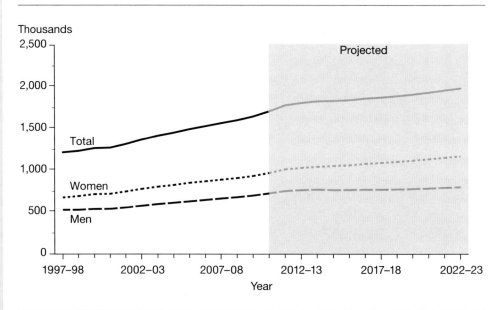

NOTE: Some data have been revised from previously published figures. Mean absolute percentage errors of selected education statistics can be found in table A-2, appendix A. SOURCE: U.S. Department of Education, National Center for Education Statistics, Integrated Postsecondary Education Data System (IPEDS), "Completions Survey" (IPEDS-C:98–99); IPEDS Fall 2000 through Fall 2011 Completions component; and Degrees Conferred Model, 1980–81 through 2010–11. (This figure was prepared March 2013.)

Figure 26. Actual and projected numbers for master's degrees conferred by postsecondary degree-granting institutions, by sex of recipient: Academic years 1997–98 through 2022–23

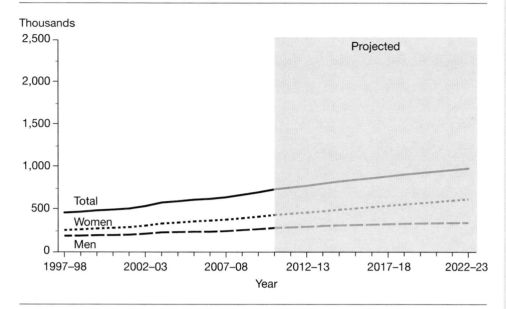

NOTE: Includes some degrees formerly classified as first professional such as divinity degrees (M.Div. and M.H.L./Rav). Some data have been revised from previously published figures. SOURCE: U.S. Department of Education, National Center for Education Statistics, Integrated Postsecondary Education Data System (IPEDS), "Completions Survey" (IPEDS-C:98–99); IPEDS Fall 2000 through Fall 2011 Completions component; and Degrees Conferred Model, 1980–81 through 2010–11. (This figure was prepared March 2013.)

Master's degrees

The total number of master's degrees

▲ increased 68 percent between 1997–98 and 2010–11; and

▲ is projected to increase 36 percent between 2010–11 and 2022–23.

The number of master's degrees awarded to men

▲ increased 54 percent between 1997–98 and 2010–11; and

▲ is projected to increase 22 percent between 2010–11 and 2022–23.

The number of master's degrees awarded to women

▲ increased 78 percent between 1997–98 and 2010–11; and

▲ is projected to increase 45 percent between 2010–11 and 2022–23.

For more information:
Table 34

Figure 27. Actual and projected numbers for doctor's degrees conferred by postsecondary degree-granting institutions, by sex of recipient: Academic years 1997–98 through 2022–23

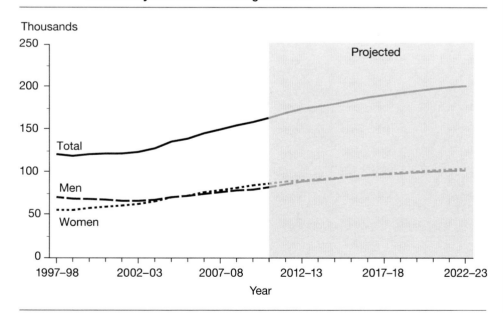

NOTE: Doctor's degrees include Ph.D., Ed.D., and comparable degrees at the doctoral level. Includes most degrees formerly classified as first-professional, such as M.D., D.D.S., and law degrees. Some data have been revised from previously published figures. Mean absolute percentage errors of selected education statistics can be found in table A-2, appendix A. SOURCE: U.S. Department of Education, National Center for Education Statistics, Integrated Postsecondary Education Data System (IPEDS), "Completions Survey" (IPEDS-C:98–99); IPEDS Fall 2000 through Fall 2011 Completions component; and Degrees Conferred Model, 1980–81 through 2010–11. (This figure was prepared March 2013.)

Doctor's degrees

The total number of doctor's degrees

▲ increased 38 percent between 1997–98 and 2010–11; and

▲ is projected to increase 24 percent between 2010–11 and 2022–23.

The number of doctor's degrees awarded to men

▲ increased 18 percent between 1997–98 and 2010–11; and

▲ is projected to increase 26 percent between 2010–11 and 2022–23.

The number of doctor's degrees awarded to women

▲ increased 63 percent between 1997–98 and 2010–11; and

▲ is projected to increase 22 percent between 2010–11 and 2022–23.

For more information:
Table 35

This page intentionally left blank.

Reference Tables

This page intentionally left blank.

Table 1. Actual and projected numbers for enrollment in grades preK–12, preK–8, and 9–12 in elementary and secondary schools, by control of school: Fall 1997 through fall 2022

[In thousands]

Year	Total			Public			Private		
	preK–12[1]	preK–8[1]	9–12	preK–12[1]	preK–8[1]	9–12	preK–12[1]	preK–8[1]	9–12
1	2	3	4	5	6	7	8	9	10
Actual									
1997	52,071	37,830	14,241	46,127	33,071	13,056	5,944	4,759	1,185
1998[2]	52,526	38,119	14,407	46,539	33,344	13,195	5,988	4,776	1,212
1999	52,875	38,275	14,600	46,857	33,486	13,371	6,018	4,789	1,229
2000[2]	53,373	38,592	14,781	47,204	33,686	13,517	6,169	4,906	1,264
2001	53,992	38,959	15,032	47,672	33,936	13,736	6,320	5,023	1,296
2002[2]	54,403	39,029	15,374	48,183	34,114	14,069	6,220	4,915	1,306
2003	54,639	38,989	15,651	48,540	34,201	14,339	6,099	4,788	1,311
2004[2]	54,882	38,933	15,949	48,795	34,178	14,618	6,087	4,756	1,331
2005	55,187	38,928	16,258	49,113	34,204	14,909	6,073	4,724	1,349
2006[2]	55,307	38,866	16,441	49,316	34,235	15,081	5,991	4,631	1,360
2007	55,203	38,751	16,451	49,293	34,205	15,087	5,910	4,546	1,364
2008[2]	54,973	38,650	16,322	49,266	34,286	14,980	5,707	4,365	1,342
2009	54,849	38,588	16,261	49,361	34,409	14,952	5,488	4,179	1,309
2010[2]	54,867	38,708	16,159	49,484	34,625	14,860	5,382	4,084	1,299
2011	54,790	38,750	16,040	49,522	34,773	14,749	5,268	3,977	1,291
Projected									
2012	54,814	38,855	15,959	49,636	34,953	14,684	5,178	3,903	1,275
2013	54,886	39,011	15,875	49,785	35,145	14,639	5,101	3,866	1,235
2014	55,053	39,166	15,887	50,018	35,328	14,689	5,035	3,838	1,197
2015	55,307	39,386	15,922	50,328	35,557	14,771	4,980	3,829	1,151
2016	55,600	39,675	15,926	50,654	35,843	14,811	4,947	3,832	1,114
2017	55,930	39,972	15,958	50,999	36,129	14,870	4,931	3,843	1,088
2018	56,257	40,298	15,959	51,336	36,432	14,903	4,921	3,866	1,056
2019	56,635	40,646	15,989	51,707	36,747	14,960	4,928	3,899	1,029
2020	57,066	40,998	16,068	52,124	37,067	15,057	4,943	3,931	1,011
2021	57,497	41,348	16,148	52,534	37,385	15,149	4,963	3,963	1,000
2022	57,944	41,691	16,253	52,952	37,697	15,255	4,992	3,994	998

[1]Includes private nursery and prekindergarten enrollment in schools that offer kindergarten or higher grades.
[2]Since the biennial Private School Universe Survey (PSS) is collected in the fall of odd-numbered years, private school numbers for alternate years are estimated based on data from the PSS.
NOTE: PreK = prekindergarten. Some data have been revised from previously published figures. Detail may not sum to totals because of rounding. Mean absolute percentage errors of selected education statistics can be found in table A-2, appendix A.

SOURCE: U.S. Department of Education, National Center for Education Statistics, Common Core of Data (CCD), "State Nonfiscal Survey of Public Elementary/Secondary Education," 1997–98 through 2011–12; Private School Universe Survey (PSS), selected years 1997–98 through 2011–12; and National Elementary and Secondary Enrollment Model, 1972–2011. (This table was prepared February 2013.)

Table 2. Actual and projected numbers for enrollment in public elementary and secondary schools, by grade: Fall 1997 through fall 2022

[In thousands]

Year	Total	preK	K	1	2	3	4	5	6	7	8	9	10	11	12	Elementary ungraded	Secondary ungraded
1	2	3	4	5	6	7	8	9	10	11	12	13	14	15	16	17	18
Actual																	
1997	46,127	695	3,503	3,755	3,689	3,597	3,507	3,458	3,492	3,520	3,415	3,819	3,376	2,972	2,673	440	216
1998	46,539	729	3,443	3,727	3,681	3,696	3,592	3,520	3,497	3,530	3,480	3,856	3,382	3,021	2,722	449	214
1999	46,857	751	3,397	3,684	3,656	3,691	3,686	3,604	3,564	3,541	3,497	3,935	3,415	3,034	2,782	415	205
2000	47,204	776	3,382	3,636	3,634	3,676	3,711	3,707	3,663	3,629	3,538	3,963	3,491	3,083	2,803	334	177
2001	47,672	865	3,379	3,614	3,593	3,653	3,695	3,727	3,769	3,720	3,616	4,012	3,528	3,174	2,863	304	159
2002	48,183	915	3,434	3,594	3,565	3,623	3,669	3,711	3,788	3,821	3,709	4,105	3,584	3,229	2,990	285	161
2003	48,540	950	3,503	3,613	3,544	3,611	3,619	3,685	3,772	3,841	3,809	4,190	3,675	3,277	3,046	255	150
2004	48,795	990	3,544	3,663	3,560	3,580	3,612	3,635	3,735	3,818	3,825	4,281	3,750	3,369	3,094	215	122
2005	49,113	1,036	3,619	3,691	3,606	3,586	3,578	3,633	3,670	3,777	3,802	4,287	3,866	3,454	3,180	205	121
2006	49,316	1,084	3,631	3,751	3,641	3,627	3,586	3,602	3,660	3,716	3,766	4,260	3,882	3,551	3,277	170	110
2007	49,293	1,081	3,609	3,750	3,704	3,659	3,624	3,600	3,628	3,701	3,709	4,200	3,863	3,558	3,375	139	92
2008	49,266	1,180	3,640	3,708	3,699	3,708	3,647	3,629	3,614	3,653	3,692	4,123	3,822	3,548	3,400	117	87
2009	49,361	1,223	3,678	3,729	3,665	3,707	3,701	3,652	3,644	3,641	3,651	4,080	3,809	3,541	3,432	119	90
2010	49,484	1,279	3,682	3,754	3,701	3,686	3,711	3,718	3,682	3,676	3,659	4,008	3,800	3,538	3,472	77	42
2011	49,522	1,291	3,746	3,773	3,713	3,703	3,672	3,699	3,724	3,696	3,679	3,957	3,751	3,546	3,452	77	43
Projected																	
2012	49,636	1,299	3,774	3,797	3,732	3,721	3,707	3,681	3,718	3,744	3,702	3,978	3,704	3,501	3,459	78	42
2013	49,785	1,310	3,807	3,825	3,756	3,741	3,725	3,716	3,699	3,738	3,749	4,003	3,724	3,456	3,415	78	42
2014	50,018	1,323	3,843	3,858	3,785	3,765	3,744	3,734	3,735	3,719	3,743	4,054	3,746	3,475	3,372	79	42
2015	50,328	1,336	3,881	3,895	3,817	3,793	3,769	3,754	3,753	3,755	3,725	4,048	3,795	3,496	3,390	80	43
2016	50,654	1,349	3,919	3,934	3,854	3,826	3,797	3,778	3,772	3,773	3,760	4,028	3,789	3,541	3,410	81	43
2017	50,999	1,361	3,955	3,973	3,892	3,862	3,830	3,806	3,797	3,793	3,779	4,066	3,770	3,535	3,454	81	44
2018	51,336	1,373	3,990	4,010	3,931	3,901	3,866	3,839	3,825	3,817	3,798	4,086	3,806	3,518	3,449	82	44
2019	51,707	1,384	4,021	4,045	3,967	3,939	3,905	3,876	3,858	3,846	3,823	4,107	3,825	3,552	3,432	83	45
2020	52,124	1,394	4,050	4,077	4,002	3,976	3,943	3,914	3,895	3,879	3,851	4,134	3,844	3,569	3,465	84	45
2021	52,534	1,403	4,078	4,107	4,034	4,011	3,980	3,953	3,934	3,916	3,885	4,165	3,869	3,587	3,482	84	46
2022	52,952	1,412	4,103	4,135	4,063	4,043	4,015	3,990	3,973	3,955	3,922	4,201	3,898	3,610	3,500	85	46

NOTE: PreK = prekindergarten. K = kindergarten. Elementary ungraded includes students in grades prekindergarten through 8 who are in classes or programs to which students are assigned without standard grade designations. Secondary ungraded includes students in grades 9 through 12 who are in classes or programs to which students are assigned without standard grade designations. Some data have been revised from previously published figures. Detail may not sum to totals because of rounding. Mean absolute percentage errors of selected education statistics can be found in table A-2, appendix A.
SOURCE: U.S. Department of Education, National Center for Education Statistics, Common Core of Data (CCD), "State Nonfiscal Survey of Public Elementary/Secondary Education," 1997–98 through 2011–12; and National Elementary and Secondary Enrollment Model, 1972–2011. (This table was prepared February 2013.)

Table 3. Actual and projected numbers for enrollment in public elementary and secondary schools, by race/ethnicity: Fall 1997 through fall 2022

[In thousands]

Year	Total	Race/ethnicity					
		White	Black	Hispanic	Asian/ Pacific Islander[1]	American Indian/ Alaska Native	Two or more races[2]
1	2	3	4	5	6	7	8
Actual							
1997..	46,127	29,241	7,851	6,705	1,796	535	—
1998..	46,539	29,217	7,935	7,007	1,846	534	—
1999..	46,857	29,032	8,054	7,337	1,892	542	—
2000..	47,204	28,873	8,099	7,733	1,949	550	—
2001..	47,672	28,731	8,176	8,175	2,026	563	—
2002..	48,183	28,614	8,297	8,601	2,088	583	—
2003..	48,540	28,438	8,347	9,018	2,144	593	—
2004..	48,795	28,186	8,400	9,415	2,204	591	—
2005..	49,113	28,001	8,443	9,794	2,278	598	—
2006..	49,316	27,797	8,421	10,171	2,331	595	—
2007..	49,293	27,454	8,392	10,457	2,396	594	—
2008[3].....................................	49,266	27,053	8,359	10,570	2,450	589	244
2009[4].....................................	49,361	26,695	8,248	10,996	2,485	600	335
2010..	49,484	25,930	7,918	11,442	2,467	566	1,161
2011..	49,522	25,604	7,827	11,761	2,512	547	1,270
Projected							
2012..	49,636	25,317	7,769	12,150	2,551	537	1,312
2013..	49,785	25,063	7,728	12,516	2,590	530	1,359
2014..	50,018	24,861	7,709	12,883	2,629	524	1,412
2015..	50,328	24,686	7,704	13,277	2,678	520	1,462
2016..	50,654	24,529	7,695	13,669	2,728	517	1,516
2017..	50,999	24,388	7,710	14,043	2,780	514	1,565
2018..	51,336	24,258	7,728	14,397	2,825	512	1,616
2019..	51,707	24,153	7,763	14,737	2,874	512	1,668
2020..	52,124	24,088	7,816	15,062	2,922	513	1,723
2021..	52,534	24,026	7,880	15,371	2,966	515	1,775
2022..	52,952	23,981	7,951	15,664	3,011	517	1,826

—Data not available. Prior to 2008, "two or more races" was not an available category.

[1]In 2008 and 2009, some students of both Asian origin and Hawaiian or Other Pacific Islander origin were included in the two or more races category. In 2010 and 2011, all students of both Asian origin and Hawaiian or Other Pacific Islander origin were included in the two or more races category. For more information, see the Elementary and Secondary Enrollment section A.1 in the appendix.

[2]A person who has identified himself or herself as a member of two or more of the following race groups: White, Black, Asian, Native Hawaiian or Other Pacific Islander, or American Indian or Alaska Native.

[3]Five states reported enrollment counts for students of two or more races.

[4]Fourteen states reported enrollment counts for students of two or more races.

NOTE: Some data have been revised from previously published figures. Race categories exclude persons of Hispanic ethnicity. The historical racial/ethnic time-series were con-structed using racial/ethnic enrollment data at the state level for individual grades. In some instances, enrollment data by race/ethnicity had to be imputed. Further, in some instances, the racial/ethnic enrollment data for individual grades had to be adjusted in order for them to sum to the state total for that grade. For additional information, see the Elementary and Secondary Enrollment section A.1 in appendix A. Detail may not sum to totals because of rounding. Mean absolute percentage errors of selected education statistics can be found in table A-2, appendix A.

SOURCE: U.S. Department of Education, National Center for Education Statistics, Common Core of Data (CCD), "State Nonfiscal Survey of Public Elementary/Secondary Education," 1997–98 through 2011–12; and National Public Elementary and Secondary Enrollment by Race/Ethnicity Model, 1994–2011. (This table was prepared February 2013.)

Table 4. Actual and projected numbers for enrollment in grades preK–8 in public elementary and secondary schools, by race/ethnicity: Fall 1997 through fall 2022

[In thousands]

| Year | Total | Race/ethnicity | | | | | |
		White	Black	Hispanic	Asian/ Pacific Islander[1]	American Indian/ Alaska Native	Two or more races[2]
1	2	3	4	5	6	7	8
Actual							
1997	33,071	20,625	5,782	5,030	1,244	390	—
1998	33,344	20,548	5,861	5,274	1,275	386	—
1999	33,486	20,313	5,948	5,529	1,305	391	—
2000	33,686	20,123	5,980	5,838	1,348	397	—
2001	33,936	19,954	6,002	6,167	1,408	405	—
2002	34,114	19,760	6,040	6,453	1,446	415	—
2003	34,201	19,554	6,013	6,736	1,482	415	—
2004	34,178	19,266	5,992	6,988	1,519	413	—
2005	34,204	19,047	5,953	7,223	1,569	412	—
2006	34,235	18,859	5,880	7,470	1,611	414	—
2007	34,205	18,678	5,821	7,636	1,660	412	—
2008[3]	34,286	18,497	5,794	7,696	1,703	410	185
2009[4]	34,409	18,310	5,716	7,982	1,731	419	251
2010	34,625	17,821	5,496	8,317	1,711	394	884
2011	34,773	17,655	5,469	8,560	1,743	384	961
Projected							
2012	34,953	17,492	5,450	8,861	1,777	379	994
2013	35,145	17,343	5,443	9,142	1,813	375	1,030
2014	35,328	17,218	5,433	9,397	1,837	371	1,072
2015	35,557	17,100	5,443	9,664	1,872	369	1,110
2016	35,843	17,032	5,465	9,922	1,903	368	1,153
2017	36,129	16,969	5,513	10,157	1,929	369	1,193
2018	36,432	16,923	5,571	10,377	1,957	371	1,234
2019	36,747	16,909	5,634	10,568	1,990	373	1,273
2020	37,067	16,912	5,692	10,746	2,029	376	1,312
2021	37,385	16,925	5,742	10,920	2,069	379	1,350
2022	37,697	16,939	5,788	11,098	2,106	382	1,384

—Data not available. Prior to 2008, "two or more races" was not an available category.

[1]In 2008 and 2009, some students of both Asian origin and Hawaiian or Other Pacific Islander origin were included in the two or more races category. In 2010 and 2011, all students of both Asian origin and Hawaiian or Other Pacific Islander origin were included in the two or more races category. For more information, see the Elementary and Secondary Enrollment section A.1 in the appendix.

[2]A person who has identified himself or herself as a member of two or more of the following race groups: White, Black, Asian, Native Hawaiian or Other Pacific Islander, or American Indian or Alaska Native.

[3]Five states reported enrollment counts for students of two or more races.

[4]Fourteen states reported enrollment counts for students of two or more races.

NOTE: PreK = prekindergarten. Some data have been revised from previously published figures. Race categories exclude persons of Hispanic ethnicity. The historical racial/ethnic time-series were constructed using racial/ethnic enrollment data at the state level for individual grades. In some instances, enrollment data by race/ethnicity had to be imputed. Further, in some instances, the racial/ethnic enrollment data for individual grades had to be adjusted in order for them to sum to the state total for that grade. For additional information, see the Elementary and Secondary Enrollment section A.1 in appendix A. Detail may not sum to totals because of rounding. Mean absolute percentage errors of selected education statistics can be found in table A-2, appendix A.

SOURCE: U.S. Department of Education, National Center for Education Statistics, Common Core of Data (CCD), "State Nonfiscal Survey of Public Elementary/Secondary Education," 1997–98 through 2011–12; and National Public Elementary and Secondary Enrollment by Race/Ethnicity Model, 1994–2011. (This table was prepared February 2013.)

Table 5. Actual and projected numbers for enrollment in grades 9–12 in public schools, by race/ethnicity: Fall 1997 through fall 2022

[In thousands]

Year	Total	Race/ethnicity					
		White	Black	Hispanic	Asian/ Pacific Islander[1]	American Indian/ Alaska Native	Two or more races[2]
1	2	3	4	5	6	7	8
Actual							
1997..	13,056	8,616	2,068	1,675	552	145	—
1998..	13,195	8,670	2,073	1,732	572	148	—
1999..	13,371	8,719	2,106	1,808	587	151	—
2000..	13,517	8,750	2,119	1,894	601	153	—
2001..	13,736	8,777	2,173	2,008	619	158	—
2002..	14,069	8,854	2,257	2,148	642	168	—
2003..	14,339	8,884	2,334	2,282	663	177	—
2004..	14,618	8,920	2,408	2,427	686	178	—
2005..	14,909	8,954	2,490	2,570	709	186	—
2006..	15,081	8,938	2,540	2,701	720	181	—
2007..	15,087	8,776	2,571	2,821	736	183	—
2008[3].......................................	14,980	8,556	2,565	2,874	746	179	59
2009[4].......................................	14,952	8,385	2,532	3,014	754	182	84
2010..	14,860	8,109	2,422	3,125	755	171	277
2011..	14,749	7,948	2,357	3,201	769	163	309
Projected							
2012..	14,684	7,825	2,319	3,289	775	158	318
2013..	14,639	7,719	2,285	3,374	777	155	329
2014..	14,689	7,643	2,276	3,486	792	152	340
2015..	14,771	7,586	2,262	3,614	806	151	352
2016..	14,811	7,497	2,230	3,747	825	148	363
2017..	14,870	7,419	2,197	3,886	851	144	372
2018..	14,903	7,336	2,157	4,020	868	141	382
2019..	14,960	7,244	2,130	4,169	883	139	395
2020..	15,057	7,176	2,124	4,316	894	137	411
2021..	15,149	7,101	2,138	4,451	897	136	426
2022..	15,255	7,042	2,163	4,566	905	136	442

—Data not available. Prior to 2008, "two or more races" was not an available category.

[1]In 2008 and 2009, some students of both Asian origin and Hawaiian or Other Pacific Islander origin were included in the two or more races category. In 2010 and 2011, all students of both Asian origin and Hawaiian or Other Pacific Islander origin were included in the two or more races category. For more information, see the Elementary and Secondary Enrollment section A.1 in the appendix.

[2]A person who has identified himself or herself as a member of two or more of the following race groups: White, Black, Asian, Native Hawaiian or Other Pacific Islander, or American Indian or Alaska Native.

[3]Five states reported enrollment counts for students of two or more races.

[4]Fourteen states reported enrollment counts for students of two or more races.

NOTE: Some data have been revised from previously published figures. Race categories exclude persons of Hispanic ethnicity. The historical racial/ethnic time-series were con-

structed using racial/ethnic enrollment data at the state level for individual grades. In some instances, enrollment data by race/ethnicity had to be imputed. Further, in some instances, the racial/ethnic enrollment data for individual grades had to be adjusted in order for them to sum to the state total for that grade. For additional information, see the Elementary and Secondary Enrollment section A.1 in appendix A. Detail may not sum to totals because of rounding. Mean absolute percentage errors of selected education statistics can be found in table A-2, appendix A.

SOURCE: U.S. Department of Education, National Center for Education Statistics, Common Core of Data (CCD), "State Nonfiscal Survey of Public Elementary/Secondary Education," 1997–98 through 2011–12; and National Public Elementary and Secondary Enrollment by Race/Ethnicity Model, 1994–2011. (This table was prepared February 2013.)

Table 6. Actual and projected numbers for enrollment in grades preK–12 in public elementary and secondary schools, by region and state: Fall 2004 through fall 2022

[In thousands]

Region and state	Actual							
	2004	2005	2006	2007	2008	2009	2010	2011
1	2	3	4	5	6	7	8	9
United States	**48,795**	**49,113**	**49,316**	**49,293**	**49,266**	**49,361**	**49,484**	**49,522**
Northeast	8,271	8,240	8,258	8,122	8,053	8,092	8,071	7,954
Connecticut	577	575	575	571	567	564	561	554
Maine	199	195	194	196	193	189	189	189
Massachusetts	976	972	969	963	959	957	956	953
New Hampshire	207	206	204	201	198	197	195	192
New Jersey	1,393	1,396	1,389	1,382	1,381	1,396	1,403	1,356
New York	2,836	2,816	2,810	2,765	2,741	2,766	2,735	2,705
Pennsylvania	1,828	1,831	1,871	1,802	1,775	1,786	1,793	1,771
Rhode Island	156	153	152	148	145	145	144	143
Vermont	98	97	95	94	94	91	97	90
Midwest	10,775	10,819	10,819	10,770	10,743	10,672	10,610	10,574
Illinois	2,098	2,112	2,118	2,113	2,120	2,104	2,092	2,083
Indiana	1,021	1,035	1,046	1,047	1,046	1,047	1,047	1,041
Iowa	478	483	483	485	488	492	496	496
Kansas	469	468	470	468	471	474	484	486
Michigan	1,751	1,742	1,723	1,693	1,660	1,649	1,587	1,574
Minnesota	839	839	841	838	836	837	838	840
Missouri	905	918	920	917	918	918	919	917
Nebraska	286	287	288	291	293	295	299	301
North Dakota	101	98	97	95	95	95	96	98
Ohio	1,840	1,840	1,837	1,827	1,817	1,764	1,754	1,740
South Dakota	123	122	121	122	126	124	126	128
Wisconsin	865	875	877	875	874	872	872	871
South	17,892	18,103	18,294	18,425	18,491	18,652	18,805	18,956
Alabama	730	742	744	745	746	749	756	745
Arkansas	463	474	476	479	479	481	482	483
Delaware	119	121	122	123	125	127	129	129
District of Columbia	77	77	73	78	69	69	71	74
Florida	2,639	2,675	2,672	2,667	2,631	2,635	2,643	2,668
Georgia	1,553	1,598	1,629	1,650	1,656	1,668	1,677	1,685
Kentucky	675	680	683	666	670	680	673	682
Louisiana	724	655	676	681	685	691	697	703
Maryland	866	860	852	846	844	848	852	854
Mississippi	495	495	495	494	492	492	491	491
North Carolina	1,386	1,416	1,444	1,489	1,489	1,483	1,491	1,508
Oklahoma	629	635	639	642	645	655	660	666
South Carolina	704	702	708	712	718	723	726	727
Tennessee	941	954	978	964	972	973	987	1,000
Texas	4,405	4,525	4,600	4,675	4,752	4,850	4,936	5,000
Virginia	1,205	1,214	1,220	1,231	1,236	1,245	1,251	1,258
West Virginia	280	281	282	283	283	283	283	283
West	11,857	11,951	11,945	11,976	11,979	11,945	11,998	12,038
Alaska	133	133	133	131	131	132	132	131
Arizona	1,043	1,094	1,068	1,087	1,088	1,078	1,072	1,080
California	6,442	6,437	6,407	6,343	6,323	6,263	6,290	6,288
Colorado	766	780	794	802	818	832	843	854
Hawaii	183	183	181	180	179	180	180	183
Idaho	256	262	267	272	275	276	276	280
Montana	147	145	144	143	142	142	142	142
Nevada	400	412	425	429	433	429	437	440
New Mexico	326	327	328	329	330	334	338	337
Oregon	553	552	563	566	575	583	571	568
Utah	504	508	523	576	560	572	586	599
Washington	1,020	1,032	1,027	1,030	1,037	1,035	1,044	1,045
Wyoming	85	84	85	86	87	88	89	90

See notes at end of table.

[In thousands]

Region and state	Projected										
	2012	2013	2014	2015	2016	2017	2018	2019	2020	2021	2022
1	10	11	12	13	14	15	16	17	18	19	20
United States	**49,636**	**49,785**	**50,018**	**50,328**	**50,654**	**50,999**	**51,336**	**51,707**	**52,124**	**52,534**	**52,952**
Northeast	7,904	7,864	7,848	7,848	7,854	7,868	7,884	7,903	7,930	7,950	7,972
Connecticut	549	545	541	539	538	538	538	540	542	544	547
Maine	188	188	188	189	190	190	191	192	193	194	195
Massachusetts	949	945	942	941	938	937	937	937	939	940	943
New Hampshire	190	188	187	186	185	186	186	187	189	190	192
New Jersey	1,347	1,337	1,330	1,326	1,323	1,321	1,322	1,323	1,325	1,327	1,330
New York	2,691	2,679	2,677	2,682	2,688	2,695	2,700	2,707	2,713	2,717	2,721
Pennsylvania	1,759	1,753	1,752	1,756	1,761	1,767	1,773	1,780	1,789	1,796	1,802
Rhode Island	141	140	140	140	141	142	143	144	145	146	147
Vermont	90	90	90	90	90	90	91	92	93	94	95	96
Midwest	10,556	10,545	10,552	10,579	10,599	10,623	10,643	10,659	10,685	10,708	10,724
Illinois	2,087	2,083	2,086	2,094	2,098	2,103	2,106	2,108	2,109	2,110	2,110
Indiana	1,037	1,033	1,029	1,027	1,025	1,024	1,023	1,020	1,021	1,024	1,026
Iowa	496	498	499	501	502	503	504	504	505	504	503
Kansas	488	490	493	496	499	501	503	505	506	507	508
Michigan	1,558	1,547	1,537	1,533	1,528	1,525	1,522	1,519	1,519	1,521	1,521
Minnesota	846	853	863	874	887	900	913	925	938	950	960
Missouri	916	916	917	920	921	923	926	928	932	935	938
Nebraska	303	306	308	310	313	315	317	318	319	320	319
North Dakota	98	99	100	101	102	103	104	104	105	105	105
Ohio	1,728	1,721	1,716	1,713	1,709	1,705	1,700	1,696	1,693	1,690	1,686
South Dakota	128	129	130	131	132	133	134	135	136	137	137
Wisconsin	870	871	875	879	884	888	892	897	902	906	910
South	19,090	19,224	19,377	19,543	19,706	19,868	20,017	20,177	20,357	20,544	20,742
Alabama	740	737	734	732	729	726	723	720	719	719	719
Arkansas	484	485	486	486	487	487	488	488	489	490	491
Delaware	129	130	131	133	134	136	137	138	139	140	141
District of Columbia	73	72	72	72	71	71	71	70	70	69	69
Florida	2,694	2,715	2,740	2,765	2,796	2,828	2,862	2,899	2,944	2,990	3,038
Georgia	1,695	1,704	1,714	1,726	1,736	1,747	1,757	1,769	1,785	1,802	1,821
Kentucky	681	681	681	683	683	682	681	679	679	678	678
Louisiana	706	708	708	710	710	710	706	703	701	697	694
Maryland	858	863	872	882	894	909	922	938	952	965	979
Mississippi	488	486	484	483	481	479	475	473	470	468	464
North Carolina	1,515	1,525	1,537	1,551	1,564	1,578	1,591	1,607	1,626	1,647	1,678
Oklahoma	669	674	678	683	686	689	691	693	695	696	697
South Carolina	731	735	739	745	750	754	757	760	764	768	772
Tennessee	1,005	1,010	1,018	1,026	1,032	1,039	1,045	1,052	1,060	1,069	1,078
Texas	5,078	5,151	5,225	5,300	5,376	5,448	5,514	5,581	5,648	5,716	5,783
Virginia	1,262	1,269	1,279	1,290	1,303	1,315	1,328	1,341	1,355	1,369	1,384
West Virginia	281	279	277	276	273	271	268	265	262	259	256
West	12,086	12,151	12,241	12,357	12,494	12,640	12,792	12,968	13,152	13,331	13,513
Alaska	132	133	135	137	140	143	145	149	152	155	158
Arizona	1,090	1,102	1,117	1,138	1,160	1,185	1,209	1,234	1,261	1,287	1,314
California	6,287	6,293	6,314	6,350	6,404	6,466	6,532	6,621	6,710	6,797	6,884
Colorado	865	875	887	899	910	921	931	941	951	959	969
Hawaii	182	183	184	184	185	185	185	186	186	186	186
Idaho	284	288	292	297	302	306	310	314	318	321	325
Montana	143	143	144	145	146	147	148	148	149	149	149
Nevada	443	448	454	461	470	478	488	499	511	525	539
New Mexico	339	341	344	347	350	352	353	354	355	356	356
Oregon	570	573	577	582	588	594	600	607	616	624	633
Utah	612	625	637	649	659	669	678	687	696	704	712
Washington	1,049	1,054	1,062	1,073	1,086	1,100	1,115	1,132	1,152	1,172	1,193
Wyoming	91	92	93	94	95	96	96	96	96	96	95

NOTE: PreK = prekindergarten. Some data have been revised from previously published figures. Detail may not sum to totals because of rounding. Mean absolute percentage errors of preK–12 enrollment in public elementary and secondary schools by state and region can be found in table A-7, appendix A.

SOURCE: U.S. Department of Education, National Center for Education Statistics, Common Core of Data (CCD), "State Nonfiscal Survey of Public Elementary/Secondary Education," 2004–05 through 2011–12; and State Public Elementary and Secondary Enrollment Model, 1980–2011. (This table was prepared February 2013.)

Table 7. Actual and projected percentage changes in grades preK–12 enrollment in public elementary and secondary schools, by region and state: Fall 2004 through fall 2022

Region and state	Actual 2004–2011	Projected		
		2011–2017	2017–2022	2011–2022
1	2	3	4	5
United States	**1.5**	**3.0**	**3.8**	**6.9**
Northeast	-3.8	-1.1	1.3	0.2
Connecticut	-4.0	-3.0	1.8	-1.3
Maine	-5.0	0.8	2.2	3.0
Massachusetts	-2.3	-1.7	0.5	-1.1
New Hampshire	-7.2	-3.2	3.6	0.2
New Jersey	-2.6	-2.6	0.6	-2.0
New York	-4.6	-0.3	0.9	0.6
Pennsylvania	-3.1	-0.2	2.0	1.7
Rhode Island	-8.7	-0.4	3.3	2.8
Vermont	-8.6	1.2	5.4	6.6
Midwest	-1.9	0.5	1.0	1.4
Illinois	-0.7	0.9	0.3	1.3
Indiana	1.9	-1.6	0.2	-1.4
Iowa	3.7	1.5	#	1.5
Kansas	3.6	3.1	1.5	4.6
Michigan	-10.1	-3.1	-0.2	-3.3
Minnesota	0.1	7.1	6.7	14.3
Missouri	1.2	0.7	1.6	2.3
Nebraska	5.4	4.6	1.3	6.0
North Dakota	-2.9	5.0	2.4	7.6
Ohio	-5.4	-2.0	-1.1	-3.1
South Dakota	4.2	4.2	2.9	7.2
Wisconsin	0.7	2.0	2.4	4.4
South	5.9	4.8	4.4	9.4
Alabama	2.0	-2.5	-1.0	-3.5
Arkansas	4.3	0.9	0.8	1.6
Delaware	8.3	5.4	3.8	9.4
District of Columbia	-3.7	-3.6	-3.9	-7.3
Florida	1.1	6.0	7.4	13.9
Georgia	8.5	3.6	4.3	8.1
Kentucky	1.1	#	-0.7	-0.6
Louisiana	-2.9	0.9	-2.2	-1.3
Maryland	-1.3	6.4	7.8	14.6
Mississippi	-1.0	-2.4	-3.0	-5.3
North Carolina	8.8	4.7	6.3	11.3
Oklahoma	5.8	3.4	1.3	4.7
South Carolina	3.3	3.7	2.4	6.2
Tennessee	6.2	3.9	3.8	7.9
Texas	13.5	8.9	6.1	15.6
Virginia	4.4	4.6	5.2	10.0
West Virginia	1.0	-4.2	-5.5	-9.4
West	1.5	5.0	6.9	12.3
Alaska	-1.4	8.7	10.8	20.5
Arizona	3.5	9.7	10.9	21.6
California	-2.4	2.8	6.5	9.5
Colorado	11.5	7.9	5.2	13.5
Hawaii	-0.3	1.4	0.3	1.7
Idaho	9.3	9.3	6.1	16.0
Montana	-3.0	3.1	1.6	4.7
Nevada	9.9	8.8	12.7	22.6
New Mexico	3.4	4.2	1.3	5.6
Oregon	2.8	4.5	6.7	11.5
Utah	18.9	11.7	6.4	18.8
Washington	2.5	5.2	8.4	14.1
Wyoming	6.3	6.1	-0.5	5.5

\# Rounds to zero.
NOTE: PreK = prekindergarten. Calculations are based on unrounded numbers. Mean absolute percentage errors of preK–12 enrollment in public elementary and secondary schools by state and region can be found in table A-7, appendix A.

SOURCE: U.S. Department of Education, National Center for Education Statistics, Common Core of Data (CCD), "State Nonfiscal Survey of Public Elementary/Secondary Education," selected years, 2004–05 through 2011–12; and State Public Elementary and Secondary Enrollment Model, 1980–2011. (This table was prepared February 2013.)

This page intentionally left blank.

Table 8. Actual and projected numbers for enrollment in grades preK–8 in public schools, by region and state: Fall 2004 through fall 2022

[In thousands]

Region and state	Actual							
	2004	2005	2006	2007	2008	2009	2010	2011
1	2	3	4	5	6	7	8	9
United States	**34,178**	**34,204**	**34,235**	**34,205**	**34,286**	**34,409**	**34,625**	**34,773**
Northeast................................	5,689	5,623	5,574	5,504	5,476	5,494	5,540	5,479
Connecticut.............................	404	400	398	394	392	390	387	383
Maine	136	133	132	131	129	129	129	130
Massachusetts........................	682	675	671	667	667	667	666	666
New Hampshire	140	139	136	134	133	133	132	130
New Jersey	976	971	963	954	957	968	981	948
New York.................................	1,943	1,909	1,887	1,856	1,843	1,847	1,869	1,858
Pennsylvania...........................	1,235	1,228	1,220	1,205	1,194	1,200	1,210	1,205
Rhode Island...........................	107	104	102	99	98	98	98	98
Vermont	66	65	64	63	63	62	68	62
Midwest	7,439	7,425	7,405	7,359	7,373	7,362	7,349	7,359
Illinois....................................	1,484	1,480	1,478	1,473	1,479	1,464	1,455	1,453
Indiana	720	724	730	730	730	731	729	725
Iowa	324	326	326	330	336	341	348	350
Kansas	321	321	326	327	331	333	343	347
Michigan	1,212	1,191	1,171	1,137	1,119	1,115	1,076	1,071
Minnesota	558	558	558	558	560	565	570	576
Missouri	629	635	634	632	635	638	643	645
Nebraska	195	195	196	200	203	207	210	214
North Dakota...........................	67	66	64	63	64	65	66	68
Ohio	1,267	1,261	1,253	1,241	1,239	1,225	1,223	1,217
South Dakota	84	84	83	83	87	86	88	91
Wisconsin	578	584	585	585	590	593	598	603
South	12,780	12,882	12,990	13,086	13,167	13,301	13,435	13,578
Alabama..................................	522	529	529	527	528	529	534	527
Arkansas.................................	328	336	337	340	342	344	346	346
Delaware	84	85	85	85	87	88	90	91
District of Columbia..................	57	56	52	56	51	52	54	56
Florida....................................	1,858	1,873	1,867	1,856	1,849	1,851	1,858	1,876
Georgia...................................	1,118	1,145	1,167	1,179	1,186	1,195	1,202	1,211
Kentucky	486	487	487	469	472	484	480	488
Louisiana	534	482	492	500	504	510	512	519
Maryland	597	589	579	576	576	582	588	594
Mississippi	361	358	356	354	352	352	351	353
North Carolina	986	1,003	1,027	1,072	1,059	1,054	1,058	1,074
Oklahoma	453	457	460	463	468	477	483	490
South Carolina	504	498	501	505	508	512	516	519
Tennessee...............................	671	677	692	682	685	687	702	713
Texas	3,184	3,268	3,320	3,375	3,447	3,520	3,587	3,637
Virginia...................................	840	841	842	850	855	864	871	881
West Virginia...........................	198	197	198	199	199	200	201	202
West.......................................	8,270	8,274	8,267	8,256	8,269	8,253	8,300	8,357
Alaska	92	91	90	89	89	91	92	92
Arizona...................................	722	740	760	771	772	760	752	759
California.................................	4,507	4,466	4,410	4,329	4,306	4,264	4,294	4,308
Colorado	541	550	559	566	580	591	601	611
Hawaii	129	127	126	126	126	127	128	131
Idaho......................................	178	183	187	191	194	195	194	198
Montana..................................	99	98	97	96	97	98	98	100
Nevada...................................	289	296	303	308	308	306	307	309
New Mexico	228	230	230	230	231	235	239	239
Oregon	377	380	381	384	395	404	393	391
Utah	355	358	371	410	404	413	425	435
Washington	695	699	695	697	705	705	714	718
Wyoming.................................	57	57	58	59	61	62	63	64

See notes at end of table.

Table 8. Actual and projected numbers for enrollment in grades preK–8 in public schools, by region and state: Fall 2004 through fall 2022—Continued

[In thousands]

Region and state	Projected										
	2012	2013	2014	2015	2016	2017	2018	2019	2020	2021	2022
1	10	11	12	13	14	15	16	17	18	19	20
United States	**34,953**	**35,145**	**35,328**	**35,557**	**35,843**	**36,129**	**36,432**	**36,747**	**37,067**	**37,385**	**37,696**
Northeast	5,474	5,472	5,471	5,477	5,493	5,504	5,518	5,542	5,569	5,596	5,622
Connecticut	380	378	377	377	378	378	381	383	387	390	393
Maine	130	131	131	132	133	134	135	136	136	137	137
Massachusetts	663	661	658	657	656	655	656	657	660	663	668
New Hampshire	128	128	127	128	128	129	130	132	134	136	138
New Jersey	944	940	938	936	936	936	936	939	944	949	954
New York	1,861	1,865	1,866	1,870	1,875	1,876	1,879	1,883	1,889	1,895	1,900
Pennsylvania	1,207	1,208	1,210	1,215	1,222	1,229	1,234	1,241	1,248	1,254	1,258
Rhode Island	97	98	99	99	99	100	101	102	103	104	104
Vermont	63	63	64	65	65	66	67	68	69	70	70
Midwest	7,364	7,373	7,380	7,388	7,409	7,430	7,445	7,473	7,499	7,521	7,539
Illinois	1,457	1,459	1,460	1,460	1,461	1,461	1,460	1,465	1,469	1,473	1,477
Indiana	722	719	716	712	712	712	713	716	719	722	726
Iowa	352	353	354	355	356	356	356	356	355	354	353
Kansas	349	351	353	354	356	356	357	358	359	360	361
Michigan	1,063	1,057	1,052	1,049	1,050	1,052	1,053	1,058	1,063	1,066	1,068
Minnesota	584	592	600	609	618	627	635	643	652	661	668
Missouri	646	647	648	650	653	656	658	660	663	664	666
Nebraska	216	218	220	221	222	222	222	222	222	222	222
North Dakota	68	69	71	71	72	72	72	72	72	72	72
Ohio	1,213	1,208	1,203	1,199	1,197	1,195	1,193	1,193	1,193	1,192	1,191
South Dakota	91	92	93	94	95	96	96	96	96	96	96
Wisconsin	605	608	611	614	619	623	627	632	635	638	641
South	13,682	13,784	13,868	13,962	14,081	14,208	14,346	14,478	14,615	14,757	14,902
Alabama	525	522	518	515	514	513	513	512	512	512	512
Arkansas	346	346	346	346	346	346	346	347	347	349	350
Delaware	92	93	94	95	96	97	98	98	99	99	100
District of Columbia	55	56	55	55	55	55	55	54	54	53	52
Florida	1,893	1,909	1,928	1,948	1,977	2,010	2,042	2,076	2,110	2,145	2,179
Georgia	1,216	1,221	1,225	1,231	1,240	1,252	1,265	1,278	1,292	1,306	1,321
Kentucky	489	489	488	486	485	484	483	482	482	481	481
Louisiana	520	521	518	516	514	513	511	508	506	503	500
Maryland	601	610	618	629	639	649	660	670	681	691	701
Mississippi	352	351	348	346	345	343	341	339	336	334	331
North Carolina	1,080	1,086	1,092	1,098	1,107	1,118	1,140	1,155	1,173	1,193	1,214
Oklahoma	492	495	497	498	500	500	501	501	502	502	503
South Carolina	523	526	528	530	533	536	539	541	544	546	549
Tennessee	717	720	723	726	731	737	743	748	755	763	771
Texas	3,693	3,745	3,791	3,837	3,886	3,935	3,983	4,032	4,079	4,127	4,174
Virginia	887	895	901	909	919	928	938	949	960	971	983
West Virginia	201	200	197	196	193	191	189	186	183	181	179
West	8,433	8,517	8,610	8,730	8,859	8,988	9,124	9,255	9,384	9,511	9,633
Alaska	94	95	97	99	102	104	107	109	111	114	116
Arizona	774	789	805	821	838	856	873	893	912	933	953
California	4,333	4,364	4,402	4,463	4,528	4,595	4,665	4,727	4,789	4,847	4,902
Colorado	619	627	634	641	647	652	659	665	672	679	687
Hawaii	131	132	132	133	133	133	133	133	133	133	132
Idaho	202	205	208	211	215	218	221	223	225	227	228
Montana	100	101	102	103	104	104	104	105	105	105	105
Nevada	313	317	323	328	335	343	352	362	373	384	395
New Mexico	242	244	246	247	249	250	251	252	252	251	251
Oregon	393	396	400	404	410	416	422	429	436	442	449
Utah	443	451	458	464	471	476	481	486	490	495	501
Washington	724	730	738	748	760	774	788	804	820	835	851
Wyoming	65	66	67	67	68	67	67	67	66	65	64

NOTE: PreK = prekindergarten. Some data have been revised from previously published figures. Detail may not sum to totals because of rounding. Mean absolute percentage errors of preK–8 enrollment in public schools by state and region can be found in table A-8, appendix A.

SOURCE: U.S. Department of Education, National Center for Education Statistics, Common Core of Data (CCD), "State Nonfiscal Survey of Public Elementary/Secondary Education," 2004–05 through 2011–12; and State Public Elementary and Secondary Enrollment Model, 1980–2011. (This table was prepared February 2013.)

Table 9. Actual and projected percentage changes in grades preK–8 enrollment in public schools, by region and state: Fall 2004 through fall 2022

Region and state	Actual 2004–2011	Projected 2011–2017	Projected 2017–2022	Projected 2011–2022
1	2	3	4	5
United States	1.7	3.9	4.3	8.4
Northeast	-3.7	0.4	2.2	2.6
Connecticut	-5.1	-1.3	3.9	2.6
Maine	-4.6	3.4	1.7	5.2
Massachusetts	-2.3	-1.6	1.9	0.2
New Hampshire	-7.6	-0.4	6.7	6.2
New Jersey	-2.9	-1.3	1.9	0.6
New York	-4.4	1.0	1.3	2.3
Pennsylvania	-2.4	2.0	2.4	4.4
Rhode Island	-8.8	2.4	4.4	6.9
Vermont	-5.7	6.7	6.2	13.3
Midwest	-1.1	1.0	1.5	2.5
Illinois	-2.1	0.6	1.1	1.6
Indiana	0.6	-1.7	1.9	0.2
Iowa	8.0	1.8	-1.1	0.7
Kansas	8.1	2.8	1.0	3.9
Michigan	-11.6	-1.8	1.5	-0.3
Minnesota	3.1	8.9	6.6	16.1
Missouri	2.7	1.6	1.6	3.2
Nebraska	9.6	4.1	-0.1	4.1
North Dakota	1.1	6.8	-1.1	5.6
Ohio	-3.9	-1.8	-0.3	-2.2
South Dakota	7.9	5.6	0.2	5.8
Wisconsin	4.3	3.4	2.8	6.3
South	6.2	4.6	4.9	9.7
Alabama	1.0	-2.6	-0.2	-2.8
Arkansas	5.4	-0.1	1.4	1.3
Delaware	8.4	6.7	3.3	10.2
District of Columbia	-1.6	-1.6	-5.7	-7.2
Florida	1.0	7.1	8.4	16.2
Georgia	8.3	3.4	5.5	9.1
Kentucky	0.5	-0.8	-0.6	-1.5
Louisiana	-2.8	-1.2	-2.4	-3.6
Maryland	-0.5	9.3	7.9	17.9
Mississippi	-2.2	-2.7	-3.5	-6.1
North Carolina	9.0	4.1	8.6	13.0
Oklahoma	8.2	2.1	0.6	2.7
South Carolina	3.0	3.3	2.3	5.7
Tennessee	6.2	3.4	4.6	8.1
Texas	14.2	8.2	6.1	14.8
Virginia	4.9	5.4	5.9	11.5
West Virginia	2.3	-5.4	-6.3	-11.4
West	1.1	7.6	7.2	15.3
Alaska	0.1	13.1	11.0	25.5
Arizona	5.2	12.6	11.4	25.5
California	-4.4	6.6	6.7	13.8
Colorado	13.0	6.8	5.2	12.4
Hawaii	1.7	1.8	-0.7	1.1
Idaho	11.1	10.0	4.8	15.3
Montana	1.1	4.4	0.4	4.8
Nevada	7.1	10.9	15.2	27.7
New Mexico	5.1	4.4	0.2	4.6
Oregon	3.8	6.2	8.0	14.7
Utah	22.3	9.5	5.2	15.2
Washington	3.3	7.7	10.0	18.5
Wyoming	11.8	5.4	-4.5	0.6

NOTE: PreK = prekindergarten. Calculations are based on unrounded numbers. Mean absolute percentage errors of preK–8 enrollment in public schools by state and region can be found in table A-8, appendix A.

SOURCE: U.S. Department of Education, National Center for Education Statistics, Common Core of Data (CCD), "State Nonfiscal Survey of Public Elementary/Secondary Education," selected years, 2004–05 through 2011–12; and State Public Elementary and Secondary Enrollment Model, 1980–2011. (This table was prepared February 2013.)

This page intentionally left blank.

Table 10. Actual and projected numbers for enrollment in grades 9–12 in public schools, by region and state: Fall 2004 through fall 2022

[In thousands]

Region and state	Actual							
	2004	2005	2006	2007	2008	2009	2010	2011
1	2	3	4	5	6	7	8	9
United States	**14,618**	**14,909**	**15,081**	**15,087**	**14,980**	**14,952**	**14,860**	**14,749**
Northeast......................	2,582	2,617	2,684	2,618	2,577	2,598	2,531	2,475
Connecticut..............................	173	175	177	177	175	174	173	171
Maine	63	62	62	66	64	61	60	59
Massachusetts..........................	293	297	298	296	292	291	289	287
New Hampshire	67	67	67	66	65	64	63	62
New Jersey	417	425	425	428	425	428	421	409
New York..................................	894	907	922	909	898	919	866	847
Pennsylvania............................	593	603	651	597	581	586	584	567
Rhode Island............................	49	50	50	48	47	47	46	45
Vermont	32	32	32	31	31	29	29	28
Midwest	3,337	3,394	3,415	3,411	3,370	3,310	3,260	3,215
Illinois......................................	614	631	641	640	641	640	637	630
Indiana	301	311	316	317	316	316	318	316
Iowa	154	157	157	156	152	151	148	146
Kansas	148	147	143	142	140	141	141	139
Michigan	540	551	552	556	541	534	511	503
Minnesota	280	281	282	279	276	272	268	264
Missouri	277	283	286	285	282	280	276	271
Nebraska	91	92	92	91	90	89	88	88
North Dakota............................	33	33	32	32	31	30	30	30
Ohio	573	578	584	586	578	539	531	523
South Dakota	39	38	38	38	39	38	38	37
Wisconsin	287	291	292	289	284	279	274	268
South	5,112	5,221	5,304	5,338	5,324	5,351	5,370	5,378
Alabama....................................	208	212	215	218	218	219	222	218
Arkansas	135	138	140	139	137	136	136	137
Delaware	35	36	37	38	39	39	39	38
District of Columbia..................	20	21	20	23	18	18	18	18
Florida	782	802	805	811	782	784	785	792
Georgia	435	453	463	471	470	473	475	474
Kentucky	189	192	196	197	198	196	193	194
Louisiana	191	172	184	181	181	181	184	185
Maryland	268	271	273	269	267	267	264	260
Mississippi	134	137	139	141	140	141	140	138
North Carolina	400	413	417	417	430	430	432	434
Oklahoma	177	178	179	179	177	178	176	176
South Carolina	199	204	207	208	211	211	210	208
Tennessee................................	270	277	286	283	287	286	286	287
Texas..	1,221	1,257	1,280	1,300	1,306	1,330	1,349	1,364
Virginia.....................................	365	372	379	380	381	381	380	377
West Virginia............................	83	84	84	84	83	82	81	81
West............................	3,587	3,677	3,678	3,720	3,710	3,692	3,698	3,681
Alaska	41	42	42	42	41	41	40	39
Arizona.....................................	321	355	309	316	316	317	320	321
California..................................	1,934	1,972	1,997	2,015	2,016	1,999	1,996	1,979
Colorado	225	230	235	236	238	241	242	243
Hawaii	54	55	55	54	54	53	52	52
Idaho..	78	79	80	81	81	82	82	82
Montana....................................	48	48	47	46	45	44	43	43
Nevada.....................................	111	116	122	122	125	123	130	130
New Mexico	98	97	98	99	99	99	99	98
Oregon......................................	176	173	182	182	180	178	178	177
Utah..	148	151	152	166	155	158	161	164
Washington...............................	325	333	332	333	332	330	330	327
Wyoming...................................	27	27	27	27	27	26	26	26

See notes at end of table.

Table 10. Actual and projected numbers for enrollment in grades 9–12 in public schools, by region and state: Fall 2004 through fall 2022—Continued

[In thousands]

Region and state	Projected										
	2012	2013	2014	2015	2016	2017	2018	2019	2020	2021	2022
1	10	11	12	13	14	15	16	17	18	19	20
United States	**14,684**	**14,639**	**14,689**	**14,771**	**14,811**	**14,870**	**14,903**	**14,960**	**15,057**	**15,149**	**15,255**
Northeast	2,431	2,393	2,377	2,371	2,361	2,365	2,366	2,361	2,361	2,354	2,350
Connecticut	169	166	164	163	160	159	158	156	155	154	154
Maine	58	57	57	57	56	56	56	56	57	57	58
Massachusetts	286	285	284	284	282	282	282	280	279	277	275
New Hampshire	61	60	59	58	57	57	56	55	55	55	55
New Jersey	402	397	392	389	386	386	387	384	382	379	376
New York	830	814	812	812	813	820	821	823	825	822	821
Pennsylvania	553	545	542	541	539	539	539	539	541	543	544
Rhode Island	45	43	41	42	41	42	43	43	42	42	42
Vermont	27	26	26	25	25	25	25	25	25	25	25
Midwest	3,193	3,173	3,173	3,191	3,190	3,193	3,198	3,186	3,186	3,187	3,185
Illinois	630	625	626	633	638	641	646	643	640	637	633
Indiana	315	314	312	315	314	312	310	305	302	301	300
Iowa	145	145	145	146	146	147	147	148	150	150	151
Kansas	139	139	140	142	143	144	145	146	147	147	148
Michigan	495	489	485	484	478	473	468	460	457	455	454
Minnesota	262	261	263	266	269	273	278	281	286	289	291
Missouri	270	270	270	270	268	268	267	268	269	271	272
Nebraska	88	87	88	89	91	93	95	96	97	97	97
North Dakota	30	30	29	29	30	30	31	32	33	33	33
Ohio	516	512	512	514	512	510	507	503	500	497	496
South Dakota	37	37	37	37	37	38	38	39	40	41	41
Wisconsin	265	264	264	265	265	265	265	265	266	268	269
South	5,408	5,441	5,509	5,581	5,625	5,660	5,672	5,699	5,742	5,787	5,840
Alabama	216	215	216	217	215	213	210	208	207	207	206
Arkansas	138	139	140	141	141	142	142	142	141	141	141
Delaware	37	37	37	38	38	39	40	40	41	41	41
District of Columbia	17	17	17	16	16	16	16	16	16	16	16
Florida	801	805	812	818	819	818	820	823	834	846	859
Georgia	478	483	489	495	496	495	492	491	493	496	501
Kentucky	193	192	194	197	198	198	198	197	197	197	196
Louisiana	186	187	190	194	196	197	196	195	195	195	194
Maryland	257	254	253	253	255	259	263	268	271	274	278
Mississippi	136	135	136	137	137	135	134	134	134	134	133
North Carolina	435	439	445	452	457	460	451	452	453	454	464
Oklahoma	177	179	182	185	186	188	190	192	193	194	194
South Carolina	208	209	211	216	217	217	218	218	220	222	223
Tennessee	288	290	295	299	301	302	302	303	305	306	308
Texas	1,385	1,406	1,434	1,463	1,490	1,513	1,531	1,549	1,569	1,589	1,608
Virginia	375	374	377	381	384	387	390	392	395	398	401
West Virginia	80	80	80	80	80	80	80	80	79	78	77
West	3,652	3,633	3,631	3,628	3,635	3,652	3,668	3,713	3,768	3,820	3,880
Alaska	38	38	38	38	38	39	39	39	40	41	42
Arizona	315	312	312	317	322	329	336	342	348	354	361
California	1,954	1,930	1,913	1,887	1,876	1,871	1,867	1,893	1,921	1,949	1,982
Colorado	246	248	253	258	263	269	273	276	279	280	283
Hawaii	51	51	51	51	51	52	52	53	53	53	53
Idaho	82	83	84	86	87	88	89	91	93	95	96
Montana	42	42	42	42	42	43	43	43	44	44	45
Nevada	130	130	131	133	135	135	136	137	138	141	144
New Mexico	97	98	99	100	101	101	102	103	104	105	106
Oregon	177	177	177	178	178	178	178	178	180	182	184
Utah	168	173	180	185	189	193	197	201	205	208	211
Washington	325	324	325	326	325	326	327	328	332	336	342
Wyoming	26	26	27	27	28	28	29	29	30	30	31

NOTE: Some data have been revised from previously published figures. Detail may not sum to totals because of rounding. Mean absolute percentage errors of grades 9–12 enrollment in public schools by state and region can be found in table A-9, appendix A.

SOURCE: U.S. Department of Education, National Center for Education Statistics, Common Core of Data (CCD), "State Nonfiscal Survey of Public Elementary/Secondary Education," 2004–05 through 2011–12; and State Public Elementary and Secondary Enrollment Model, 1980–2011. (This table was prepared February 2013.)

Table 11. Actual and projected percentage changes in grades 9–12 enrollment in public schools, by region and state: Fall 2004 through fall 2022

Region and state	Actual 2004–2011	Projected 2011–2017	Projected 2017–2022	Projected 2011–2022
1	2	3	4	5
United States	**0.9**	**0.8**	**2.6**	**3.4**
Northeast	-4.2	-4.5	-0.6	-5.0
Connecticut	-1.2	-6.8	-3.3	-9.9
Maine	-5.8	-5.1	3.4	-1.9
Massachusetts	-2.2	-1.7	-2.6	-4.3
New Hampshire	-6.5	-9.1	-3.5	-12.3
New Jersey	-2.1	-5.7	-2.5	-8.0
New York	-5.2	-3.2	0.2	-3.1
Pennsylvania	-4.5	-4.9	1.0	-4.0
Rhode Island	-8.6	-6.7	0.6	-6.1
Vermont	-14.4	-11.0	3.0	-8.3
Midwest	-3.6	-0.7	-0.3	-0.9
Illinois	2.6	1.8	-1.3	0.5
Indiana	4.9	-1.3	-3.9	-5.1
Iowa	-5.5	0.8	2.6	3.5
Kansas	-6.1	3.7	2.6	6.4
Michigan	-6.8	-6.0	-4.0	-9.8
Minnesota	-5.7	3.2	6.9	10.3
Missouri	-2.0	-1.3	1.4	0.1
Nebraska	-3.5	5.7	4.7	10.6
North Dakota	-10.9	1.1	10.9	12.1
Ohio	-8.8	-2.4	-2.8	-5.2
South Dakota	-3.6	0.8	9.7	10.5
Wisconsin	-6.5	-1.3	1.6	0.3
South	5.2	5.3	3.2	8.6
Alabama	4.4	-2.1	-3.1	-5.1
Arkansas	1.6	3.2	-0.7	2.5
Delaware	8.0	2.4	4.8	7.3
District of Columbia	-9.6	-9.8	2.4	-7.6
Florida	1.3	3.3	4.9	8.4
Georgia	8.9	4.4	1.2	5.6
Kentucky	2.4	2.2	-0.7	1.5
Louisiana	-3.1	6.8	-1.6	5.1
Maryland	-3.1	-0.2	7.3	7.1
Mississippi	2.5	-1.6	-1.7	-3.3
North Carolina	8.4	6.1	0.9	7.0
Oklahoma	-0.3	7.1	3.0	10.3
South Carolina	4.2	4.6	2.6	7.3
Tennessee	6.2	5.2	2.0	7.3
Texas	11.7	11.0	6.3	18.0
Virginia	3.2	2.7	3.5	6.3
West Virginia	-2.1	-1.1	-3.5	-4.6
West	2.6	-0.8	6.2	5.4
Alaska	-4.6	-1.4	10.2	8.6
Arizona	-0.1	2.6	9.7	12.6
California	2.3	-5.5	6.0	0.2
Colorado	8.0	10.5	5.1	16.1
Hawaii	-5.0	0.3	2.9	3.2
Idaho	5.1	7.7	9.4	17.8
Montana	-11.3	-0.1	4.5	4.5
Nevada	17.0	4.0	6.3	10.5
New Mexico	-0.5	3.8	4.0	8.0
Oregon	0.8	0.6	3.6	4.2
Utah	10.9	17.4	9.4	28.4
Washington	0.8	-0.4	4.8	4.4
Wyoming	-5.1	7.8	9.1	17.7

NOTE: Calculations are based on unrounded numbers. Mean absolute percentage errors of grades 9–12 enrollment in public schools by state and region can be found in table A-9, appendix A.

SOURCE: U.S. Department of Education, National Center for Education Statistics, Common Core of Data (CCD), "State Nonfiscal Survey of Public Elementary/Secondary Education," selected years, 2004–05 through 2011–12; and State Public Elementary and Secondary Enrollment Model, 1980–2011. (This table was prepared February 2013.)

Table 12. Actual and projected numbers for high school graduates, by control of school: School years 1997–98 through 2022–23

School year	Total	Public	Private
1	2	3	4
Actual			
1997–98[1]	2,704,133	2,439,050	265,083
1998–99	2,758,655	2,485,630	273,025
1999–2000[1]	2,832,656	2,553,844	278,812
2000–01	2,847,973	2,569,200	278,773
2001–02[1]	2,906,287	2,621,534	284,753
2002–03	3,015,702	2,719,947	295,755
2003–04[1]	3,054,247	2,753,438	300,809
2004–05	3,106,499	2,799,250	307,249
2005–06[1]	3,119,258	2,815,544	303,714
2006–07	3,199,650	2,893,045	306,605
2007–08[1]	3,312,870	3,001,337	311,533
2008–09	3,347,828	3,039,015	308,813
2009–10[1]	3,440,185	3,128,022	312,163
2010–11[2]	3,427,470	3,121,630	305,840
Projected			
2011–12	3,408,360	3,103,680	304,680
2012–13	3,408,590	3,110,140	298,450
2013–14	3,365,530	3,070,410	295,120
2014–15	3,322,730	3,031,410	291,320
2015–16	3,322,610	3,047,810	274,800
2016–17	3,328,740	3,066,370	262,370
2017–18	3,366,110	3,106,010	260,100
2018–19	3,348,670	3,100,960	247,710
2019–20	3,326,640	3,085,660	240,980
2020–21	3,352,730	3,115,190	237,540
2021–22	3,360,260	3,130,440	229,820
2022–23	3,369,470	3,146,620	222,850

[1]Since the biennial Private School Universe Survey (PSS) is collected in the fall of odd-numbered years and the numbers collected for high school graduates are for the preceding year, private school numbers for odd years are estimated based on data from the PSS.
[2]The number of high school graduates in public schools is a projection.
NOTE: Some data have been revised from previously published figures. Detail may not sum to totals because of rounding. Mean absolute percentage errors of selected education statistics can be found in table A-2, appendix A.

SOURCE: U.S. Department of Education, National Center for Education Statistics, Common Core of Data (CCD), "State Nonfiscal Survey of Public Elementary/Secondary Education," 1998–99 through 2010–11; Private School Universe Survey (PSS), selected years, 1999–2000 through 2011–12; and National High School Graduates Model, 1972–73 through 2010–11. (This table was prepared February 2013.)

Table 13. Actual and projected numbers for public high school graduates, by race/ethnicity: School years 1997–98 through 2022–23

School year	Total	Race/ethnicity				
		White	Black	Hispanic	Asian/ Pacific Islander	American Indian/ Alaska Native
1	2	3	4	5	6	7
Actual						
1997–98	2,439,050	1,733,478	317,846	252,023	112,089	23,614
1998–99	2,485,630	1,754,617	322,532	268,539	115,930	24,012
1999–2000	2,553,844	1,787,322	334,206	283,738	123,231	25,347
2000–01	2,569,200	1,782,294	336,375	297,696	126,847	25,988
2001–02	2,621,534	1,801,175	345,854	314,989	132,347	27,169
2002–03	2,719,947	1,857,954	359,051	339,555	135,614	27,773
2003–04	2,753,438	1,851,136	373,307	362,467	137,913	28,615
2004–05	2,799,250	1,856,760	385,180	382,964	143,751	30,595
2005–06	2,815,544	1,854,776	392,180	388,718	150,567	29,303
2006–07	2,893,045	1,884,020	412,698	410,587	154,935	30,805
2007–08	3,001,337	1,917,973	435,569	454,057	161,434	32,304
2008–09[1]	3,039,015	1,901,056	456,049	484,844	164,656	32,410
2009–10[2]	3,128,022	1,895,225	478,024	550,769	169,523	34,481
Projected						
2010–11	3,121,630	1,846,330	479,820	594,080	169,080	32,330
2011–12	3,103,680	1,811,480	472,300	615,890	172,140	31,870
2012–13	3,110,140	1,793,610	464,310	644,120	177,890	30,220
2013–14	3,070,410	1,757,870	447,580	657,250	178,870	28,850
2014–15	3,031,410	1,716,540	438,520	670,690	178,640	27,020
2015–16	3,047,810	1,709,560	442,150	690,440	178,070	27,600
2016–17	3,066,370	1,704,320	437,870	714,930	181,350	27,910
2017–18	3,106,010	1,695,690	440,830	749,540	192,860	27,090
2018–19	3,100,960	1,673,960	431,160	776,910	192,410	26,520
2019–20	3,085,660	1,639,240	421,150	802,630	196,800	25,840
2020–21	3,115,190	1,638,590	414,910	831,070	205,480	25,130
2021–22	3,130,440	1,625,420	410,040	861,090	209,030	24,870
2022–23	3,146,620	1,600,970	410,360	902,410	208,310	24,570

[1]In the 2008–09 school year, five states reported high school graduate counts for graduates of two or more races. These high school graduate counts were proportioned across the other racial/ethnic categories. When more complete sets of data for high school graduates of two or more races are compiled, separate projections for that category will be presented.
[2]The high school graduate numbers by race/ethnicity for 2009–10 are projected numbers.
NOTE: Some data have been revised from previously published figures. Detail may not sum to totals because of rounding. The historical racial/ethnic time-series were constructed using racial/ethnic high school graduate data at the state level. In some instances, high school graduate data by race/ethnicity had to be imputed. Further, in some instances, the racial/ethnic

data had to be adjusted in order for them to sum to the state total for high school graduates. Race categories exclude persons of Hispanic ethnicity. For additional information see the High School Graduates section A.2 in appendix A. Mean absolute percentage errors of selected education statistics can be found in table A-2, appendix A.
SOURCE: U.S. Department of Education, National Center for Education Statistics, Common Core of Data (CCD), "State Nonfiscal Survey of Public Elementary/Secondary Education," 1998–99 through 2010–11; and National Public High School Graduates by Race/Ethnicity Model, 1995–96 through 2008–09. (This table was prepared February 2013.)

This page intentionally left blank.

Table 14. Actual and projected numbers for public high school graduates, by region and state: School years 2004–05 through 2022–23

Region and state	Actual					
	2004–05	2005–06	2006–07	2007–08	2008–09	2009–10
1	2	3	4	5	6	7
United States	2,799,250	2,815,544	2,893,045	3,001,337	3,039,015	3,128,022
Northeast	503,528	521,015	536,697	552,289	552,973	556,400
Connecticut	35,515	36,222	37,541	38,419	34,968	34,495
Maine	13,077	12,950	13,151	14,350	14,093	14,069
Massachusetts	59,665	61,272	63,903	65,197	65,258	64,462
New Hampshire	13,775	13,988	14,452	14,982	14,757	15,034
New Jersey	86,502	90,049	93,013	94,994	95,085	96,225
New York	153,203	161,817	168,333	176,310	180,917	183,826
Pennsylvania	124,758	127,830	128,603	130,298	130,658	131,182
Rhode Island	9,881	10,108	10,384	10,347	10,028	9,908
Vermont	7,152	6,779	7,317	7,392	7,209	7,199
Midwest	676,786	684,049	702,987	721,220	717,536	726,844
Illinois	123,615	126,817	130,220	135,143	131,670	139,035
Indiana	55,444	57,920	59,887	61,901	63,663	64,551
Iowa	33,547	33,693	34,127	34,573	33,926	34,462
Kansas	30,355	29,818	30,139	30,737	30,368	31,642
Michigan	101,582	102,582	111,838	115,183	112,742	110,682
Minnesota	58,391	58,898	59,497	60,409	59,729	59,667
Missouri	57,841	58,417	60,275	61,717	62,969	63,994
Nebraska	19,940	19,764	19,873	20,035	19,501	19,370
North Dakota	7,555	7,192	7,159	6,999	7,232	7,155
Ohio	116,702	117,356	117,658	120,758	122,203	123,437
South Dakota	8,585	8,589	8,346	8,582	8,123	8,162
Wisconsin	63,229	63,003	63,968	65,183	65,410	64,687
South	953,206	962,327	986,801	1,031,773	1,068,270	1,104,770
Alabama	37,453	37,918	38,912	41,346	42,082	43,166
Arkansas	26,621	28,790	27,166	28,725	28,057	28,276
Delaware	6,934	7,275	7,205	7,388	7,839	8,133
District of Columbia	2,781	3,150	2,944	3,352	3,517	3,602
Florida	133,318	134,686	142,284	149,046	153,461	156,130
Georgia	70,834	73,498	77,829	83,505	88,003	91,561
Kentucky	38,399	38,449	39,099	39,339	41,851	42,664
Louisiana	36,009	33,275	34,274	34,401	35,622	36,573
Maryland	54,170	55,536	57,564	59,171	58,304	59,078
Mississippi	23,523	23,848	24,186	24,795	24,505	25,478
North Carolina	75,010	76,710	76,031	83,307	86,712	88,704
Oklahoma	36,227	36,497	37,100	37,630	37,219	38,503
South Carolina	33,439	34,970	35,108	35,303	39,114	40,438
Tennessee	47,967	50,880	54,502	57,486	60,368	62,408
Texas	239,717	240,485	241,193	252,121	264,275	280,894
Virginia	73,667	69,597	73,997	77,369	79,651	81,511
West Virginia	17,137	16,763	17,407	17,489	17,690	17,651
West	665,730	648,153	666,560	696,055	700,236	740,008
Alaska	6,909	7,361	7,666	7,855	8,008	8,245
Arizona	59,498	54,091	55,954	61,667	62,374	61,145
California	355,217	343,515	356,641	374,561	372,310	404,987
Colorado	44,532	44,424	45,628	46,082	47,459	49,321
Hawaii	10,813	10,922	11,063	11,613	11,508	10,998
Idaho	15,768	16,096	16,242	16,567	16,807	17,793
Montana	10,335	10,283	10,122	10,396	10,077	10,075
Nevada	15,740	16,455	17,149	18,815	19,904	20,956
New Mexico	17,353	17,822	16,131	18,264	17,931	18,595
Oregon	32,602	32,394	33,446	34,949	35,138	34,671
Utah	30,253	29,050	28,276	28,167	30,463	31,481
Washington	61,094	60,213	62,801	61,625	62,764	66,046
Wyoming	5,616	5,527	5,441	5,494	5,493	5,695

See notes at end of table.

Table 14. **Actual and projected numbers for public high school graduates, by region and state: School years 2004–05 through 2022–23—Continued**

Region and state	Projected												
	2010–11	2011–12	2012–13	2013–14	2014–15	2015–16	2016–17	2017–18	2018–19	2019–20	2020–21	2021–22	2022–23
1	8	9	10	11	12	13	14	15	16	17	18	19	20
United States	**3,121,630**	**3,103,680**	**3,110,140**	**3,070,410**	**3,031,410**	**3,047,810**	**3,066,370**	**3,106,010**	**3,100,960**	**3,085,660**	**3,115,190**	**3,130,440**	**3,146,620**
Northeast	556,050	547,550	541,790	524,560	511,640	510,350	507,520	509,230	506,200	501,740	509,280	508,810	502,760
Connecticut	36,910	36,290	35,820	35,200	34,280	34,300	33,790	33,420	33,080	32,330	32,960	32,090	31,800
Maine	14,040	13,650	13,250	12,850	12,660	12,810	12,610	12,560	12,490	12,330	12,350	12,580	12,740
Massachusetts	63,320	63,090	63,370	62,250	61,490	62,440	61,730	61,660	61,650	60,910	61,510	61,250	60,370
New Hampshire	14,330	14,230	14,160	13,770	13,710	13,450	13,170	12,980	12,690	12,660	12,460	12,410	12,030
New Jersey	94,280	91,100	90,870	88,030	86,950	86,110	85,340	83,940	84,400	83,260	84,200	84,430	81,870
New York	185,630	184,900	184,490	176,890	171,440	170,400	170,290	173,720	171,570	171,540	175,330	174,530	173,620
Pennsylvania	130,950	127,790	123,540	119,990	116,150	115,720	116,570	116,860	115,670	114,170	115,930	116,870	115,890
Rhode Island	9,730	9,820	9,810	9,430	9,020	9,220	8,190	8,460	9,000	8,980	8,950	9,040	8,800
Vermont	6,850	6,670	6,480	6,140	5,960	5,900	5,840	5,630	5,660	5,560	5,590	5,620	5,640
Midwest	702,910	691,940	689,850	678,520	664,430	672,330	671,900	678,090	680,600	672,400	675,100	681,670	671,610
Illinois	136,400	134,660	141,290	135,860	132,500	135,230	135,830	136,970	138,510	139,070	139,010	140,870	136,320
Indiana	65,750	65,090	65,670	66,570	64,860	64,520	64,640	65,190	66,750	63,860	63,170	63,550	62,040
Iowa	33,370	32,820	32,150	31,960	31,770	32,010	32,100	32,530	32,270	32,220	32,680	32,840	33,290
Kansas	31,120	30,470	30,790	30,220	29,650	30,530	30,740	31,200	31,370	31,230	31,900	31,840	32,150
Michigan	107,080	105,580	102,770	101,970	98,030	99,420	97,710	98,100	97,490	94,450	93,630	94,170	91,050
Minnesota	58,890	57,240	56,690	55,060	55,330	55,230	55,950	56,610	57,700	57,420	59,510	61,060	60,570
Missouri	62,170	60,760	60,190	59,720	58,810	59,990	59,360	59,780	59,310	58,480	58,820	59,220	59,680
Nebraska	19,230	19,320	19,450	19,470	18,990	19,150	19,360	19,940	20,180	20,600	20,870	21,510	21,350
North Dakota	7,060	6,840	6,830	6,720	6,660	6,790	6,730	6,480	6,790	6,870	7,180	7,520	7,560
Ohio	110,360	109,370	106,100	103,810	101,340	102,980	102,710	103,610	103,130	101,650	101,170	100,990	99,610
South Dakota	8,460	8,090	8,030	8,040	8,000	7,880	7,990	8,080	7,920	8,070	8,300	8,470	8,880
Wisconsin	63,020	61,710	59,890	59,140	58,500	58,610	58,780	59,590	59,180	58,480	58,850	59,640	59,120
South	1,107,200	1,104,730	1,121,490	1,118,200	1,116,330	1,130,470	1,146,240	1,172,090	1,178,000	1,171,250	1,177,880	1,181,630	1,198,830
Alabama	44,210	44,030	43,050	42,560	41,760	42,430	42,550	42,990	42,860	41,190	40,770	40,790	40,690
Arkansas	28,110	28,210	28,210	28,540	28,810	28,810	29,210	29,200	29,480	29,470	29,380	29,380	29,310
Delaware	8,220	8,320	8,140	7,950	7,820	7,610	7,770	7,970	8,160	8,100	8,560	8,380	8,510
District of Columbia	3,290	3,080	3,100	3,020	3,090	2,970	2,780	2,900	2,920	2,760	2,700	2,710	2,930
Florida	160,570	157,050	164,790	163,860	166,890	165,210	168,260	169,610	171,040	166,750	167,980	170,560	172,920
Georgia	93,410	91,780	92,890	93,770	93,390	95,300	96,430	98,350	98,220	96,670	95,860	96,180	96,930
Kentucky	41,540	41,750	41,700	40,130	39,350	40,700	40,790	41,730	42,250	41,120	41,190	41,470	41,690
Louisiana	34,330	34,920	35,510	36,510	34,150	35,870	35,850	38,490	37,580	37,260	37,350	37,140	37,190
Maryland	58,010	57,770	57,220	55,910	55,390	55,190	54,310	55,520	54,930	56,960	57,740	58,440	59,170
Mississippi	26,160	25,670	26,020	25,200	24,720	24,610	25,020	25,780	25,020	24,710	24,170	24,790	24,540
North Carolina	86,580	88,940	89,120	89,170	88,620	90,120	91,620	93,600	95,130	94,050	94,620	87,310	94,670
Oklahoma	37,830	37,660	37,520	37,310	37,330	38,740	39,100	39,580	39,800	40,130	40,790	40,820	41,430
South Carolina	40,050	40,050	39,830	39,420	38,580	39,680	40,250	41,410	41,760	40,980	40,850	41,490	42,100
Tennessee	62,880	63,080	62,670	61,490	61,780	63,430	64,650	65,570	65,750	65,110	65,410	65,730	66,530
Texas	282,670	282,960	292,560	295,600	298,360	302,280	309,670	319,290	323,230	325,870	330,110	334,350	338,510
Virginia	82,080	82,140	82,070	81,050	79,710	80,730	81,400	83,160	83,220	83,260	83,960	85,400	85,110
West Virginia	17,260	17,320	17,100	16,710	16,590	16,800	16,570	16,950	16,650	16,880	16,450	16,690	16,600
West	755,490	759,460	757,010	749,140	739,010	734,670	740,720	746,600	736,160	740,280	752,930	758,330	773,420
Alaska	7,750	7,970	7,230	7,210	7,100	7,050	7,280	7,260	7,240	7,180	7,350	7,480	7,650
Arizona	65,010	64,910	64,090	63,380	60,610	60,690	61,450	63,030	64,120	65,010	66,930	68,110	68,860
California	414,180	415,600	415,370	409,660	403,390	394,320	394,770	395,410	382,140	384,890	390,060	391,910	403,250
Colorado	51,000	51,430	52,150	52,110	52,180	53,280	54,290	55,930	56,830	57,640	59,260	58,980	59,700
Hawaii	11,090	11,360	11,000	10,900	10,630	10,790	10,960	11,070	10,530	11,050	11,190	11,170	11,310
Idaho	17,440	17,500	17,330	17,620	17,150	17,600	18,180	18,340	18,620	18,830	19,070	19,460	20,050
Montana	9,700	9,600	9,260	9,350	9,180	9,190	9,280	9,140	9,340	9,350	9,480	9,650	9,610
Nevada	23,460	24,360	24,350	23,820	23,630	24,030	24,580	24,560	25,240	25,130	25,000	25,100	25,570
New Mexico	18,900	18,980	18,470	18,130	18,310	18,280	18,850	18,980	19,140	19,170	19,190	19,440	19,580
Oregon	34,690	34,460	34,010	34,160	33,650	34,300	34,260	34,430	34,370	33,820	34,430	34,630	34,580
Utah	30,850	31,620	31,990	32,350	33,390	34,850	36,000	37,100	37,410	38,020	39,330	40,120	40,350
Washington	65,830	66,140	66,350	65,080	64,260	64,660	65,130	65,600	65,410	64,330	65,480	66,110	66,430
Wyoming	5,600	5,550	5,440	5,390	5,530	5,630	5,700	5,770	5,780	5,870	6,160	6,190	6,470

NOTE: Some data have been revised from previously published figures. Detail may not sum to totals because of rounding. Mean absolute percentage errors of public high school graduates by state and region can be found in table A-10, appendix A.

SOURCE: U.S. Department of Education, National Center for Education Statistics, Common Core of Data (CCD), "State Nonfiscal Survey of Public Elementary/Secondary Education," 2005–06 through 2010–11; and State Public High School Graduates Model, 1980–81 through 2009–10. (This table was prepared February 2013.)

Table 15. Actual and projected percentage changes in public high school graduates, by region and state: School years 2004–05 through 2022–23

Region and state	Actual 2004–05 to 2009–10	Projected		
		2009–10 to 2016–17	2016–17 to 2022–23	2009–10 to 2022–23
1	2	3	4	5
United States	**11.7**	**-2.0**	**2.6**	**0.6**
Northeast	10.5	-8.8	-0.9	-9.6
Connecticut	-2.9	-2.0	-5.9	-7.8
Maine	7.6	-10.4	1.0	-9.4
Massachusetts	8.0	-4.2	-2.2	-6.3
New Hampshire	9.1	-12.4	-8.7	-20.0
New Jersey	11.2	-11.3	-4.1	-14.9
New York	20.0	-7.4	2.0	-5.6
Pennsylvania	5.1	-11.1	-0.6	-11.7
Rhode Island	0.3	-17.3	7.4	-11.2
Vermont	0.7	-18.9	-3.4	-21.7
Midwest	7.4	-7.6	#	-7.6
Illinois	12.5	-2.3	0.4	-2.0
Indiana	16.4	0.1	-4.0	-3.9
Iowa	2.7	-6.9	3.7	-3.4
Kansas	4.2	-2.9	4.6	1.6
Michigan	9.0	-11.7	-6.8	-17.7
Minnesota	2.2	-6.2	8.3	1.5
Missouri	10.6	-7.2	0.5	-6.7
Nebraska	-2.9	-0.1	10.3	10.2
North Dakota	-5.3	-5.9	12.3	5.7
Ohio	5.8	-16.8	-3.0	-19.3
South Dakota	-4.9	-2.1	11.1	8.8
Wisconsin	2.3	-9.1	0.6	-8.6
South	15.9	3.8	4.6	8.5
Alabama	15.3	-1.4	-4.4	-5.7
Arkansas	6.2	3.3	0.3	3.7
Delaware	17.3	-4.5	9.5	4.6
District of Columbia	29.5	-22.8	5.4	-18.7
Florida	17.1	7.8	2.8	10.8
Georgia	29.3	5.3	2.8	5.9
Kentucky	11.1	-4.4	2.2	-2.3
Louisiana	1.6	-2.0	3.7	1.7
Maryland	9.1	-8.1	8.9	0.2
Mississippi	8.3	-1.8	-1.9	-3.7
North Carolina	18.3	3.3	3.3	6.7
Oklahoma	6.3	1.6	6.0	7.6
South Carolina	20.9	-0.5	4.6	4.1
Tennessee	30.1	3.6	2.9	6.6
Texas	17.2	10.2	9.3	20.5
Virginia	10.6	-0.1	4.6	4.4
West Virginia	3.0	-6.1	0.2	-6.0
West	11.2	0.1	4.4	4.5
Alaska	19.3	-11.7	5.1	-7.2
Arizona	2.8	0.5	12.1	12.6
California	14.0	-2.5	2.1	-0.4
Colorado	10.8	10.1	10.0	21.0
Hawaii	1.7	-0.3	3.2	2.8
Idaho	12.8	2.2	10.3	12.7
Montana	-2.5	-7.9	3.6	-4.6
Nevada	33.1	17.3	4.0	22.0
New Mexico	7.2	1.4	3.9	5.3
Oregon	6.3	-1.2	0.9	-0.3
Utah	4.1	14.4	12.1	28.2
Washington	8.1	-1.4	2.0	0.6
Wyoming	1.4	0.1	13.5	13.6

Rounds to zero.
NOTE: Calculations are based on unrounded numbers. Mean absolute percentage errors of public high school graduates by state and region can be found in table A-10, appendix A.

SOURCE: U.S. Department of Education, National Center for Education Statistics, Common Core of Data (CCD), "State Nonfiscal Survey of Public Elementary/Secondary Education," 2005–06 and 2010–11; and State Public High School Graduates Model, 1980–81 through 2009–10. (This table was prepared February 2013.)

Table 16. Actual and projected numbers for elementary and secondary teachers and elementary and secondary new teacher hires, by control of school: Fall 1997 through fall 2022

[In thousands]

Year	Number of teachers			Number of new teacher hires		
	Total	Control		Total	Control	
		Public	Private		Public	Private
1	2	3	4	5	6	7
Actual						
1997............................	3,138	2,746	391	—	—	—
1998[1]............................	3,230	2,830	400	—	—	—
1999............................	3,319	2,911	408	305	222	83
2000[1]............................	3,366	2,941	424	—	—	—
2001............................	3,440	3,000	441	—	—	—
2002[1]............................	3,476	3,034	442	—	—	—
2003............................	3,490	3,049	441	311	236	74
2004[1]............................	3,536	3,091	445	—	—	—
2005............................	3,593	3,143	450	—	—	—
2006[1]............................	3,619	3,166	453	—	—	—
2007............................	3,634	3,178	456	327	246	80
2008[1,2]............................	3,670	3,222	448	386	310	76
2009[2]............................	3,647	3,210	437	358	289	69
2010[1,2]............................	3,529	3,099	429	260	190	70
2011[2]............................	3,524	3,103	421	352	284	68
Projected						
2012............................	3,511	3,100	411	365	300	65
2013............................	3,514	3,109	405	370	303	67
2014............................	3,524	3,124	400	376	309	66
2015............................	3,577	3,177	400	419	348	71
2016............................	3,625	3,225	401	420	348	72
2017............................	3,676	3,273	403	424	351	73
2018............................	3,724	3,319	405	427	353	74
2019............................	3,773	3,365	408	432	357	75
2020............................	3,830	3,418	412	443	366	77
2021............................	3,881	3,465	416	444	367	78
2022............................	3,931	3,510	421	446	367	79

—Not available.

[1]Since the biennial Private School Universe Survey (PSS) is collected in the fall of odd numbered years, private school numbers for alternate years are estimated based on data from the PSS.

[2]Public and private new teacher hire numbers are estimated using the New Teacher Hires Model. For more information about the New Teacher Hires model, see appendix A.3.

NOTE: Number of teachers reported in full-time equivalents. Some data have been revised from previously published figures. Detail may not sum to totals because of rounding. Mean absolute percentage errors of selected education statistics can be found in table A-2, appendix A.

SOURCE: U.S. Department of Education, National Center for Education Statistics, Common Core of Data (CCD), "State Nonfiscal Survey of Public Elementary/Secondary Education," 1997–98 through 2011–12; Private School Universe Survey (PSS), selected years, 1997–98 through 2011–12; Schools and Staffing Survey (SASS), "Public School Teacher Questionnaire," 1999–2000 through 2007–08 and "Private School Teacher Questionnaire," 1999–2000 through 2007–08; Elementary and Secondary Teacher Model, 1973–2011; and New Teacher Hires Model, 1988–2007. (This table was prepared April 2013.)

Table 17. Actual and projected numbers for the pupil/teacher ratios in elementary and secondary schools, by control of school: Fall 1997 through fall 2022

Year	Total	Public	Private
1	2	3	4
Actual			
1997	16.6	16.8	15.2
1998[1]	16.3	16.4	15.0
1999	15.9	16.1	14.7
2000[1]	15.9	16.0	14.5
2001	15.7	15.9	14.3
2002[1]	15.7	15.9	14.1
2003	15.7	15.9	13.8
2004[1]	15.5	15.8	13.7
2005	15.4	15.6	13.5
2006[1]	15.3	15.6	13.2
2007	15.2	15.5	13.0
2008[1]	15.0	15.3	12.8
2009	15.0	15.4	12.5
2010[1]	15.5	16.0	12.5
2011	15.5	16.0	12.5
Projected			
2012	15.6	16.0	12.6
2013	15.6	16.0	12.6
2014	15.6	16.0	12.6
2015	15.5	15.8	12.5
2016	15.3	15.7	12.3
2017	15.2	15.6	12.2
2018	15.1	15.5	12.2
2019	15.0	15.4	12.1
2020	14.9	15.3	12.0
2021	14.8	15.2	11.9
2022	14.7	15.1	11.9

[1]Since the biennial Private School Universe Survey (PSS) is collected in the fall of odd numbered years, private school numbers for alternate years are estimated based on data from the PSS.
NOTE: The pupil/teacher ratios were derived from tables 1 and 16. Teachers reported in full-time equivalents. Some data have been revised from previously published figures. Mean absolute percentage errors of selected education statistics can be found in table A-2, appendix A.

SOURCE: U.S. Department of Education, National Center for Education Statistics, Common Core of Data (CCD), "State Nonfiscal Survey of Public Elementary/Secondary Education," 1997–98 through 2011–12; Private School Universe Survey (PSS), selected years, 1997–98 through 2011–12; National Elementary and Secondary Enrollment Model, 1972–2011; and Elementary and Secondary Teacher Model, 1973–2011. (This table was prepared April 2013.)

Table 18. Actual and projected numbers for current expenditures and current expenditures per pupil in fall enrollment for public elementary and secondary education: School years 1997–98 through 2022–23

School year	Fall enrollment (in thousands)	Current expenditures			
		Constant 2011–12 dollars[1]		Current dollars	
		Total (in billions)	Per pupil in fall enrollment	Total (in billions)	Per pupil in fall enrollment
1	2	3	4	5	6
Actual					
1997–98.............................	46,127	$401.7	$8,709	$285.5	$6,189
1998–99.............................	46,539	418.9	9,002	302.9	6,508
1999–2000.........................	46,857	435.4	9,293	323.9	6,912
2000–01.............................	47,204	452.9	9,595	348.4	7,380
2001–02.............................	47,672	470.6	9,871	368.4	7,727
2002–03.............................	48,183	484.5	10,055	387.6	8,044
2003–04.............................	48,540	493.3	10,163	403.4	8,310
2004–05.............................	48,795	504.6	10,342	425.0	8,711
2005–06.............................	49,113	513.8	10,462	449.1	9,145
2006–07[2].........................	49,262	531.7	10,793	476.8	9,679
2007–08[2].........................	49,221	545.0	11,073	506.9	10,298
2008–09[2].........................	49,235	550.2	11,175	518.9	10,540
2009–10[2].........................	49,463	551.7	11,154	525.4	10,623
Projected					
2010–11[3].........................	49,484	542.7	10,966	527.2	10,653
2011–12[3].........................	49,520	546.7	11,041	546.7	11,041
2012–13.............................	49,636	554.0	11,160	563.0	11,342
2013–14.............................	49,785	563.7	11,322	582.0	11,690
2014–15.............................	50,018	578.6	11,568	607.1	12,138
2015–16.............................	50,328	594.9	11,820	634.4	12,605
2016–17.............................	50,654	610.5	12,052	—	—
2017–18.............................	50,999	625.5	12,265	—	—
2018–19.............................	51,336	639.6	12,460	—	—
2019–20.............................	51,707	654.7	12,662	—	—
2020–21.............................	52,124	670.0	12,853	—	—
2021–22.............................	52,534	685.1	13,042	—	—
2022–23.............................	52,952	698.8	13,197	—	—

—Not available: projections in current dollars are not shown after 2015–16 due to uncertain behavior of inflation over time.

[1]Based on the Consumer Price Index (CPI) for all urban consumers, Bureau of Labor Statistics, U.S. Department of Labor. For more detail about CPI, see table B-6 in appendix B.

[2]Fall enrollment pertains only to students for whom finance data were collected. This enrollment count differs slightly from enrollment counts reported on other tables.

[3]The fall enrollment numbers for 2010–11 and 2011–12 are actual numbers.

NOTE: Calculations were made using unrounded numbers. Some data have been revised from previously published figures. Mean absolute percentage errors of selected education statistics can be found in table A-2, appendix A.

SOURCE: U.S. Department of Education, National Center for Education Statistics, Common Core of Data (CCD), "State Nonfiscal Survey of Public Elementary/Secondary Education," 1997–98 through 2011–12; "National Public Education Financial Survey," 1997–98 through 2009–10; National Elementary and Secondary Enrollment Model, 1972–2011; and Elementary and Secondary Education Current Expenditures Model, 1969–70 through 2009–10. (This table was prepared March 2013.)

Table 19. Actual and projected numbers for current expenditures and current expenditures per pupil in average daily attendance (ADA) for public elementary and secondary education: School years 1997–98 through 2022–23

School year	ADA (in thousands)	Current expenditures			
		Constant 2011–12 dollars[1]		Current dollars	
		Total (in billions)	Per pupil in ADA	Total (in billions)	Per pupil in ADA
1	2	3	4	5	6
Actual					
1997–98	42,766	$401.7	$9,393	$285.5	$6,676
1998–99	43,187	418.9	9,700	302.9	7,013
1999–2000	43,807	435.4	9,940	323.9	7,394
2000–01	44,076	452.9	10,275	348.4	7,904
2001–02	44,605	470.6	10,550	368.4	8,259
2002–03	45,017	484.5	10,762	387.6	8,610
2003–04	45,326	493.3	10,884	403.4	8,900
2004–05	45,625	504.6	11,061	425.0	9,316
2005–06	45,932	513.8	11,187	449.1	9,778
2006–07	46,133	531.7	11,525	476.8	10,336
2007–08	46,156	545.0	11,808	506.9	10,982
2008–09	46,173	550.2	11,916	518.9	11,239
2009–10	45,919	551.7	12,015	525.4	11,442
Projected					
2010–11	46,252	542.7	11,733	527.2	11,398
2011–12	46,286	546.7	11,812	546.7	11,812
2012–13	46,394	554.0	11,940	563.0	12,134
2013–14	46,533	563.7	12,113	582.0	12,507
2014–15	46,751	578.6	12,377	607.1	12,986
2015–16	47,040	594.9	12,647	634.4	13,486
2016–17	47,345	610.5	12,894	—	—
2017–18	47,668	625.5	13,122	—	—
2018–19	47,983	639.6	13,330	—	—
2019–20	48,330	654.7	13,546	—	—
2020–21	48,719	670.0	13,752	—	—
2021–22	49,102	685.1	13,953	—	—
2022–23	49,493	698.8	14,120	—	—

—Not available: projections in current dollars are not shown after 2015–16 due to uncertain behavior of inflation over time.

[1]Based on the Consumer Price Index (CPI) for all urban consumers, Bureau of Labor Statistics, U.S. Department of Labor. For more detail about CPI, see table B-6 in appendix B.

NOTE: Calculations were made using unrounded numbers. Some data have been revised from previously published figures. Mean absolute percentage errors of selected education statistics can be found in table A-2, appendix A.

SOURCE: U.S. Department of Education, National Center for Education Statistics, Common Core of Data (CCD), "National Public Education Financial Survey," 1997–98 through 2009–10; National Elementary and Secondary Average Daily Attendance Model, 1994–95 through 2009–10; and Elementary and Secondary Education Current Expenditures Model, 1969–70 through 2009–10. (This table was prepared March 2013.)

Table 20. Actual and projected numbers for total enrollment in all postsecondary degree-granting institutions, by sex, attendance status, and control of institution: Fall 1997 through fall 2022

[In thousands]

Year	Total	Sex		Attendance status		Control	
		Men	Women	Full-time	Part-time	Public	Private
1	2	3	4	5	6	7	8
Actual							
1997	14,502	6,396	8,106	8,438	6,064	11,196	3,306
1998	14,507	6,369	8,138	8,563	5,944	11,138	3,369
1999	14,850	6,515	8,335	8,803	6,047	11,376	3,474
2000	15,312	6,722	8,591	9,010	6,303	11,753	3,560
2001	15,928	6,961	8,967	9,448	6,480	12,233	3,695
2002	16,612	7,202	9,410	9,946	6,665	12,752	3,860
2003	16,911	7,260	9,651	10,326	6,585	12,859	4,053
2004	17,272	7,387	9,885	10,610	6,662	12,980	4,292
2005	17,487	7,456	10,032	10,797	6,690	13,022	4,466
2006	17,759	7,575	10,184	10,957	6,802	13,180	4,579
2007	18,248	7,816	10,432	11,270	6,978	13,491	4,757
2008	19,103	8,189	10,914	11,748	7,355	13,972	5,131
2009	20,428	8,770	11,658	12,723	7,705	14,811	5,617
2010	21,016	9,045	11,971	13,082	7,934	15,143	5,873
2011	20,994	9,027	11,968	13,001	7,993	15,110	5,884
Projected							
2012	20,968	8,998	11,970	13,014	7,953	15,078	5,890
2013	21,216	9,070	12,146	13,107	8,109	15,256	5,960
2014	21,575	9,142	12,433	13,297	8,278	15,509	6,066
2015	21,805	9,163	12,642	13,400	8,405	15,671	6,134
2016	22,076	9,216	12,860	13,532	8,544	15,863	6,213
2017	22,376	9,297	13,079	13,688	8,687	16,077	6,299
2018	22,698	9,389	13,309	13,867	8,831	16,308	6,390
2019	23,025	9,493	13,533	14,068	8,957	16,545	6,481
2020	23,309	9,588	13,721	14,247	9,062	16,751	6,558
2021	23,630	9,700	13,931	14,451	9,180	16,982	6,649
2022	23,888	9,796	14,092	14,616	9,273	17,168	6,720

NOTE: Detail may not sum to totals because of rounding. Some data have been revised from previously published figures. Mean absolute percentage errors of selected education statistics can be found in table A-2, appendix A.

SOURCE: U.S. Department of Education, National Center for Education Statistics, Integrated Postsecondary Education Data System (IPEDS), "Fall Enrollment Survey" (IPEDS-EF:97–99); IPEDS Spring 2001 through Spring 2012, Enrollment component; and Enrollment in Degree-Granting Institutions Model, 1980–2011. (This table was prepared February 2013.)

Table 21. Actual and projected numbers for total enrollment in all postsecondary degree-granting institutions, by age group, sex, and attendance status: Fall 1997 through fall 2022

[In thousands]

Age group, sex, and attendance status	Actual														
	1997	1998	1999	2000	2001	2002	2003	2004	2005	2006	2007	2008	2009	2010	2011
1	2	3	4	5	6	7	8	9	10	11	12	13	14	15	16
Total enrollment	**14,502**	**14,507**	**14,850**	**15,312**	**15,928**	**16,612**	**16,911**	**17,272**	**17,487**	**17,759**	**18,248**	**19,103**	**20,428**	**21,016**	**20,994**
14 to 17 years old	174	142	138	140	161	163	184	184	210	204	211	199	222	214	208
18 and 19 years old	3,164	3,251	3,474	3,473	3,578	3,562	3,560	3,560	3,640	3,777	3,909	4,020	4,299	4,385	4,261
20 and 21 years old	2,782	2,876	2,962	3,104	3,296	3,425	3,523	3,634	3,676	3,717	3,748	3,885	4,196	4,357	4,451
22 to 24 years old	2,406	2,416	2,470	2,602	2,772	3,072	3,140	3,211	3,104	3,191	3,308	3,480	3,592	3,661	3,750
25 to 29 years old	2,051	1,944	1,921	1,963	2,009	2,100	2,181	2,306	2,397	2,421	2,560	2,741	2,980	3,029	3,164
30 to 34 years old	1,171	1,145	1,187	1,244	1,274	1,341	1,322	1,354	1,365	1,391	1,422	1,510	1,630	1,705	1,698
35 years old and over	2,754	2,733	2,698	2,786	2,839	2,949	3,001	3,022	3,095	3,058	3,090	3,269	3,509	3,665	3,463
Men	**6,396**	**6,369**	**6,515**	**6,722**	**6,961**	**7,202**	**7,260**	**7,387**	**7,456**	**7,575**	**7,816**	**8,189**	**8,770**	**9,045**	**9,027**
14 to 17 years old	65	56	61	63	67	66	74	73	79	78	92	95	107	94	99
18 and 19 years old	1,443	1,470	1,577	1,559	1,613	1,605	1,585	1,569	1,608	1,690	1,766	1,804	1,912	1,964	1,915
20 and 21 years old	1,327	1,367	1,396	1,427	1,525	1,557	1,606	1,672	1,727	1,680	1,709	1,800	1,977	2,085	2,105
22 to 24 years old	1,172	1,136	1,164	1,234	1,319	1,429	1,431	1,453	1,401	1,451	1,498	1,574	1,618	1,670	1,719
25 to 29 years old	961	917	867	895	881	923	947	991	1,024	1,016	1,110	1,174	1,339	1,325	1,387
30 to 34 years old	462	474	490	530	523	558	545	550	539	586	597	640	657	679	659
35 years old and over	967	950	961	1,014	1,033	1,063	1,073	1,080	1,078	1,073	1,044	1,103	1,160	1,229	1,142
Women	**8,106**	**8,138**	**8,335**	**8,591**	**8,967**	**9,410**	**9,651**	**9,885**	**10,032**	**10,184**	**10,432**	**10,914**	**11,658**	**11,971**	**11,968**
14 to 17 years old	110	86	77	77	94	97	111	111	131	125	119	103	115	120	108
18 and 19 years old	1,720	1,782	1,897	1,914	1,964	1,957	1,975	1,991	2,031	2,087	2,144	2,216	2,387	2,421	2,346
20 and 21 years old	1,455	1,509	1,566	1,677	1,770	1,868	1,918	1,963	1,949	2,037	2,039	2,086	2,218	2,272	2,346
22 to 24 years old	1,234	1,280	1,306	1,368	1,452	1,642	1,709	1,759	1,703	1,740	1,811	1,906	1,975	1,992	2,031
25 to 29 years old	1,090	1,028	1,054	1,068	1,128	1,177	1,234	1,315	1,373	1,405	1,450	1,567	1,641	1,704	1,777
30 to 34 years old	709	670	697	714	752	782	776	804	826	805	825	870	973	1,026	1,039
35 years old and over	1,787	1,783	1,737	1,772	1,806	1,886	1,929	1,942	2,018	1,984	2,046	2,166	2,349	2,436	2,320
Full-time, total	**8,438**	**8,563**	**8,803**	**9,010**	**9,448**	**9,946**	**10,326**	**10,610**	**10,797**	**10,957**	**11,270**	**11,748**	**12,723**	**13,082**	**13,001**
14 to 17 years old	127	114	118	124	136	136	150	139	155	150	169	165	179	167	170
18 and 19 years old	2,619	2,704	2,890	2,859	2,945	2,958	3,006	3,006	3,065	3,181	3,299	3,403	3,593	3,646	3,481
20 and 21 years old	2,211	2,301	2,357	2,434	2,621	2,739	2,848	2,897	2,951	2,991	3,033	3,124	3,343	3,438	3,472
22 to 24 years old	1,594	1,611	1,619	1,690	1,768	1,941	2,043	2,113	2,095	2,096	2,180	2,331	2,497	2,549	2,476
25 to 29 years old	907	877	861	880	909	996	1,058	1,127	1,170	1,193	1,256	1,317	1,456	1,487	1,562
30 to 34 years old	379	360	369	420	451	492	480	523	552	563	540	548	642	714	741
35 years old and over	601	597	589	603	618	684	741	805	809	782	793	861	1,013	1,081	1,098
Men	**3,890**	**3,934**	**4,034**	**4,111**	**4,300**	**4,501**	**4,638**	**4,739**	**4,803**	**4,879**	**5,029**	**5,234**	**5,671**	**5,837**	**5,793**
14 to 17 years old	53	49	53	53	53	53	60	50	55	53	75	72	78	61	75
18 and 19 years old	1,175	1,202	1,279	1,255	1,305	1,327	1,336	1,324	1,356	1,420	1,492	1,548	1,607	1,641	1,544
20 and 21 years old	1,053	1,104	1,132	1,133	1,220	1,253	1,307	1,353	1,392	1,366	1,381	1,443	1,561	1,651	1,613
22 to 24 years old	800	783	796	829	875	945	974	988	972	984	1,031	1,092	1,165	1,181	1,167
25 to 29 years old	448	441	407	419	419	461	486	491	503	530	561	570	649	653	718
30 to 34 years old	149	151	154	191	193	214	203	229	224	235	224	236	275	286	291
35 years old and over	213	203	213	233	234	247	272	305	301	292	265	273	337	364	385
Women	**4,548**	**4,630**	**4,770**	**4,899**	**5,148**	**5,445**	**5,688**	**5,871**	**5,994**	**6,078**	**6,240**	**6,513**	**7,052**	**7,245**	**7,208**
14 to 17 years old	74	65	65	72	83	82	90	89	100	97	95	93	102	106	95
18 and 19 years old	1,444	1,502	1,611	1,604	1,639	1,632	1,670	1,682	1,709	1,761	1,806	1,855	1,986	2,005	1,937
20 and 21 years old	1,158	1,197	1,226	1,302	1,401	1,486	1,542	1,544	1,559	1,625	1,652	1,680	1,782	1,787	1,859
22 to 24 years old	794	828	823	861	893	996	1,069	1,125	1,123	1,112	1,149	1,239	1,332	1,369	1,309
25 to 29 years old	458	436	454	461	490	535	572	636	667	663	695	747	807	833	845
30 to 34 years old	230	209	215	229	258	278	277	294	328	329	316	312	367	428	450
35 years old and over	389	394	375	370	384	437	468	501	507	491	528	587	676	716	713
Part-time, total	**6,064**	**5,944**	**6,047**	**6,303**	**6,480**	**6,665**	**6,585**	**6,662**	**6,690**	**6,802**	**6,978**	**7,355**	**7,705**	**7,934**	**7,993**
14 to 17 years old	47	28	21	16	25	28	34	45	55	53	42	34	43	46	38
18 and 19 years old	545	547	583	614	633	604	554	554	574	596	610	617	706	739	780
20 and 21 years old	571	575	605	670	675	686	675	737	725	726	715	761	853	919	978
22 to 24 years old	812	805	850	912	1,003	1,130	1,097	1,098	1,009	1,096	1,128	1,149	1,096	1,112	1,274
25 to 29 years old	1,144	1,067	1,060	1,083	1,100	1,104	1,123	1,179	1,227	1,228	1,304	1,424	1,524	1,542	1,602
30 to 34 years old	793	785	817	825	823	848	841	832	814	828	882	961	988	991	957
35 years old and over	2,153	2,136	2,110	2,184	2,222	2,265	2,261	2,217	2,287	2,275	2,297	2,408	2,496	2,584	2,364
Men	**2,506**	**2,436**	**2,482**	**2,611**	**2,661**	**2,701**	**2,622**	**2,648**	**2,653**	**2,695**	**2,786**	**2,955**	**3,099**	**3,208**	**3,233**
14 to 17 years old	11	7	9	10	13	13	13	23	24	25	18	24	29	33	25
18 and 19 years old	268	267	298	304	308	279	250	245	252	270	273	256	305	323	371
20 and 21 years old	274	262	264	294	305	304	299	319	335	314	328	356	416	434	491
22 to 24 years old	372	353	368	405	444	484	457	465	429	467	466	482	453	489	552
25 to 29 years old	513	476	460	476	462	462	461	500	521	486	549	604	691	672	669
30 to 34 years old	313	323	335	339	329	344	342	322	315	351	373	403	382	393	368
35 years old and over	754	747	748	782	799	817	800	775	776	781	779	830	823	864	757
Women	**3,559**	**3,508**	**3,565**	**3,692**	**3,820**	**3,964**	**3,963**	**4,014**	**4,038**	**4,106**	**4,192**	**4,401**	**4,606**	**4,726**	**4,760**
14 to 17 years old	36	22	12	5	11	15	21	22	31	28	24	11	14	13	13
18 and 19 years old	276	280	285	310	325	325	305	310	322	326	337	361	401	416	409
20 and 21 years old	297	313	341	376	369	382	376	419	390	412	387	405	437	485	487
22 to 24 years old	441	452	482	507	559	646	639	633	580	628	662	667	643	623	722
25 to 29 years old	632	591	600	607	638	642	662	679	706	742	755	820	833	871	933
30 to 34 years old	480	461	482	485	494	504	499	510	499	477	509	558	606	598	589
35 years old and over	1,398	1,389	1,362	1,402	1,422	1,449	1,460	1,441	1,511	1,494	1,518	1,579	1,673	1,720	1,607

See notes at end of table.

Table 21. Actual and projected numbers for total enrollment in all postsecondary degree-granting institutions, by age group, sex, and attendance status: Fall 1997 through fall 2022—Continued

[In thousands]

Age group, sex, and attendance status	Projected										
	2012	2013	2014	2015	2016	2017	2018	2019	2020	2021	2022
1	17	18	19	20	21	22	23	24	25	26	27
Total enrollment	**20,968**	**21,216**	**21,575**	**21,805**	**22,076**	**22,376**	**22,698**	**23,025**	**23,309**	**23,630**	**23,888**
14 to 17 years old	206	207	209	213	219	225	234	237	240	244	247
18 and 19 years old	4,210	4,192	4,223	4,228	4,243	4,302	4,382	4,501	4,608	4,644	4,695
20 and 21 years old	4,428	4,403	4,402	4,398	4,416	4,415	4,424	4,473	4,536	4,662	4,751
22 to 24 years old	3,847	3,940	4,018	4,033	4,038	4,048	4,059	4,056	4,054	4,082	4,124
25 to 29 years old	3,152	3,228	3,334	3,438	3,542	3,633	3,700	3,727	3,717	3,709	3,686
30 to 34 years old	1,705	1,763	1,818	1,854	1,891	1,929	1,972	2,016	2,060	2,105	2,134
35 years old and over	3,419	3,484	3,571	3,641	3,728	3,823	3,926	4,017	4,094	4,184	4,251
Men	**8,998**	**9,070**	**9,142**	**9,163**	**9,216**	**9,297**	**9,389**	**9,493**	**9,588**	**9,700**	**9,796**
14 to 17 years old	98	97	97	98	101	103	107	108	109	110	111
18 and 19 years old	1,891	1,874	1,879	1,872	1,872	1,895	1,928	1,976	2,021	2,037	2,058
20 and 21 years old	2,082	2,074	2,064	2,053	2,054	2,048	2,048	2,068	2,094	2,149	2,189
22 to 24 years old	1,755	1,797	1,818	1,813	1,805	1,804	1,803	1,796	1,792	1,801	1,818
25 to 29 years old	1,378	1,401	1,432	1,462	1,496	1,526	1,547	1,553	1,545	1,538	1,526
30 to 34 years old	660	679	692	698	706	715	725	738	752	767	777
35 years old and over	1,134	1,147	1,160	1,168	1,183	1,205	1,231	1,254	1,274	1,299	1,317
Women	**11,970**	**12,146**	**12,433**	**12,642**	**12,860**	**13,079**	**13,309**	**13,533**	**13,721**	**13,931**	**14,092**
14 to 17 years old	108	110	112	114	118	122	128	129	131	134	135
18 and 19 years old	2,319	2,318	2,344	2,356	2,371	2,407	2,455	2,525	2,586	2,608	2,637
20 and 21 years old	2,346	2,329	2,338	2,346	2,362	2,367	2,376	2,405	2,442	2,513	2,562
22 to 24 years old	2,092	2,142	2,199	2,221	2,233	2,243	2,256	2,260	2,262	2,281	2,306
25 to 29 years old	1,775	1,827	1,903	1,976	2,047	2,107	2,152	2,173	2,172	2,171	2,160
30 to 34 years old	1,044	1,084	1,126	1,156	1,185	1,214	1,247	1,278	1,308	1,338	1,358
35 years old and over	2,285	2,337	2,411	2,474	2,545	2,618	2,695	2,762	2,820	2,886	2,934
Full-time, total	**13,014**	**13,107**	**13,297**	**13,400**	**13,532**	**13,688**	**13,867**	**14,068**	**14,247**	**14,451**	**14,616**
14 to 17 years old	167	167	170	173	178	183	191	193	196	199	201
18 and 19 years old	3,440	3,422	3,450	3,456	3,470	3,521	3,588	3,688	3,775	3,806	3,848
20 and 21 years old	3,461	3,435	3,437	3,435	3,451	3,451	3,460	3,500	3,550	3,650	3,719
22 to 24 years old	2,550	2,601	2,651	2,661	2,665	2,672	2,681	2,679	2,679	2,700	2,728
25 to 29 years old	1,557	1,596	1,649	1,698	1,750	1,795	1,828	1,842	1,838	1,835	1,824
30 to 34 years old	749	775	800	816	831	848	868	887	907	927	940
35 years old and over	1,090	1,112	1,140	1,161	1,187	1,217	1,250	1,279	1,304	1,333	1,355
Men	**5,774**	**5,815**	**5,862**	**5,875**	**5,913**	**5,970**	**6,034**	**6,108**	**6,177**	**6,255**	**6,323**
14 to 17 years old	72	71	71	72	74	76	78	79	80	81	82
18 and 19 years old	1,524	1,508	1,514	1,511	1,514	1,535	1,563	1,604	1,641	1,654	1,672
20 and 21 years old	1,597	1,592	1,587	1,580	1,584	1,582	1,584	1,601	1,622	1,666	1,697
22 to 24 years old	1,193	1,223	1,240	1,238	1,236	1,238	1,240	1,236	1,234	1,241	1,254
25 to 29 years old	714	729	746	763	783	802	815	820	816	813	807
30 to 34 years old	292	301	308	311	316	321	327	333	340	347	352
35 years old and over	383	390	395	399	406	415	426	435	443	452	459
Women	**7,240**	**7,292**	**7,436**	**7,524**	**7,619**	**7,718**	**7,833**	**7,960**	**8,070**	**8,196**	**8,293**
14 to 17 years old	95	96	98	101	104	108	113	114	116	118	119
18 and 19 years old	1,916	1,913	1,935	1,945	1,956	1,986	2,025	2,084	2,133	2,152	2,176
20 and 21 years old	1,864	1,843	1,850	1,855	1,867	1,869	1,876	1,899	1,927	1,984	2,022
22 to 24 years old	1,357	1,377	1,412	1,423	1,428	1,434	1,441	1,443	1,445	1,459	1,475
25 to 29 years old	843	867	903	935	967	993	1,013	1,023	1,022	1,022	1,016
30 to 34 years old	458	474	492	504	516	527	541	554	567	580	588
35 years old and over	707	722	745	762	781	802	824	844	861	882	896
Part-time, total	**7,953**	**8,109**	**8,278**	**8,405**	**8,544**	**8,687**	**8,831**	**8,957**	**9,062**	**9,180**	**9,273**
14 to 17 years old	39	39	40	40	41	42	43	44	44	45	45
18 and 19 years old	770	771	773	772	772	781	794	813	833	838	847
20 and 21 years old	967	968	965	963	966	964	964	973	986	1,012	1,032
22 to 24 years old	1,298	1,339	1,366	1,372	1,373	1,375	1,378	1,376	1,375	1,382	1,395
25 to 29 years old	1,595	1,633	1,686	1,739	1,793	1,838	1,871	1,884	1,880	1,874	1,863
30 to 34 years old	955	987	1,018	1,038	1,059	1,081	1,104	1,129	1,154	1,178	1,194
35 years old and over	2,328	2,372	2,431	2,480	2,540	2,606	2,676	2,737	2,790	2,851	2,897
Men	**3,224**	**3,255**	**3,281**	**3,288**	**3,303**	**3,326**	**3,355**	**3,385**	**3,411**	**3,444**	**3,473**
14 to 17 years old	26	26	26	26	27	27	28	28	29	29	29
18 and 19 years old	367	366	364	361	358	360	364	372	380	382	386
20 and 21 years old	485	481	477	472	470	466	464	467	472	483	492
22 to 24 years old	562	574	578	574	569	566	563	560	557	559	564
25 to 29 years old	664	673	686	699	712	724	732	734	729	724	718
30 to 34 years old	368	378	384	387	390	393	398	405	412	420	425
35 years old and over	750	757	765	769	777	789	805	819	832	847	859
Women	**4,729**	**4,854**	**4,997**	**5,117**	**5,241**	**5,361**	**5,476**	**5,572**	**5,651**	**5,735**	**5,799**
14 to 17 years old	13	13	13	14	14	15	15	15	16	16	16
18 and 19 years old	403	405	409	411	414	421	429	441	453	456	461
20 and 21 years old	481	486	488	491	495	498	500	507	514	529	540
22 to 24 years old	736	765	788	798	804	810	815	816	817	823	831
25 to 29 years old	931	960	1,000	1,040	1,080	1,114	1,139	1,151	1,151	1,150	1,144
30 to 34 years old	587	610	634	652	669	687	706	724	741	758	769
35 years old and over	1,578	1,615	1,666	1,712	1,763	1,817	1,871	1,918	1,958	2,004	2,038

NOTE: Detail may not sum to totals because of rounding. Some data have been revised from previously published figures. Data by age are based on the distribution by age from the Census Bureau. For additional information see section A.4 in appendix A. Mean absolute percentage errors of selected education statistics can be found in table A-2, appendix A.
SOURCE: U.S. Department of Education, National Center for Education Statistics, Integrated Postsecondary Education Data System (IPEDS), "Fall Enrollment Survey" (IPEDS-EF:97–99); IPEDS Spring 2001 through Spring 2012, Enrollment component; Enrollment in Degree-Granting Institutions Model, 1980–2011; and U.S. Department of Commerce, Census Bureau, Current Population Reports, "Social and Economic Characteristics of Students," various years. (This table was prepared February 2013.)

Table 22. Actual and projected numbers for enrollment in all postsecondary degree-granting institutions, by sex and attendance status: Fall 1997 through fall 2022

[In thousands]

Year	Total	Men		Women	
		Full-time	Part-time	Full-time	Part-time
1	2	3	4	5	6
Actual					
1997	14,502	3,890	2,506	4,548	3,559
1998	14,507	3,934	2,436	4,630	3,508
1999	14,850	4,034	2,482	4,770	3,565
2000	15,312	4,111	2,611	4,899	3,692
2001	15,928	4,300	2,661	5,148	3,820
2002	16,612	4,501	2,701	5,445	3,964
2003	16,911	4,638	2,622	5,688	3,963
2004	17,272	4,739	2,648	5,871	4,014
2005	17,487	4,803	2,653	5,994	4,038
2006	17,759	4,879	2,695	6,078	4,106
2007	18,248	5,029	2,786	6,240	4,192
2008	19,103	5,234	2,955	6,513	4,401
2009	20,428	5,671	3,099	7,052	4,606
2010	21,016	5,837	3,208	7,245	4,726
2011	20,994	5,793	3,233	7,208	4,760
Projected					
2012	20,968	5,774	3,224	7,240	4,729
2013	21,216	5,815	3,255	7,292	4,854
2014	21,575	5,862	3,281	7,436	4,997
2015	21,805	5,875	3,288	7,524	5,117
2016	22,076	5,913	3,303	7,619	5,241
2017	22,376	5,970	3,326	7,718	5,361
2018	22,698	6,034	3,355	7,833	5,476
2019	23,025	6,108	3,385	7,960	5,572
2020	23,309	6,177	3,411	8,070	5,651
2021	23,630	6,255	3,444	8,196	5,735
2022	23,888	6,323	3,473	8,293	5,799

NOTE: Detail may not sum to totals because of rounding. Some data have been revised from previously published figures. Mean absolute percentage errors of selected education statistics can be found in table A-2, appendix A.

SOURCE: U.S. Department of Education, National Center for Education Statistics, Integrated Postsecondary Education Data System (IPEDS), "Fall Enrollment Survey" (IPEDS-EF:97–99); IPEDS Spring 2001 through Spring 2012, Enrollment component; and Enrollment in Degree-Granting Institutions Model, 1980–2011. (This table was prepared February 2013.)

Table 23. Actual and projected numbers for enrollment in public 4-year postsecondary degree-granting institutions, by sex and attendance status: Fall 1997 through fall 2022

[In thousands]

Year	Total	Men		Women	
		Full-time	Part-time	Full-time	Part-time
1	2	3	4	5	6
Actual					
1997..	5,835	1,951	687	2,214	984
1998..	5,892	1,959	685	2,260	988
1999..	5,978	1,985	687	2,312	994
2000..	6,055	2,009	683	2,363	1,001
2001..	6,236	2,082	687	2,450	1,017
2002..	6,482	2,167	706	2,557	1,052
2003..	6,649	2,225	713	2,639	1,072
2004..	6,737	2,260	717	2,684	1,076
2005..	6,838	2,295	724	2,726	1,091
2006..	6,955	2,339	740	2,765	1,111
2007..	7,167	2,418	773	2,827	1,149
2008..	7,332	2,488	789	2,890	1,165
2009..	7,709	2,626	833	3,024	1,226
2010..	7,925	2,707	861	3,104	1,252
2011..	8,048	2,743	886	3,146	1,273
Projected					
2012..	8,045	2,732	879	3,162	1,271
2013..	8,131	2,753	889	3,182	1,307
2014..	8,264	2,774	898	3,242	1,349
2015..	8,345	2,780	902	3,278	1,384
2016..	8,443	2,797	908	3,317	1,420
2017..	8,551	2,823	916	3,357	1,455
2018..	8,668	2,851	925	3,405	1,488
2019..	8,790	2,884	934	3,458	1,513
2020..	8,896	2,916	941	3,505	1,534
2021..	9,020	2,953	950	3,561	1,556
2022..	9,120	2,986	958	3,604	1,572

NOTE: Detail may not sum to totals because of rounding. Some data have been revised from previously published figures. Mean absolute percentage errors of selected education statistics can be found in table A-2, appendix A.

SOURCE: U.S. Department of Education, National Center for Education Statistics, Integrated Postsecondary Education Data System (IPEDS), "Fall Enrollment Survey" (IPEDS-EF:97–99); IPEDS Spring 2001 through Spring 2012, Enrollment component; and Enrollment in Degree-Granting Institutions Model, 1980–2011. (This table was prepared February 2013.)

Table 24. Actual and projected numbers for enrollment in public 2-year postsecondary degree-granting institutions, by sex and attendance status: Fall 1997 through fall 2022

[In thousands]

Year	Total	Men		Women	
		Full-time	Part-time	Full-time	Part-time
1	2	3	4	5	6
Actual					
1997	5,361	842	1,444	1,049	2,026
1998	5,246	841	1,383	1,040	1,981
1999	5,398	878	1,419	1,074	2,026
2000	5,697	891	1,549	1,109	2,148
2001	5,997	962	1,596	1,194	2,245
2002	6,270	1,035	1,605	1,299	2,332
2003	6,209	1,060	1,515	1,346	2,288
2004	6,244	1,065	1,518	1,360	2,300
2005	6,184	1,055	1,514	1,332	2,283
2006	6,225	1,067	1,533	1,325	2,300
2007	6,324	1,099	1,568	1,343	2,314
2008	6,640	1,152	1,672	1,396	2,420
2009	7,101	1,318	1,733	1,563	2,488
2010	7,218	1,342	1,769	1,610	2,497
2011	7,062	1,258	1,769	1,518	2,517
Projected					
2012	7,033	1,250	1,772	1,521	2,490
2013	7,125	1,255	1,786	1,533	2,551
2014	7,245	1,264	1,796	1,564	2,621
2015	7,326	1,266	1,797	1,584	2,678
2016	7,420	1,274	1,802	1,606	2,738
2017	7,526	1,287	1,812	1,630	2,797
2018	7,640	1,303	1,825	1,658	2,854
2019	7,755	1,323	1,840	1,688	2,904
2020	7,855	1,341	1,854	1,713	2,947
2021	7,961	1,357	1,873	1,739	2,992
2022	8,048	1,372	1,889	1,759	3,027

NOTE: Detail may not sum to totals because of rounding. Some data have been revised from previously published figures. Mean absolute percentage errors of selected education statistics can be found in table A-2, appendix A.

SOURCE: U.S. Department of Education, National Center for Education Statistics, Integrated Postsecondary Education Data System (IPEDS), "Fall Enrollment Survey" (IPEDS-EF:97–99); IPEDS Spring 2001 through Spring 2012, Enrollment component; and Enrollment in Degree-Granting Institutions Model, 1980–2011. (This table was prepared February 2013.)

Table 25. Actual and projected numbers for enrollment in private 4-year postsecondary degree-granting institutions, by sex and attendance status: Fall 1997 through fall 2022

[In thousands]

Year	Total	Men		Women	
		Full-time	Part-time	Full-time	Part-time
1	2	3	4	5	6
Actual					
1997..	3,061	1,008	360	1,170	523
1998..	3,126	1,038	353	1,220	514
1999..	3,218	1,069	360	1,270	519
2000..	3,308	1,107	365	1,315	522
2001..	3,441	1,151	365	1,389	536
2002..	3,601	1,199	377	1,468	557
2003..	3,768	1,250	382	1,561	574
2004..	3,990	1,313	400	1,670	607
2005..	4,162	1,354	402	1,774	632
2006..	4,285	1,381	411	1,830	664
2007..	4,464	1,422	433	1,911	698
2008..	4,800	1,496	480	2,041	782
2009..	5,197	1,596	518	2,228	855
2010..	5,410	1,646	565	2,260	940
2011..	5,446	1,662	564	2,291	930
Projected					
2012..	5,455	1,663	559	2,304	930
2013..	5,521	1,678	565	2,322	956
2014..	5,620	1,693	572	2,369	987
2015..	5,684	1,699	574	2,397	1,013
2016..	5,757	1,711	578	2,428	1,040
2017..	5,836	1,727	584	2,459	1,066
2018..	5,920	1,745	590	2,494	1,090
2019..	6,003	1,765	596	2,533	1,110
2020..	6,073	1,783	600	2,566	1,125
2021..	6,157	1,804	607	2,605	1,141
2022..	6,223	1,823	611	2,636	1,153

NOTE: Detail may not sum to totals because of rounding. Some data have been revised from previously published figures. Mean absolute percentage errors of selected education statistics can be found in table A-2, appendix A.

SOURCE: U.S. Department of Education, National Center for Education Statistics, Integrated Postsecondary Education Data System (IPEDS), "Fall Enrollment Survey" (IPEDS-EF:97–99); IPEDS Spring 2001 through Spring 2012, Enrollment component; and Enrollment in Degree-Granting Institutions Model, 1980–2011. (This table was prepared February 2013.)

Table 26. Actual and projected numbers for enrollment in private 2-year postsecondary degree-granting institutions, by sex and attendance status: Fall 1997 through fall 2022

[In thousands]

| Year | Total | Men | | Women | |
		Full-time	Part-time	Full-time	Part-time
1	2	3	4	5	6
Actual					
1997....................................	245	89	14	115	26
1998....................................	243	95	14	109	25
1999....................................	255	101	15	114	26
2000....................................	251	105	13	112	21
2001....................................	254	105	12	114	22
2002....................................	259	101	13	122	23
2003....................................	285	103	13	142	28
2004....................................	302	101	13	156	31
2005....................................	304	99	12	161	32
2006....................................	293	93	11	159	30
2007....................................	294	91	12	159	31
2008....................................	331	98	14	186	33
2009....................................	420	131	16	237	36
2010....................................	463	141	13	271	37
2011....................................	438	130	14	253	40
Projected					
2012....................................	435	129	14	254	38
2013....................................	439	130	14	256	39
2014....................................	446	130	14	261	40
2015....................................	450	131	14	264	41
2016....................................	456	131	14	268	42
2017....................................	462	133	15	272	43
2018....................................	470	135	15	277	44
2019....................................	477	137	15	282	44
2020....................................	484	138	15	286	45
2021....................................	491	140	15	290	46
2022....................................	497	142	15	294	46

NOTE: Detail may not sum to totals because of rounding. Some data have been revised from previously published figures. Mean absolute percentage errors of selected education statistics can be found in table A-2, appendix A.

SOURCE: U.S. Department of Education, National Center for Education Statistics, Integrated Postsecondary Education Data System (IPEDS), "Fall Enrollment Survey" (IPEDS-EF:97–99); IPEDS Spring 2001 through Spring 2012, Enrollment component; and Enrollment in Degree-Granting Institutions Model, 1980–2011. (This table was prepared February 2013.)

Table 27. Actual and projected numbers for undergraduate enrollment in all postsecondary degree-granting institutions, by sex, attendance status, and control of institution: Fall 1997 through fall 2022

[In thousands]

Year	Total	Sex		Attendance status		Control	
		Men	Women	Full-time	Part-time	Public	Private
1	2	3	4	5	6	7	8
Actual							
1997...................................	12,451	5,469	6,982	7,419	5,032	10,007	2,443
1998...................................	12,437	5,446	6,991	7,539	4,898	9,950	2,487
1999...................................	12,739	5,584	7,155	7,754	4,986	10,174	2,565
2000...................................	13,155	5,778	7,377	7,923	5,232	10,539	2,616
2001...................................	13,716	6,004	7,711	8,328	5,388	10,986	2,730
2002...................................	14,257	6,192	8,065	8,734	5,523	11,433	2,824
2003...................................	14,480	6,227	8,253	9,045	5,435	11,523	2,957
2004...................................	14,781	6,340	8,441	9,284	5,496	11,651	3,130
2005...................................	14,964	6,409	8,555	9,446	5,518	11,698	3,266
2006...................................	15,184	6,514	8,671	9,571	5,613	11,847	3,337
2007...................................	15,604	6,728	8,876	9,841	5,763	12,138	3,466
2008...................................	16,366	7,067	9,299	10,255	6,111	12,591	3,775
2009...................................	17,565	7,595	9,970	11,144	6,422	13,387	4,179
2010...................................	18,079	7,835	10,244	11,452	6,627	13,704	4,374
2011...................................	18,063	7,817	10,246	11,359	6,704	13,689	4,374
Projected							
2012...................................	18,006	7,771	10,235	11,334	6,672	13,642	4,364
2013...................................	18,187	7,820	10,368	11,390	6,797	13,788	4,400
2014...................................	18,467	7,872	10,595	11,536	6,931	14,002	4,465
2015...................................	18,639	7,881	10,758	11,609	7,030	14,136	4,503
2016...................................	18,848	7,918	10,930	11,711	7,138	14,299	4,550
2017...................................	19,086	7,980	11,106	11,836	7,250	14,482	4,603
2018...................................	19,349	8,055	11,295	11,986	7,363	14,685	4,664
2019...................................	19,634	8,146	11,487	12,169	7,465	14,900	4,733
2020...................................	19,887	8,234	11,653	12,336	7,551	15,092	4,795
2021...................................	20,169	8,335	11,834	12,521	7,648	15,303	4,865
2022...................................	20,399	8,423	11,976	12,673	7,726	15,476	4,923

NOTE: Detail may not sum to totals because of rounding. Some data have been revised from previously published figures. Mean absolute percentage errors of selected education statistics can be found in table A-2, appendix A.

SOURCE: U.S. Department of Education, National Center for Education Statistics, Integrated Postsecondary Education Data System (IPEDS), "Fall Enrollment Survey" (IPEDS-EF:97–99); IPEDS Spring 2001 through Spring 2012, Enrollment component; and Enrollment in Degree-Granting Institutions Model, 1980–2011. (This table was prepared February 2013.)

Table 28. Actual and projected numbers for postbaccalaureate enrollment in all postsecondary degree-granting institutions, by sex, attendance status, and control of institution: Fall 1997 through fall 2022

[In thousands]

Year	Total	Sex		Attendance status		Control	
		Men	Women	Full-time	Part-time	Public	Private
1	2	3	4	5	6	7	8
Actual							
1997	2,052	927	1,124	1,019	1,032	1,189	863
1998	2,070	923	1,147	1,025	1,045	1,188	882
1999	2,110	931	1,179	1,050	1,061	1,202	909
2000	2,157	944	1,213	1,087	1,070	1,213	943
2001	2,212	956	1,256	1,120	1,093	1,247	965
2002	2,355	1,010	1,345	1,212	1,143	1,319	1,035
2003	2,431	1,033	1,398	1,281	1,150	1,336	1,096
2004	2,491	1,047	1,444	1,326	1,166	1,330	1,162
2005	2,524	1,047	1,476	1,351	1,173	1,324	1,199
2006	2,575	1,061	1,514	1,386	1,188	1,333	1,242
2007	2,644	1,088	1,556	1,429	1,215	1,353	1,291
2008	2,737	1,122	1,615	1,493	1,244	1,381	1,356
2009	2,862	1,174	1,688	1,579	1,283	1,424	1,438
2010	2,937	1,210	1,728	1,631	1,307	1,439	1,499
2011	2,931	1,210	1,722	1,642	1,289	1,421	1,510
Projected							
2012	2,962	1,227	1,735	1,680	1,282	1,436	1,526
2013	3,029	1,250	1,778	1,717	1,312	1,468	1,560
2014	3,108	1,270	1,837	1,761	1,347	1,507	1,601
2015	3,166	1,282	1,883	1,790	1,375	1,534	1,631
2016	3,228	1,298	1,929	1,822	1,406	1,565	1,663
2017	3,290	1,317	1,973	1,852	1,437	1,595	1,695
2018	3,349	1,334	2,014	1,881	1,468	1,623	1,725
2019	3,392	1,346	2,046	1,900	1,492	1,644	1,747
2020	3,422	1,354	2,068	1,911	1,510	1,659	1,763
2021	3,462	1,365	2,097	1,930	1,531	1,678	1,783
2022	3,489	1,373	2,116	1,943	1,546	1,692	1,797

NOTE: Detail may not sum to totals because of rounding. Some data have been revised from previously published figures. Mean absolute percentage errors of selected education statistics can be found in table A-2, appendix A.

SOURCE: U.S. Department of Education, National Center for Education Statistics, Integrated Postsecondary Education Data System (IPEDS), "Fall Enrollment Survey" (IPEDS-EF:97–99); IPEDS Spring 2001 through Spring 2012, Enrollment component; and Enrollment in Degree-Granting Institutions Model, 1980–2011. (This table was prepared February 2013.)

Table 29. Actual and projected numbers for enrollment of U.S. residents in all postsecondary degree-granting institutions, by race/ethnicity: Fall 1997 through fall 2022

[In thousands]

| Year | Total | Race/ethnicity | | | | |
		White	Black	Hispanic	Asian/Pacific Islander	American Indian/ Alaska Native
1	2	3	4	5	6	7
Actual						
1997	14,037	10,266	1,551	1,218	859	142
1998	14,064	10,179	1,583	1,257	901	144
1999	14,362	10,329	1,649	1,324	914	146
2000	14,784	10,463	1,730	1,462	978	151
2001	15,363	10,775	1,850	1,561	1,019	158
2002	16,021	11,141	1,979	1,662	1,074	166
2003	16,320	11,284	2,070	1,717	1,076	173
2004	16,683	11,423	2,165	1,810	1,109	176
2005	16,903	11,496	2,215	1,882	1,134	176
2006	17,164	11,573	2,280	1,964	1,166	181
2007	17,624	11,756	2,383	2,076	1,218	190
2008	18,443	12,089	2,585	2,273	1,303	193
2009	19,743	12,731	2,920	2,547	1,338	208
2010	20,308	12,931	3,088	2,786	1,303	200
2011	20,255	12,666	3,135	2,953	1,311	190
Projected						
2012	20,198	12,781	3,083	2,828	1,314	191
2013	20,423	12,798	3,191	2,925	1,320	191
2014	20,749	12,901	3,298	3,024	1,334	192
2015	20,951	12,913	3,391	3,119	1,337	191
2016	21,192	12,948	3,487	3,220	1,345	191
2017	21,459	13,010	3,581	3,321	1,355	191
2018	21,747	13,099	3,666	3,423	1,369	191
2019	22,037	13,191	3,743	3,526	1,385	191
2020	22,282	13,249	3,817	3,624	1,400	191
2021	22,565	13,393	3,886	3,697	1,398	191
2022	22,780	13,492	3,940	3,757	1,400	190

NOTE: Race categories exclude persons of Hispanic ethnicity. Because of underreporting and nonreporting of racial/ethnic data and nonresident aliens, totals are lower than corresponding data in other published tables. Enrollment data in the "race/ethnicity unknown" (all years) and "two or more races" (2008 through 2011 only) categories of the Integrated Postsecondary Education Data System (IPEDS) "Enrollment component" have been prorated to the other racial/ethnic categories at the institutional level. Detail may not sum to totals because of rounding. Mean absolute percentage errors of selected education statistics can be found in table A-2, appendix A. Some data have been revised from previously published figures.
SOURCE: U.S. Department of Education, National Center for Education Statistics, Integrated Postsecondary Education Data System (IPEDS), "Fall Enrollment Survey" (IPEDS-EF:97–99); IPEDS Spring 2001 through Spring 2012, Enrollment component; and Enrollment in Degree-Granting Institutions by Race/Ethnicity Model, 1980–2011. (This table was prepared March 2013.)

Table 30. Actual and projected numbers for first-time freshmen fall enrollment in all postsecondary degree-granting institutions, by sex: Fall 1997 through fall 2022

[In thousands]

Year	Total	Men	Women
1	2	3	4
Actual			
1997..	2,219	1,026	1,193
1998..	2,213	1,023	1,190
1999..	2,358	1,095	1,263
2000..	2,428	1,124	1,304
2001..	2,497	1,153	1,344
2002..	2,571	1,171	1,400
2003..	2,592	1,176	1,416
2004..	2,630	1,190	1,440
2005..	2,657	1,200	1,457
2006..	2,707	1,229	1,479
2007..	2,776	1,267	1,509
2008..	3,025	1,389	1,635
2009..	3,210	1,480	1,730
2010..	3,157	1,462	1,695
2011..	3,093	1,425	1,668
Projected			
2012..	3,165	1,454	1,711
2013..	3,196	1,463	1,733
2014..	3,244	1,473	1,771
2015..	3,273	1,475	1,798
2016..	3,309	1,482	1,827
2017..	3,350	1,493	1,857
2018..	3,395	1,507	1,888
2019..	3,445	1,524	1,920
2020..	3,489	1,541	1,948
2021..	3,538	1,560	1,978
2022..	3,578	1,576	2,002

NOTE: Detail may not sum to totals because of rounding. Some data have been revised from previously published figures. Mean absolute percentage errors of selected education statistics can be found in table A-2, appendix A.
SOURCE: U.S. Department of Education, National Center for Education Statistics, Integrated Postsecondary Education Data System (IPEDS), "Fall Enrollment Survey" (IPEDS-EF:97–99); IPEDS Spring 2001 through Spring 2012, Enrollment component; Enrollment in Degree-Granting Institutions Model, 1980–2011; and First-Time Freshman Model, 1975–2011. (This table was prepared February 2013.)

Table 31. Actual and projected numbers for full-time-equivalent enrollment in all postsecondary degree-granting institutions, by control and level of institution: Fall 1997 through fall 2022

[In thousands]

| Year | Total | Public | | Private | |
		4-year	2-year	4-year	2-year
1	2	3	4	5	6
Actual					
1997.......................................	10,615	4,814	3,056	2,525	220
1998.......................................	10,699	4,869	3,011	2,599	220
1999.......................................	10,975	4,950	3,109	2,684	231
2000.......................................	11,267	5,026	3,241	2,770	231
2001.......................................	11,766	5,194	3,445	2,894	233
2002.......................................	12,331	5,406	3,655	3,033	237
2003.......................................	12,689	5,558	3,684	3,186	260
2004.......................................	13,001	5,641	3,707	3,377	276
2005.......................................	13,201	5,728	3,662	3,533	277
2006.......................................	13,403	5,825	3,679	3,631	268
2007.......................................	13,783	5,994	3,745	3,775	268
2008.......................................	14,394	6,140	3,922	4,030	302
2009.......................................	15,496	6,452	4,298	4,357	389
2010.......................................	15,943	6,636	4,385	4,490	433
2011.......................................	15,886	6,733	4,216	4,532	405
Projected					
2012.......................................	15,886	6,736	4,201	4,545	404
2013.......................................	16,036	6,794	4,243	4,591	407
2014.......................................	16,287	6,896	4,310	4,668	413
2015.......................................	16,436	6,953	4,352	4,713	417
2016.......................................	16,619	7,025	4,404	4,768	422
2017.......................................	16,827	7,108	4,464	4,828	428
2018.......................................	17,058	7,199	4,531	4,893	434
2019.......................................	17,305	7,300	4,603	4,961	442
2020.......................................	17,521	7,389	4,666	5,019	448
2021.......................................	17,767	7,494	4,730	5,089	455
2022.......................................	17,966	7,579	4,782	5,145	460

NOTE: Detail may not sum to totals because of rounding. Some data have been revised from previously published figures. Mean absolute percentage errors of selected education statistics can be found in table A-2, appendix A.

SOURCE: U.S. Department of Education, National Center for Education Statistics, Integrated Postsecondary Education Data System (IPEDS), "Fall Enrollment Survey" (IPEDS-EF:97–99); IPEDS Spring 2001 through Spring 2012, Enrollment component; and Enrollment in Degree-Granting Institutions Model, 1980–2011. (This table was prepared February 2013.)

Table 32. Actual and projected numbers for associate's degrees conferred by postsecondary degree-granting institutions, by sex of recipient: Academic years 1997–98 through 2022–23

Year	Total	Men	Women
1	2	3	4
Actual			
1997–98	558,555	217,613	340,942
1998–99	564,984	220,508	344,476
1999–2000	564,933	224,721	340,212
2000–01	578,865	231,645	347,220
2001–02	595,133	238,109	357,024
2002–03	634,016	253,451	380,565
2003–04	665,301	260,033	405,268
2004–05	696,660	267,536	429,124
2005–06	713,066	270,095	442,971
2006–07	728,114	275,187	452,927
2007–08	750,164	282,521	467,643
2008–09	787,325	298,141	489,184
2009–10	849,452	322,916	526,536
2010–11	942,327	361,309	581,018
Projected			
2011–12	1,002,000	383,000	618,000
2012–13	1,028,000	401,000	627,000
2013–14	1,039,000	411,000	629,000
2014–15	1,074,000	427,000	646,000
2015–16	1,111,000	444,000	666,000
2016–17	1,151,000	462,000	688,000
2017–18	1,190,000	480,000	709,000
2018–19	1,231,000	499,000	732,000
2019–20	1,275,000	519,000	756,000
2020–21	1,319,000	538,000	781,000
2021–22	1,364,000	558,000	806,000
2022–23	1,407,000	578,000	830,000

NOTE: Some data have been revised from previously published figures. Detail may not sum to totals because of rounding. Mean absolute percentage errors of selected education statistics can be found in table A-2, appendix A.

SOURCE: U.S. Department of Education, National Center for Education Statistics, Integrated Postsecondary Education Data System (IPEDS), "Completions Survey" (IPEDS-C:98–99); IPEDS Fall 2000 through Fall 2011, Completions component; and Degrees Conferred Model, 1980–81 through 2010–11. (This table was prepared March 2013.)

Table 33. Actual and projected numbers for bachelor's degrees conferred by postsecondary degree-granting institutions, by sex of recipient: Academic years 1997–98 through 2022–23

Year	Total	Men	Women
1	2	3	4
Actual			
1997–98..................................	1,184,406	519,956	664,450
1998–99..................................	1,202,239	519,961	682,278
1999–2000..............................	1,237,875	530,367	707,508
2000–01..................................	1,244,171	531,840	712,331
2001–02..................................	1,291,900	549,816	742,084
2002–03..................................	1,348,811	573,258	775,553
2003–04..................................	1,399,542	595,425	804,117
2004–05..................................	1,439,264	613,000	826,264
2005–06..................................	1,485,242	630,600	854,642
2006–07..................................	1,524,092	649,570	874,522
2007–08..................................	1,563,069	667,928	895,141
2008–09..................................	1,601,368	685,382	915,986
2009–10..................................	1,650,014	706,633	943,381
2010–11..................................	1,715,913	734,133	981,780
Projected			
2011–12..................................	1,795,000	765,000	1,030,000
2012–13..................................	1,825,000	777,000	1,048,000
2013–14..................................	1,846,000	784,000	1,062,000
2014–15..................................	1,851,000	778,000	1,073,000
2015–16..................................	1,861,000	779,000	1,082,000
2016–17..................................	1,882,000	782,000	1,100,000
2017–18..................................	1,895,000	783,000	1,113,000
2018–19..................................	1,913,000	786,000	1,127,000
2019–20..................................	1,934,000	792,000	1,143,000
2020–21..................................	1,958,000	798,000	1,160,000
2021–22..................................	1,986,000	807,000	1,180,000
2022–23..................................	2,012,000	815,000	1,198,000

NOTE: Some data have been revised from previously published figures. Detail may not sum to totals because of rounding. Mean absolute percentage errors of selected education statistics can be found in table A-2, appendix A.

SOURCE: U.S. Department of Education, National Center for Education Statistics, Integrated Postsecondary Education Data System (IPEDS), "Completions Survey" (IPEDS-C:98–99); IPEDS Fall 2000 through Fall 2011, Completions component; and Degrees Conferred Model, 1980–81 through 2010–11. (This table was prepared March 2013.)

Table 34. Actual and projected numbers for master's degrees conferred by postsecondary degree-granting institutions, by sex of recipient: Academic years 1997–98 through 2022–23

Year	Total	Men	Women
1	2	3	4
Actual			
1997–98................................	436,037	188,718	247,319
1998–99................................	446,038	190,230	255,808
1999–2000............................	463,185	196,129	267,056
2000–01................................	473,502	197,770	275,732
2001–02................................	487,313	202,604	284,709
2002–03................................	518,699	215,172	303,527
2003–04................................	564,272	233,056	331,216
2004–05................................	580,151	237,155	342,996
2005–06................................	599,731	241,656	358,075
2006–07................................	610,597	242,189	368,408
2007–08................................	630,666	250,169	380,497
2008–09................................	662,079	263,538	398,541
2009–10................................	693,025	275,197	417,828
2010–11................................	730,635	291,551	439,084
Projected			
2011–12................................	754,000	299,000	455,000
2012–13................................	776,000	306,000	471,000
2013–14................................	804,000	317,000	487,000
2014–15................................	830,000	324,000	506,000
2015–16................................	852,000	329,000	522,000
2016–17................................	873,000	334,000	539,000
2017–18................................	895,000	340,000	556,000
2018–19................................	918,000	345,000	573,000
2019–20................................	938,000	349,000	589,000
2020–21................................	957,000	352,000	605,000
2021–22................................	976,000	354,000	622,000
2022–23................................	995,000	357,000	638,000

NOTE: Includes some degrees that, prior to *Projections of Education Statistics to 2021*, were classified as first professional, such as divinity degrees (M.Div. and M.H.L./Rav). Some data have been revised from previously published figures. Detail may not sum to totals because of rounding. Mean absolute percentage errors of selected education statistics can be found in table A-2, appendix A.

SOURCE: U.S. Department of Education, National Center for Education Statistics, Integrated Postsecondary Education Data System (IPEDS), "Completions Survey" (IPEDS-C:98–99); IPEDS Fall 2000 through Fall 2011, Completions component; and Degrees Conferred Model, 1980–81 through 2010–11. (This table was prepared March 2013.)

Table 35. Actual and projected numbers for doctor's degrees conferred by postsecondary degree-granting institutions, by sex of recipient: Academic years 1997–98 through 2022–23

Year	Total	Men	Women
1	2	3	4
Actual			
1997–98..................................	118,735	67,232	51,503
1998–99..................................	116,700	65,340	51,360
1999–2000..............................	118,736	64,930	53,806
2000–01..................................	119,585	64,171	55,414
2001–02..................................	119,663	62,731	56,932
2002–03..................................	121,579	62,730	58,849
2003–04..................................	126,087	63,981	62,106
2004–05..................................	134,387	67,257	67,130
2005–06..................................	138,056	68,912	69,144
2006–07..................................	144,690	71,308	73,382
2007–08..................................	149,378	73,453	75,925
2008–09..................................	154,425	75,639	78,786
2009–10..................................	158,558	76,605	81,953
2010–11..................................	163,765	79,654	84,111
Projected			
2011–12..................................	169,800	83,100	86,600
2012–13..................................	174,900	86,700	88,200
2013–14..................................	177,800	88,400	89,400
2014–15..................................	181,100	90,100	90,900
2015–16..................................	185,400	92,800	92,600
2016–17..................................	189,200	94,500	94,700
2017–18..................................	192,000	95,700	96,300
2018–19..................................	194,700	96,700	98,000
2019–20..................................	197,300	98,000	99,400
2020–21..................................	199,800	99,200	100,600
2021–22..................................	201,900	100,100	101,800
2022–23..................................	203,200	100,600	102,700

NOTE: Doctor's degrees include Ph.D., Ed.D., and comparable degrees at the doctoral level. Includes most degrees that, prior to *Projections of Education Statistics to 2021*, were classified as first professional, such as M.D., D.D.S., and law degrees. See Glossary. Some data have been revised from previously published figures. Detail may not sum to totals because of rounding. Mean absolute percentage errors of selected education statistics can be found in table A-2, appendix A.

SOURCE: U.S. Department of Education, National Center for Education Statistics, Integrated Postsecondary Education Data System (IPEDS), "Completions Survey" (IPEDS-C:98–99); IPEDS Fall 2000 through Fall 2011 Completions component; and Degrees Conferred Model, 1980–81 through 2010–11. (This table was prepared March 2013.)

This page intentionally left blank.

Technical Appendixes

This page intentionally left blank.

Appendix A
Introduction to Projection Methodology

A.0. INTRODUCTION TO PROJECTION METHODOLOGY

Content of appendix A

Since its inception in 1964, the *Projections of Education Statistics* series has been providing projections of key education statistics to policy makers, educators, researchers, the press, and the general public. This edition of *Projections of Education Statistics* is the forty-first in the series.

Appendix A contains this introduction, which provides a general overview of the projection methodology, as well as six additional sections, which discuss the specific methodology for the different statistics projected:

> » A.0. Introduction to Projection Methodology;
> » A.1. Elementary and Secondary Enrollment;
> » A.2. High School Graduates;
> » A.3. Elementary and Secondary Teachers;
> » A.4. Expenditures for Public Elementary and Secondary Education;
> » A.5. Enrollment in Postsecondary Degree-Granting Institutions; and
> » A.6. Postsecondary Degrees Conferred.

This introduction

> » outlines the two major techniques used to make the projections;
> » summarizes key demographic and economic assumptions underlying the projections;
> » examines the accuracy of the projections; and
> » introduces the subsequent sections of appendix A.

Projection techniques

Two main projection techniques were used to develop the projections presented in this publication:

> » Exponential smoothing was the technique used in the projections of elementary and secondary enrollments and high school graduates. This technique also played a role in the projections of teachers at the elementary and secondary level, as well as enrollments and degrees conferred at the postsecondary level.
> » Multiple linear regression was the primary technique used in the projections of teachers and expenditures at the elementary and secondary level, as well as enrollments and degrees conferred at the postsecondary level.

Exponential smoothing

Two different types of exponential smoothing, single exponential smoothing and double exponential smoothing, were used in producing the projections presented in this publication.

Single exponential smoothing was used when the historical data had a basically horizontal pattern. Single exponential smoothing produces a single forecast for all years in the forecast period. In developing projections of elementary and secondary enrollments, for example, the rate at which students progress from one particular grade to the next (e.g., from grade 2 to grade 3) was projected using single exponential smoothing. Thus, this percentage was assumed to be constant over the forecast period.

In general, exponential smoothing places more weight on recent observations than on earlier ones. The weights for observations decrease exponentially as one moves further into the past. As a result, the older data have less influence on the projections. The rate at which the weights of older observations decrease is determined by the smoothing constant.

When using single exponential smoothing for a time series, P_t, a smoothed series, $\hat{P}$, is computed recursively by evaluating

$$\hat{P}_t = \alpha\, P_t + (1-\alpha)\, \hat{P}_{t-1}$$

where $0 < \alpha \leq 1$ is the smoothing constant.

By repeated substitution, we can rewrite the equation as

$$\hat{P}_t = \alpha \sum_{s=0}^{t-1} (1-\alpha)^s P_{t-s}$$

where time, s, goes from the first period in the time series, 0, to time period t-1.

The forecasts are constant for all years in the forecast period. The constant equals

$$\hat{P}_{T+k} = \hat{P}_T$$

where T is the last year of actual data and k is the kth year in the forecast period where $k > 0$.

These equations illustrate that the projection is a weighted average based on exponentially decreasing weights. For higher smoothing constants, weights for earlier observations decrease more rapidly than for lower smoothing constants.

For each of the approximately 1,200 single exponential smoothing equations in this edition of *Projections of Education Statistics*, a smoothing constant was individually chosen to minimize the sum of squared forecast errors for that equation. The smoothing constants used to produce the projections in this report ranged from 0.001 to 0.999.

Double exponential smoothing is an extension of single exponential smoothing that allows the forecasting of data with trends. It produces different forecasts for different years in the forecast period. Double exponential smoothing with two smoothing constants was used to forecast the number of doctor's degrees awarded to men and women.

The smoothing forecast using double exponential smoothing is found using the three equations:

$$\hat{P}_{t+k} = a_t + b_t k$$

$$a_t = \alpha\, P_t + (1-\alpha)\,(a_{t-1} + b_{t-1})$$

$$b_t = \beta\,(a_t - a_{t-1}) + (1-\beta)\, b_{t-1}$$

where a_t denotes an estimate of the level of the series at time t, b_t denotes an estimate of the level of the series at time t, and $0 < \alpha, \beta < 1$ are the smoothing constants.

Forecasts from double smoothing are computed as

$$\hat{P}_{T+k} = a_T + b_T k$$

where T is the last year of actual data and k is the kth year in the forecast period where $k > 0$. The last expression shows that forecasts from double smoothing lie on a linear trend with intercept a_T and slope b_T. Single exponential smoothing can be viewed as a special case of double exponential smoothing where the impact that time has on the forecasts has been eliminated (i.e., requiring the slope term b_t to equal 0.0).

The smoothing constants for each of the two double exponential smoothing equations used for this report were selected using a search algorithm that finds the pair of smoothing constants that together minimizes the sum of forecast errors for their equation.

Beginning with the *Projections of Education Statistics to 2020*, each smoothing constant was chosen separately. In earlier editions all the smoothing constants had been set to 0.4. Also beginnings with that edition, two smoothing constants, rather than one, were used for double exponential smoothing.

Multiple linear regression

Multiple linear regression was used in cases where a strong relationship exists between the variable being projected (the dependent variable) and independent variables. This technique can be used only when accurate data and reliable projections of the independent variables are available. Key independent variables for this publication include demographic and economic factors. For example, current expenditures for public elementary and secondary education are related to economic factors such as disposable income and education revenues from state sources. The sources of the demographic and economic projections used for this publication are discussed below, under "Assumptions."

The equations in this appendix should be viewed as forecasting rather than structural equations. That is, the equations are intended only to project values for the dependent variables, not to reflect all elements of underlying social, political, and economic structures. Lack of available data precluded the building of large-scale structural models. The particular equations shown were selected on the basis of their statistical properties, such as coefficients of determination (R^2s), the t-statistics of the coefficients, the Durbin-Watson statistic, the Breusch-Godfrey Serial Correlation LM test statistic, and residual plots.

The functional form primarily used is the multiplicative model. When used with two independent variables, this model takes the form:

$$Y = a \cdot X_1^{b_1} \cdot X_2^{b_2}$$

This equation can easily be transformed into the linear form by taking the natural log (ln) of both sides of the equation:

$$ln(Y) = ln(a) + b_1 ln X_1 + b_2 ln X_2$$

One property of this model is that the coefficient of an independent variable shows how responsive in percentage terms the dependent variable is to a one percent change in that independent variable (also called the elasticity). For example, a 1 percent change in X_1 in the above equation would lead to a b_1 percent change in Y.

Assumptions

All projections are based on underlying assumptions, and these assumptions determine projection results to a large extent. It is important that users of projections understand the assumptions to determine the acceptability of projected time series for their purposes. All the projections in this publication are to some extent dependent on demographic and/or economic assumptions.

Demographic assumptions

Many of the projections in this publication are demographically based on the U.S. Census Bureau's 2012 National Population Projections (December 2012) and the Interim State Population Projections (April 2005).

The two sets of Census Bureau population projections are produced using cohort-component models. In order for the national-level population projections by age, sex, and race/ethnicity to be consistent with the most recent historical estimates released by the Census Bureau, the projections were ratio-adjusted by applying the ratio of the last historical estimate to the corresponding projections year to the projections for each age, sex, and race/ethnicity combination. This allows for a consistent set of historical estimates and projections. For more information on the methodology used for Census Bureau population projections, see appendix C, Data Sources.

The enrollment projections in this publication depend on Census Bureau population projections for the various age groups that attend school. The future fertility rate assumption (along with corresponding projections of female populations) determines projections of the number of births, a key factor for population projections. The fertility rate assumption plays a major role in determining population projections for the age groups enrolled in nursery school, kindergarten, and elementary grades. The effects of the fertility rate assumption are more pronounced toward the end of the forecast period, while immigration assumptions affect all years. For enrollments in secondary grades and college, the fertility rate assumption is of no consequence, since all the population cohorts for these enrollment ranges have already been born.

Economic assumptions

Various economic variables are used in the forecasting models for numbers of elementary and secondary teachers, public elementary and secondary school expenditures, and postsecondary enrollment.

The source of these variables is the trend scenario of the "U.S. Monthly Model January 2013: Short-Term Projections" developed by the economic consulting firm IHS Global Insight. The trend scenario depicts a mean of possible paths that the economy could take over the forecast period, barring major shocks. The economy, in this scenario, evolves smoothly, without major fluctuations.

More information about specific assumptions

For details about the primary assumptions used in this edition of *Projections of Education Statistics*, see table A-1 on page 81.

Accuracy of the projections

Projections of time series usually differ from the final reported data due to errors from many sources. This is because of the inherent nature of the statistical universe from which the basic data are obtained and the properties of projection methodologies, which depend on the validity of many assumptions.

The mean absolute percentage error (MAPE) is one way to express the forecast accuracy of past projections. This measure expresses the average absolute value of errors over past projections in percentage terms. For example, an analysis of projection errors over the past 29 editions of *Projections of Education Statistics* indicates that the MAPEs for public school enrollment in grades preK–12 for lead times of 1, 2, 5, and 10 years were 0.3, 0.6, 1.3, and 2.5 percent, respectively. For the 1-year-out projection, this means that one would expect the projection to be within 0.3 percent of the actual value, on average.

For a list of MAPEs for selected national statistics in this publication, see table A-2 on page 82. Sections A.1 through A.5 each contains at least one text table (tables A through F) that presents the MAPEs for the key national statistics of that section. Each text table appears directly after the discussion of accuracy of that section's national projections. For a list of MAPEs by state and region for public elementary and secondary enrollment, see tables A-7 through A-9 on pages 91–93 and for a list of MAPEs by state and region for the number of high school graduates in public schools, see table A-10 on page 98.

Tables A-3 and A-4 present an example of how the MAPEs were constructed using actual values for national public elementary and secondary enrollment projections for schools years 2008–09 through 2011–12 and enrollment projections from the last four editions of *Projections of Education Statistics*. The top two panels of table A-3 shows the actual values for school years 2008–09 through 2011–12 and enrollment projections for each year from *Projections of Education Statistics to 2018* with the number of projections generally decreasing by one for each subsequent edition. The bottom panel of table A-3 shows the percentage differences between the actual values and the projected values. For example, the projected value for 2008–09 presented in *Projections of Education Statistics to 2018* was 0.7 higher than the actual value for that year.

The top panel of table A-4 shows the absolute value of the percent differences from table A-3 arranged by lead time rather than year. For example, in the *Projections of Education Statistics to 2018*, the last year of actual data reported was 2006–07 and thus the lead time for the projection of 2008–09 data was 2 years. Thus, the 0.7 appearing in the 2008–09 column of Table A-3 for *Projections of Education Statistics to 2018* appears in the column for lead times of 2 years in Table A-4, indicating that projection of the two-years-out forecast from *Projections of Education Statistics to 2018* differed by 0.7 percent in absolute terms from its actual value. The MAPEs for each lead time shown in the bottom panel of table A-4 were calculated by computing the average of the absolute values of the percentage differences for that lead time. For example, actual values are available to calculate the absolute values of the percentage differences for a lead time of 3 years for the first three editions of the *Projections of Education Statistics* listed in table A-4. These absolute values are 0.9, 0.2, and 0.2. The MAPE for a lead time of 3 years was then calculated by taking the average of these numbers, or 0.4. This matches the MAPE that appears in the bottom panel for a lead time of 3 years. (Calculations for table A-3 are based on unrounded numbers.) These MAPEs are different from the MAPEs for public elementary and secondary enrollment projections elsewhere in this report because the MAPEs in the example were calculated using only the last 4 editions of *Projections of Education Statistics*.

The number of years used in the analyses of the projection errors differ both because projections of additional education statistics have been added to the report over time and because, in some cases, there have been substantial changes in the methodology used to produce the projections that the MAPES for the earlier projections are no longer relevant. MAPEs are presented for a statistic only after it has been produced using substantially the same methodology in five previous editions of *Projections of Education Statistics*.

Table A-1. Summary of forecast assumptions to 2022

Variable	Assumption
1	2
Demographic assumptions	
Population...	Projections are consistent with the Census Bureau estimates[1]
18- to 24-year-old population...	Census Bureau projection: average annual growth rate of -0.3%
25- to 29-year-old population...	Census Bureau projection: average annual growth rate of 0.6%
30- to 34-year-old population...	Census Bureau projection: average annual growth rate of 1.3%
35- to 44-year-old population...	Census Bureau projection: average annual growth rate of 0.6%
Economic assumptions	
Disposable income per capita in constant dollars....................................	Annual percent changes range between -0.4% and 2.5% with an annual growth rate of 1.4%
Education revenue receipts from state sources per capita in constant dollars	Annual percent changes range between 0.1% and 2.6% with an annual growth rate of 1.5%
Inflation rate...	Inflation rate ranges between 1.5% and 2.9%
Unemployment rate (men)	
Ages 18 and 19	Remains between 17.3% and 25.4%
Ages 20 to 24	Remains between 9.7% and 14.0%
Age 25 and over	Remains between 4.6% and 6.7%
Unemployment rate (women)	
Ages 18 and 19	Remains between 13.5% and 18.8%
Ages 20 to 24	Remains between 8.3% and 12.4%
Age 25 and over	Remains between 4.6% and 6.6%

[1]As the Census Bureau projections were not updated to reflect the most recent 2012 Census Bureau population estimates, the Census Bureau age-specific population projections for each year were adjusted by multiplying the ratio of the total Census Bureau estimate for 2012 to the total Census Bureau projection for 2012.

SOURCE: U.S. Department of Commerce, Census Bureau, Population Estimates, retrieved December 19, 2012, from http://www.census.gov/popest/data/index.html; and Population Projections, retrieved December 12, 2012, from http://www.census.gov/population/projections/data/national/2012/downloadablefiles.html; and IHS Global Insight, "U.S. Monthly Model January 2013 Short-Term Projections." (This table was prepared March 2013.)

Table A-2. Mean absolute percentage errors (MAPEs), by lead time for selected statistics in all elementary and secondary schools and postsecondary degree-granting institutions: 2013

Statistic	Lead time (years)									
	1	2	3	4	5	6	7	8	9	10
1	2	3	4	5	6	7	8	9	10	11
Public elementary and secondary schools										
Prekindergarten–12 enrollment[1]	0.3	0.6	0.8	1.1	1.3	1.5	1.7	1.9	2.2	2.5
Prekindergarten–8 enrollment[1]	0.3	0.6	1.0	1.2	1.5	1.7	2.0	2.3	2.7	3.1
9–12 enrollment[1]	0.4	0.7	0.9	1.1	1.2	1.4	1.8	2.1	2.3	2.5
High school graduates[2]	1.0	1.1	1.6	1.8	1.7	2.1	2.8	3.8	4.4	4.6
Elementary and secondary teachers[3]	0.8	1.6	1.8	2.3	3.0	3.7	4.4	4.8	4.7	5.2
Total current expenditures[4]	1.3	2.1	2.1	2.0	2.6	3.4	4.0	4.0	3.9	3.9
Current expenditures per pupil in fall enrollment[4]	1.3	2.0	2.1	2.0	2.9	3.6	4.4	4.6	5.0	4.9
Private elementary and secondary schools[5]										
Prekindergarten–12 enrollment[5]	2.2	5.5	3.7	8.4	8.3	11.7	12.1	15.1	16.2	15.2
Prekindergarten–8 enrollment	2.6	5.8	4.3	9.5	10.0	14.0	15.0	17.4	19.3	17.9
9–12 enrollment	2.7	4.2	2.5	4.5	3.0	4.6	4.0	7.8	6.2	6.6
High school graduates	0.7	1.2	1.6	2.8	4.1	5.2	3.3	5.6	4.6	4.9
Postsecondary degree-granting institutions[6]										
Total enrollment	1.6	2.5	3.8	5.0	5.8	6.5	7.8	9.4	11.5	13.1
Men	1.7	2.9	4.3	5.7	6.6	7.4	8.5	9.8	11.8	13.3
Women	1.7	2.5	3.9	4.7	5.1	5.7	7.3	9.0	11.2	12.9
4-year institutions	1.7	3.0	4.3	5.7	6.6	7.3	8.9	10.6	13.1	14.8
2-year institutions	2.3	3.1	4.2	4.9	5.2	5.1	5.9	7.1	8.7	10.1
White	1.0	2.4	3.7	5.1	6.4	5.8	5.2	—	—	—
Black	4.1	8.8	12.7	16.4	19.3	19.9	20.0	—	—	—
Hispanic	3.8	8.6	13.3	16.9	20.0	22.1	24.0	—	—	—
Asian/Pacific Islander	2.3	5.0	5.5	5.5	4.8	2.5	2.9	—	—	—
American Indian/Alaska Native	5.5	4.1	5.1	6.8	4.7	8.2	11.9	—	—	—
Nonresident alien	2.9	4.8	6.6	9.5	11.7	9.0	3.9	—	—	—

—Not available.

[1]MAPEs for public prekindergarten–12 enrollments were calculated using the last 29 editions of *Projections of Education Statistics*.

[2]MAPEs for public high school graduates were calculated from the past 22 editions of *Projections of Education Statistics*.

[3]Data for teachers expressed in full-time equivalents. MAPEs for teachers were calculated from the past 22 editions containing teachers projections.

[4]In constant dollars based on the Consumer Price Index for all urban consumers, Bureau of Labor Statistics, U.S. Department of Labor. MAPEs for current expenditures were calculated using projections from the last 21 editions containing current expenditure projections.

[5]MAPEs for private prekindergarten–12 enrollments and high school graduates were calculated from the past 11 editions.

[6]MAPEs for postsecondary degree-granting institution enrollments were calculated using the last 15 editions of *Projections of Education Statistics*, with the exception of the enrollment projections by race/ethnicity, which were calculated using the last 7 editions of *Projections of Education Statistics*.

NOTE: Mean absolute percentage error (MAPE) is the average value over past projections of the absolute values of errors expressed in percentage terms. No MAPEs are presented for degrees conferred as the current models used for producing these projections have only been used for four other editions of *Projections of Education Statistics*. Calculations were made using unrounded numbers. Some data have been revised from previously published figures.

SOURCE: U.S. Department of Education, National Center for Education Statistics, *Projections of Education Statistics*, various issues. (This table was prepared March 2013.)

Table A-3. Example of constructing mean absolute percentage errors (MAPEs), part 1

Source	Year of data			
	2008–09	2009–10	2010–11	2011–12
1	2	3	4	5
	Enrollment in thousands			
Actual..	49,266	49,361	49,484	49,520
	Projected enrollment in thousands			
Projections of Education Statistics to 2018	49,623	49,788	50,034	50,349
Projections of Education Statistics to 2019	49,265	49,312	49,386	49,554
Projections of Education Statistics to 2020	†	49,282	49,306	49,422
Projections of Education Statistics to 2021	†	†	†	49,636
	Percentage difference between actual and projected values			
Projections of Education Statistics to 2018	0.7	0.9	1.1	1.7
Projections of Education Statistics to 2019	#	-0.1	-0.2	0.1
Projections of Education Statistics to 2020	†	-0.2	-0.4	-0.2
Projections of Education Statistics to 2021	†	†	†	0.2

† Not applicable.
# Rounds to zero.
NOTE: Some data have been revised from previously published figures. Calculations are based on unrounded numbers.

SOURCE: U.S. Department of Education, National Center for Education Statistics, Common Core of Data (CCD), "State Nonfiscal Survey of Public Elementary/Secondary Education," 2008–09 through 2011–12; and *Projections of Education Statistics*, various editions. (This table was prepared March 2013.)

Table A-4. Example of constructing mean absolute percentage errors (MAPEs), part 2

Source	Lead time (years)			
	1	2	3	4
1	2	3	4	5
	Absolute value of percentage difference between actual and projected values			
Projections of Education Statistics to 2018	†	0.7	0.9	1.1
Projections of Education Statistics to 2019	#	0.1	0.2	0.1
Projections of Education Statistics to 2020	0.2	0.4	0.2	†
Projections of Education Statistics to 2021	0.2	†	†	†
	Mean absolute percentage error			
Example..	0.1	0.4	0.4	0.6

† Not applicable.
# Rounds to zero.
NOTE: The MAPEs presented in this table are for illustrative purpose only. Calculations are based on unrounded numbers.

SOURCE: U.S. Department of Education, National Center for Education Statistics, Common Core of Data (CCD), "State Nonfiscal Survey of Public Elementary/Secondary Education," 2008–09 through 2011–12; and *Projections of Education Statistics*, various editions. (This table was prepared March 2013.)

A.1. ELEMENTARY AND SECONDARY ENROLLMENT

Projections in this edition

This edition of *Projections of Education Statistics* presents projected trends in elementary and secondary enrollment from 2012 to 2022. These projections were made using three models:

» The *National Elementary and Secondary Enrollment Model* was used to project total, public, and private school enrollments for the nation by grade level and for ungraded elementary and ungraded secondary programs.

» The *State Public Elementary and Secondary Enrollment Model* was used to project total public school enrollments by grade level for individual states and regions.

» The *National Public Elementary and Secondary Enrollment by Race/Ethnicity Model* was used to project public school enrollments for the nation by race/ethnicity and grade level.

All three elementary and secondary enrollment models used the following same methods.

Overview of approach

Two methods were used in all the elementary and secondary enrollment models:

» The *grade progression rate method* was used to project enrollments in grades 2 through 12. In this method, a rate of progression from each grade (1 through 11) to the next grade (2 through 12) was projected using single exponential smoothing. (For example, the rate of progression from grade 2 to grade 3 is the current year's grade 3 enrollment expressed as a percentage of the previous year's grade 2 enrollment.) To calculate enrollment for each year in the forecast period, the progression rate for each grade was applied to the previous year's enrollment in the previous grade.

» The *enrollment rate method* was used to project prekindergarten, kindergarten, and first-grade enrollments as well as elementary special and ungraded and secondary special and ungraded enrollments. For each of these enrollment categories, the enrollment rate for the last year of actual data was used as the projected enrollment rate. To calculate enrollment for each year in the forecast period, the enrollment rate for each category was applied to the projected population in the appropriate age group.

Assumptions underlying these methods

The grade progression and enrollment rate methods assume that past trends in factors affecting public and private elementary and secondary school enrollments will continue over the forecast period. This assumption implies that all factors influencing enrollments will display future patterns consistent with past patterns. This method implicitly includes the net effect of such factors as migration, dropouts, deaths, nonpromotion, and transfers between public and private schools.

For more details on the use of the grade progression and enrollment rate methods, see "Procedures and equations used in all three elementary and secondary enrollment models," below.

Procedures and equations used in all three elementary and secondary enrollment models

The notation and equations that follow describe the basic procedures used to project elementary and secondary enrollments in each of the three elementary and secondary enrollment models.

Let:

i	=	Subscript denoting age
j	=	Subscript denoting grade
t	=	Subscript denoting time
T	=	Subscript of the first year in the forecast period
N_t	=	Enrollment at the prekindergarten (nursery) level
K_t	=	Enrollment at the kindergarten level
$G_{j,t}$	=	Enrollment in grade j
E_t	=	Enrollment in elementary special and ungraded programs

S_t =   Enrollment in secondary special and ungraded programs

$P_{i,t}$ =   Population age i

$R_{j,t}$ =   Progression rate for grade j

RN_t =   Enrollment rate for prekindergarten (nursery school)

RK_t =   Enrollment rate for kindergarten

$RG_{1,t}$ =   Enrollment rate for grade 1

RE_t =   Enrollment rate for elementary special and ungraded programs

RS_t =   Enrollment rate for secondary special and ungraded programs.

Step 1. *Calculate historical grade progression rates for each of grades 2 through 12.* The first step in projecting the enrollments for grades 2 through 12 using the grade progression method was to calculate, for each grade, a progression rate for each year of actual data used to produce the projections except for the first year. The progression rate for grade j in year t equals

$$R_{j,t} = G_{j,t}/G_{j-1,t-1}$$

Step 2. *Produce a projected progression rate for each of grades 2 through 12.* Projections for each grade's progression rate were then produced for the forecast period using single exponential smoothing. A separate smoothing constant, chosen to minimize the sum of squared forecast errors, was used to calculate the projected progression rate for each grade. Single exponential smoothing produces a single forecast for all years in the forecast period. Therefore, for each grade j, the projected progression rate, $\hat{R}_j$, is the same for each year in the forecast period.

Step 3. *Calculate enrollment projections for each of grades 2 through 12.* For the first year in the forecast period, T, enrollment projections, $\hat{G}_{j,t}$, for grades 2 through 12, were produced using the projected progression rates and the enrollments of grades 1 through 11 from the last year of actual data, $T-1$. Specifically,

$$\hat{G}_{j,T} = \hat{R}_j \cdot G_{j-1,T-1}$$

This same procedure was then used to produce the projections for the following year, $T+1$, except that enrollment projections for year T were used rather than actual numbers:

$$\hat{G}_{j,T+1} = \hat{R}_j \cdot \hat{G}_{j,T}$$

The enrollment projections for grades 2 through 11 for year T were those just produced using the grade progression method. The projection for grade 1 for year T was produced using the enrollment rate method, as outlined in steps 4 and 5 below.

The same procedure was used for the remaining years in the projections period.

Step 4. *For the last year of actual data, calculate enrollment rates for prekindergarten, kindergarten, grade 1, elementary special and ungraded, and secondary special and ungraded.* The first step in projecting prekindergarten, kindergarten, first-grade, elementary special and ungraded, and secondary special and ungraded enrollments using the enrollment rate method was to calculate enrollment rates for each enrollment category for the last year of actual data, $T-1$, where:

$$RN_{T-1} \;=\; N_{T-1}/P_{5,T-1}$$
$$RK_{T-1} \;=\; K_{T-1}/P_{5,T-1}$$
$$RG_{1,T-1} \;=\; G_{1,T-1}/P_{6,T-1}$$
$$RE_{T-1} \;=\; E_{T-1}/\Sigma_{i=5}^{13}P_{i,T-1}$$
$$RS_{T-1} \;=\; S_{T-1}/\Sigma_{i=14}^{17}P_{i,T-1}$$

These enrollment rates were then used as the projected enrollment rates for each year in the forecast period ($\widehat{RN}$, $\widehat{RK}$, $\widehat{RG_1}$, $\widehat{RE}$, and $\widehat{RS}$.)

Step 5. *Using the rates for the last year of actual data as the projected enrollment rates, calculate enrollment projections for prekindergarten through grade 1 and the ungraded categories.* For each year in the forecast period, the enrollment rates were then multiplied by the appropriate population projections from the U.S. Census Bureau ($\hat{P}_{i,t}$) to calculate enrollment projections for prekindergarten (nursery school) ($\hat{N}_t$), kindergarten ($\hat{K}_t$), first grade ($\hat{G}_{1,t}$), elementary ungraded ($\hat{E}_t$), and secondary ungraded ($\hat{S}_t$)

$$\hat{N}_t = \widehat{RN} \cdot \hat{P}_{5,t}$$
$$\hat{K}_t = \widehat{RK} \cdot \hat{P}_{5,t}$$
$$\hat{G}_{1,t} = \widehat{RG_1} \cdot \hat{P}_{5,t}$$
$$\hat{E}_t = \widehat{RE} \cdot (\sum_{i=5}^{13} \hat{P}_{i,t})$$
$$\hat{S}_t = \widehat{RS} \cdot (\sum_{i=14}^{17} \hat{P}_{i,t})$$

Step 6. *Calculate total elementary and secondary enrollments by summing the projections for each grade and the ungraded categories.* To obtain projections of total enrollment, projections of enrollments for the individual grades (prekindergarten through 12), elementary ungraded, and secondary ungraded were summed.

National Elementary and Secondary Enrollment Model

This model was used to project national total, public, and private school enrollments by grade level and for ungraded elementary and ungraded secondary programs. National enrollment projections for public and private schools were developed separately, then added together to yield total elementary and secondary enrollment projections for the nation. To develop these projections, enrollment data from NCES were used, along with population estimates and projections from the U.S. Census Bureau. Below is information about the specific data used to develop the public school projections and the private school projections, as well as information about the grade progression rates and enrollment rates specific to public schools and private schools.

For details on procedures used to develop the projections, see "Procedures and equations used in all three elementary and secondary enrollment models," earlier in this section of appendix A.

Data used to develop national elementary and secondary enrollment projections

Public school enrollment data. Public school enrollment data from the NCES *Statistics of Public Elementary and Secondary School Systems* for 1972 to 1980 and the NCES Common Core of Data (CCD) for 1981 to 2011 were used to develop the national public school enrollment projections.

Private school enrollment data. Private school enrollment data from the NCES Private School Universe Survey (PSS) for 1989–90, 1991–92, 1993–94, 1995–96, 1997–98, 1999–2000, 2001–02, 2003–04, 2005–06, 2007–08, 2009–10, and 2011–12 were used to develop the national private school enrollment projections. Since the PSS is collected in the fall of odd-numbered years, data for even-numbered years without a PSS collection were estimated by interpolating grade-by-grade progression data from PSS.

Population estimates and projections used for public school enrollment projections. Population estimates for 1972 to 2011 and population projections for 2012 to 2022 from the U.S. Census Bureau were also used to develop the public school enrollment projections. The set of population projections used in this year's *Projections of Education Statistics* are the Census Bureau's 2012 National Population Projections by age and sex (December 2012), adjusted to line up with the most recent historical estimates. This was done through the use of ratio adjustments in which, for each combination of state, age, and sex, the population projections from 2012 to 2022 were multiplied by the ratio of the population estimate for 2011 to the population projection for 2012.

Population estimates and projections used for private school enrollment projections. Population estimates for 1989 to 2011 and population projections for 2012 to 2022 from the U.S. Census Bureau were used to develop the private school enrollment projections. The population projections were ratio-adjusted to line up with the most recent historical estimates.

Grade progression and enrollment rates for national elementary and secondary enrollment projections

Public school grade progression and enrollment rates. Table A-5 on page 90 shows the public school grade progression rates for 2011 and projections for 2012 through 2022. Table A-6 on page 90 shows the public school enrollment rates for 2011 and projections for 2012 through 2022.

Accuracy of national elementary and secondary enrollment projections

Mean absolute percentage errors (MAPEs) for projections of public school enrollment were calculated using the last 29 editions of *Projections of Education Statistics*, while MAPEs for projections of private school enrollment were calculated using the last 11 editions. Table A, below, shows MAPEs for both public and private school enrollment projections.

Table A.   Mean absolute percentage errors (MAPEs) of enrollment projections, by lead time, control of school, and grade in elementary and secondary schools: 2013

Statistic	Lead time (years)									
	1	2	3	4	5	6	7	8	9	10
Public elementary and secondary schools										
Prekindergarten–12 enrollment	0.3	0.6	0.8	1.1	1.3	1.5	1.7	1.9	2.2	2.5
Prekindergarten–8 enrollment	0.3	0.6	1.0	1.2	1.5	1.7	2.0	2.3	2.7	3.1
9–12 enrollment	0.4	0.7	0.9	1.1	1.2	1.4	1.8	2.1	2.3	2.5
Private elementary and secondary schools										
Prekindergarten–12 enrollment	2.2	5.5	3.7	8.4	8.3	11.7	12.1	15.1	16.2	15.2
Prekindergarten–8 enrollment	2.6	5.8	4.3	9.5	10.0	14.0	15.0	17.4	19.3	17.9
9–12 enrollment	2.7	4.2	2.5	4.5	3.0	4.6	4.0	7.8	6.2	6.6

NOTE: Mean absolute percentage error (MAPE) is the average value over past projections of the absolute values of errors expressed in percentage terms. MAPEs for public prekindergarten–12 enrollments were calculated using the last 29 editions of *Projections of Education Statistics*. MAPEs for private preK–12 enrollments were calculated from the past 11 editions. Calculations were made using unrounded numbers. Some data have been revised from previously published figures.
SOURCE: U.S. Department of Education, National Center for Education Statistics, *Projections of Education Statistics*, various issues. (This table was prepared February 2013.)

For more information about MAPEs, see Section A.0. Introduction, earlier in appendix A.

State Public Elementary and Secondary Enrollment Model

This edition of *Projections of Education Statistics* contains projected trends in public elementary and secondary enrollment by grade level from 2012 to 2022 for each of the 50 states and the District of Columbia, as well as for each region of the country. The state enrollment projections were produced in two stages:

» first, an initial set of projections for each state was produced; and

» second, these initial projections were adjusted to sum to the national public enrollment totals produced by the National Elementary and Secondary Enrollment Model.

For each region, the enrollment projections equaled the sum of enrollment projections for the states within that region.

Initial set of state projections

The same methods used to produce the national enrollment projections—namely, the grade progression rate method and the enrollment rate method—were used to produce the initial sets of public school enrollment projections for each state and the District of Columbia. A separate smoothing constant, chosen to minimize the sum of squared forecast errors, was used to calculate the projected progression rate for each combination of jurisdiction and grade.

For details on the procedures used to develop the initial sets of projections, see "Procedures and equations used in all three elementary and secondary enrollment models," earlier in this section of appendix A.

Limitations of the grade progression method for state projections

The grade progression rate method assumes that past trends in factors affecting public school enrollments will continue over the forecast period. This assumption implies that all factors influencing enrollments will display future patterns consistent with past patterns. Therefore, this method has limitations when applied to states with unanticipated changes in migration rates. This method implicitly includes the net effect of such factors as migration, dropouts, deaths, nonpromotion, and transfers to and from private schools.

Adjustments to the state projections

The initial projections of state public school enrollments were adjusted to sum to the national projections of public school prekindergarten (preK)–12, preK–8, and 9–12 enrollments shown in table 1 on page 31. This was done through the use of ratio adjustments in which all the states' initial enrollment projections for each grade level were multiplied by the ratio of the national enrollment projection for that grade level to the sum of the state enrollment projections for that grade level.

Data used to develop state elementary and secondary enrollment projections

Public school enrollment data. Public school enrollment data from the NCES *Statistics of Public Elementary and Secondary School Systems* for 1980 and from the NCES Common Core of Data (CCD) for 1981 to 2011 were used to develop these projections.

Population estimates and projections. Population estimates for 1980 to 2011 and population projections for 2012 to 2022 from the U.S. Census Bureau were used to develop the state-level enrollment projections. The set of population projections used in this year's *Projections of Education Statistics* are the Census Bureau's set of Interim State Population Projections by age and sex (April 2005). In order for the state-level population projections to be consistent with the most recent historical estimates released by the Census Bureau, these projections were adjusted to line up with the most recent historical estimate for each state. This was done through the use of ratio adjustments in which, for each combination of state, age, and sex, the population projections from 2012 to 2022 were multiplied by the ratio of the population estimate for 2011 to the population projection for 2011.

Accuracy of state elementary and secondary enrollment projections

Mean absolute percentage errors (MAPEs) for projections of public school enrollment by state were calculated using the last 17 editions of *Projections of Education Statistics*. Tables A-7 through A-9 on pages 91–93 show MAPEs for preK–12, preK–8, and 9–12 enrollment in public elementary and secondary schools by state.

National Public Elementary and Secondary Enrollment by Race/Ethnicity Model

This edition of *Projections of Education Statistics* contains projected trends in national public elementary and secondary enrollment by race/ethnicity from 2012 to 2022.

This is the first edition to include enrollment projections for students of two or more races. As 2010 is the first year in which all 50 states and the District of Columbia reported enrollment data for students of two or more races, enrollment projections for this category were produced using a different method than that used for the other five racial/ethnic groups.

Prior to 2008, there was a single category for students of Asian and/or Native Hawaiian or Other Pacific Islander origin. In 2008 and 2009, states could chose to either place these students in either single category, Asian and/or Native Hawaiian or Other Pacific Islander, or in one of three categories, (1) Asian, (2) Hawaiian or Other Pacific Islander, and (3) two or more races (for students of both Asian and Hawaiian or Other Pacific Islander origin). Beginning in 2010, the option of using the single category was eliminated and states were required to place students in one of those three categories. For students of Asian and/or Native Hawaiian or Other Pacific Islander origin, projections were calculated for a single category, Asian/Pacific Islander. For 2008 and 2009, the count of the Asian/Pacific Islander students included the total of the Asian and/or Native Hawaiian or Other Pacific Islander students for states reporting one category and the counts for Asian students and Native Hawaiian or Other Pacific Islander students for states reporting three categories. Beginning in 2010, the count of the Asian/Pacific Islander students was the sum of the counts Asian students and Native Hawaiian or Other Pacific Islander students.

The enrollment projections by race/ethnicity were produced in two stages:

   » first, an initial set of projections by race/ethnicity was produced; and

   » second, these initial projections were adjusted to sum to the national totals.

Initial set of projections by race/ethnicity

The same methods used to produce the national enrollment projections—namely, the grade progression rate method and the enrollment rate method—were used to produce initial sets of projections for each of the following five racial/ethnic groups: White, Black, Hispanic, Asian/Pacific Islander, and American Indian/Alaska Native. A separate smoothing constant, chosen to minimize the sum of squared forecast errors, was used to calculate the projected progression rate for each combination of race/ethnicity and grade.

For details on the procedures used to develop the initial sets of projections, see "Procedures and equations used in all three elementary and secondary enrollment models," earlier in this section of appendix A.

National enrollment projections for students of two or more races by grade level were produced by taking the 2011 grade level enrollment numbers for students of two or more races and applying the growth rates from 2012 to 2022 of the U.S. Census Bureau's age specific population projections for two or more races.

Adjustments to the projections by race/ethnicity

The initial projections of enrollments by race/ethnicity were adjusted to sum to the national projections of public school preK–12, preK–8, and 9–12 enrollments shown in table 1 on page 31. This was done through the use of ratio adjustments in which all the initial enrollment projections by race/ethnicity for each grade level were multiplied by the ratio of the national enrollment projection for that grade level to the sum of the initial enrollment projections by race/ethnicity for that grade level.

Data and imputations used to develop enrollment projections by race/ethnicity

Public school enrollment data. Public school enrollment data by grade level and race/ethnicity from the NCES Common Core of Data (CCD) for 1994 to 2011 were used to develop these projections. While projections by race/ethnicity were produced at the national level only, the national data used to develop these projections were constructed from state-level data on enrollment by grade level and race/ethnicity. In those instances where states did not report their enrollment data by grade level and race/ethnicity, the state-level data had to be examined and some imputations made in order to produce the national public school enrollment by grade level and race/ethnicity data. For example, in 1994, North Dakota did not report grade-level enrollment data by race/ethnicity. It did, however, report these numbers for 1995. So, to impute these numbers for 1994, North Dakota's 1994 grade-level enrollment data were multiplied by the state's 1995 racial/ethnic breakdowns at each grade level.

Population estimates and projections. Population estimates for 2000 to 2011 and population projections for 2012 to 2022 from the U.S. Census Bureau were used to develop the enrollment projections by race/ethnicity. The set of population projections used in this year's *Projections of Education Statistics* are the Census Bureau's 2012 National Population Projections by age, sex, and race/ethnicity (December 2012), ratio-adjusted to line up with the most recent historical estimates.

Accuracy of enrollment projections by race/ethnicity

Because this is the fourth edition of *Projections of Education Statistics* to include projections of elementary and secondary public school enrollments by race/ethnicity, the difference between the projections and actual data for a reasonable sample of time points cannot yet be determined.

Table A-5. Actual and projected national public school grade progression rates: Fall 2011, and fall 2012 through fall 2022

Grade	Actual 2011	Projected 2012 through 2022
1	2	3
1 to 2	98.9	98.9
2 to 3	100.1	100.2
3 to 4	99.6	100.1
4 to 5	99.7	100.2
5 to 6	100.2	100.5
6 to 7	100.4	100.5
7 to 8	100.1	100.1
8 to 9	108.1	108.1
9 to 10	93.6	93.6
10 to 11	93.3	93.3
11 to 12	97.6	97.6

NOTE: The progression rate for a particular grade in a year equals the enrollment in the grade for that year divided by the enrollment in the previous grade in the previous year, all multiplied by 100. For example, the progression rate for third-graders in 2011 equals the enrollment of third-graders in 2011 divided by the enrollment of second-graders in 2010, all multiplied by 100.

SOURCE: U.S. Department of Education, National Center for Education Statistics, Common Core of Data (CCD), "State Nonfiscal Survey of Public Elementary/Secondary Education," 2011–12; and National Elementary and Secondary Enrollment Model, 1972–2011. (This table was prepared January 2013.)

Table A-6. Actual and projected national enrollment rates in public schools, by grade level: Fall 2011, and fall 2012 through fall 2022

Grade level	Actual 2011	Projected 2012 through 2022
1	2	3
Prekindergarten	31.5	31.5
Kindergarten	91.5	91.5
Grade 1	92.1	92.1
Elementary ungraded	0.2	0.2
Secondary ungraded	0.2	0.2

NOTE: The enrollment rate for each grade level equals the enrollment at that grade level divided by the population of that grade's base age, all multiplied by 100. The base age for each grade level is as follows: kindergarten, 5 years old; grade 1, 6 years old; elementary ungraded, 5 to 13 years old; and secondary ungraded, 14 to 17 years old. Projected values for 2012 through 2022 were held constant at the actual values for 2011.

SOURCE: U.S. Department of Education, National Center for Education Statistics, Common Core of Data (CCD), "State Nonfiscal Survey of Public Elementary/Secondary Education," 2011–12; and National Elementary and Secondary Enrollment Model, 1972–2011. (This table was prepared January 2013.)

Table A-7. Mean absolute percentage errors (MAPEs) for projected preK–12 enrollment in public elementary and secondary schools, by lead time, region, and state: 2013

Region and state	Lead time (years)									
	1	2	3	4	5	6	7	8	9	10
1	2	3	4	5	6	7	8	9	10	11
United States	**0.3**	**0.6**	**0.8**	**1.1**	**1.3**	**1.5**	**1.7**	**1.9**	**2.2**	**2.5**
Northeast	0.5	0.5	0.8	0.9	0.6	0.7	0.9	0.7	0.7	1.2
Connecticut	0.6	0.8	1.0	1.4	2.0	2.5	3.3	4.1	5.1	6.1
Maine	0.8	1.3	1.4	1.8	2.0	1.9	1.6	2.0	2.6	2.6
Massachusetts	0.4	0.5	0.7	0.7	0.7	0.8	0.9	1.2	1.6	2.0
New Hampshire	0.6	0.8	0.9	1.2	1.4	1.8	2.5	2.7	3.1	3.9
New Jersey	0.8	1.2	1.7	2.0	2.2	2.8	3.3	3.9	4.9	5.6
New York	0.9	1.0	1.4	1.8	1.8	2.1	2.3	2.5	2.8	3.1
Pennsylvania	1.0	1.4	1.5	1.3	1.3	1.6	2.0	2.0	1.7	2.1
Rhode Island	1.0	1.7	2.5	3.1	3.2	3.1	3.2	3.4	3.5	3.6
Vermont	1.4	2.0	2.4	3.0	3.5	4.1	4.5	5.8	5.6	6.7
Midwest	0.3	0.4	0.5	0.7	0.8	1.0	1.2	1.4	1.5	1.7
Illinois	0.6	0.8	1.0	1.0	1.3	1.6	1.7	2.0	2.4	2.9
Indiana	0.3	0.6	0.9	1.2	1.7	2.2	2.6	2.9	3.1	3.4
Iowa	0.6	0.9	1.2	1.5	1.6	1.6	1.7	2.4	2.9	2.9
Kansas	0.8	1.1	1.5	1.7	1.8	2.0	2.1	2.4	2.3	2.4
Michigan	0.7	1.6	2.1	2.7	3.3	4.1	4.6	4.9	5.1	4.5
Minnesota	0.4	0.6	0.7	0.9	1.0	1.2	1.4	1.6	1.7	1.8
Missouri	0.4	0.5	0.6	0.7	0.9	1.0	1.1	1.2	1.2	1.5
Nebraska	0.5	0.8	1.1	1.4	1.6	2.0	2.3	2.8	3.0	2.7
North Dakota	0.8	1.4	2.1	2.7	3.4	4.3	5.6	6.9	8.0	9.1
Ohio	0.5	0.6	0.9	1.0	1.5	1.8	1.9	1.9	1.9	1.9
South Dakota	1.3	2.2	3.3	4.6	5.6	6.5	6.9	7.5	8.1	9.2
Wisconsin	0.6	1.0	1.3	1.5	1.6	1.7	2.0	2.0	2.0	2.1
South	0.4	0.9	1.3	1.8	2.2	2.5	2.8	3.3	4.2	4.8
Alabama	0.6	0.7	1.0	1.5	2.1	3.0	3.8	4.8	5.5	6.0
Arkansas	0.6	1.1	1.7	2.3	3.2	4.0	4.6	5.0	5.5	5.6
Delaware	0.7	1.2	1.8	2.4	3.2	4.1	5.3	6.5	7.7	8.0
District of Columbia	5.4	4.8	6.1	6.9	6.7	6.8	6.1	4.7	6.7	5.9
Florida	1.0	1.8	2.5	3.3	4.5	5.2	5.5	5.9	6.8	8.3
Georgia	0.7	1.3	1.9	2.7	3.3	3.7	4.0	4.6	5.8	6.7
Kentucky	1.6	1.5	2.1	2.3	2.3	3.0	3.2	3.4	4.3	4.5
Louisiana	2.0	3.2	3.9	4.9	5.8	6.5	6.1	5.9	7.2	8.6
Maryland	0.5	0.9	1.3	1.7	1.8	1.8	2.0	2.1	2.1	2.4
Mississippi	0.4	0.9	1.2	1.4	1.7	2.1	2.6	2.8	3.3	3.3
North Carolina	0.9	1.5	2.3	3.2	3.5	4.1	4.6	5.5	6.9	7.8
Oklahoma	0.9	1.4	2.0	2.5	3.2	3.9	4.8	5.8	6.6	7.1
South Carolina	0.7	1.2	1.6	2.2	2.7	3.2	4.0	4.9	5.7	5.7
Tennessee	1.0	1.4	1.8	2.2	2.4	2.6	3.2	3.9	4.1	3.7
Texas	0.8	1.4	2.0	2.6	3.2	3.8	4.6	5.7	7.1	8.3
Virginia	0.4	0.7	0.9	1.2	1.6	2.1	2.6	3.1	3.7	3.9
West Virginia	0.6	0.7	1.0	1.5	2.0	2.7	3.5	4.5	5.1	5.1
West	0.5	1.0	1.3	1.6	1.9	2.0	2.0	2.0	2.0	1.7
Alaska	1.1	1.8	2.4	2.7	3.0	4.0	5.3	6.7	8.7	10.6
Arizona	2.5	3.7	5.2	6.6	7.8	8.4	7.8	8.5	9.7	11.3
California	0.6	1.0	1.5	2.1	2.6	3.0	3.2	3.4	3.7	3.6
Colorado	0.6	0.9	1.3	1.7	2.2	3.1	4.0	4.8	5.7	6.8
Hawaii	1.8	2.7	3.8	5.2	7.0	8.6	10.5	12.1	14.2	17.2
Idaho	0.7	1.4	2.1	2.9	3.6	4.0	4.2	4.2	4.2	4.1
Montana	0.9	1.5	2.2	3.1	4.2	5.6	7.1	8.8	10.9	13.0
Nevada	1.1	2.0	3.1	4.6	6.1	7.5	8.9	10.5	12.6	15.6
New Mexico	1.4	2.3	3.1	4.2	5.5	7.0	8.7	10.0	10.9	12.5
Oregon	0.7	1.2	1.6	1.8	2.1	2.5	3.0	3.3	3.5	3.9
Utah	1.7	1.8	2.0	3.1	3.3	4.3	5.4	6.6	7.3	7.1
Washington	0.5	0.8	1.1	1.4	1.8	2.1	2.6	2.8	2.8	3.2
Wyoming	0.8	1.4	2.4	3.7	5.4	7.1	8.3	10.0	11.7	14.1

NOTE: Mean absolute percentage error (MAPE) is the average value over past projections of the absolute values of errors expressed in percentage terms. National MAPEs for public prekindergarten–12 enrollments were calculated using the last 29 editions of *Projections of Education Statistics*, and state MAPEs were calculated using the last 17 editions of *Projections of Education Statistics*. Calculations were made using unrounded numbers. Some data have been revised from previously published figures.
SOURCE: U.S. Department of Education, National Center for Education Statistics, *Projections of Education Statistics*, various issues. (This table was prepared February 2013.)

Table A-8. Mean absolute percentage errors (MAPEs) for projected preK–8 enrollment in public elementary and secondary schools, by lead time, region, and state: 2013

Region and state	Lead time (years)									
	1	2	3	4	5	6	7	8	9	10
1	2	3	4	5	6	7	8	9	10	11
United States	**0.3**	**0.6**	**1.0**	**1.2**	**1.5**	**1.7**	**2.0**	**2.3**	**2.7**	**3.1**
Northeast	0.4	0.7	0.8	0.9	0.7	0.6	0.9	0.8	0.6	1.0
Connecticut	0.6	0.9	1.3	1.7	2.3	2.9	3.8	4.3	5.2	5.6
Maine	0.6	0.9	1.2	1.7	2.1	2.8	3.4	4.3	5.5	6.6
Massachusetts	0.3	0.6	0.9	1.1	1.0	1.2	1.5	1.6	1.9	2.2
New Hampshire	0.7	1.0	1.2	1.8	2.6	3.2	4.0	4.2	4.7	5.5
New Jersey	0.9	1.3	1.7	1.9	2.0	2.4	2.9	3.3	4.0	4.4
New York	0.7	1.0	1.4	1.7	1.8	1.8	2.4	2.6	2.8	3.1
Pennsylvania	0.6	1.0	1.1	1.0	1.1	1.3	1.8	1.7	1.5	1.6
Rhode Island	1.2	1.9	2.6	3.4	3.5	3.7	4.1	4.3	4.7	5.2
Vermont	1.8	2.2	2.6	3.4	4.4	5.4	6.8	8.7	8.4	9.9
Midwest	0.3	0.4	0.6	0.7	0.8	0.9	1.1	1.1	1.2	1.4
Illinois	0.7	0.9	1.1	1.2	1.6	1.9	2.0	2.2	2.5	2.8
Indiana	0.4	0.7	1.0	1.3	1.6	2.0	2.4	2.5	2.8	3.4
Iowa	0.8	1.2	1.6	2.1	2.3	2.5	2.6	3.4	4.0	3.9
Kansas	0.9	1.2	1.5	1.8	2.1	2.4	2.6	3.1	3.1	3.2
Michigan	0.6	1.5	2.0	2.7	3.2	3.9	4.4	4.8	4.9	4.3
Minnesota	0.4	0.5	0.8	1.0	1.1	1.2	1.2	1.1	1.3	1.3
Missouri	0.5	0.8	1.0	1.2	1.4	1.5	1.5	1.3	1.1	1.3
Nebraska	0.7	1.0	1.3	1.6	1.9	2.3	2.6	3.2	3.4	3.2
North Dakota	1.1	2.0	2.9	3.7	4.6	5.8	7.4	9.2	10.3	11.4
Ohio	0.5	0.5	0.7	0.7	1.0	1.1	1.2	1.1	1.2	1.4
South Dakota	1.4	2.1	3.2	4.9	6.3	7.7	8.4	10.1	11.2	11.8
Wisconsin	0.7	0.9	1.1	1.5	1.6	1.8	1.9	2.0	1.9	1.9
South	0.6	1.1	1.7	2.3	2.7	3.0	3.3	3.7	4.6	5.3
Alabama	0.7	1.0	1.6	2.0	2.8	3.6	4.2	5.2	6.0	6.5
Arkansas	0.8	1.3	2.1	2.9	3.9	4.9	5.6	5.8	6.4	6.5
Delaware	0.9	1.4	2.0	2.8	3.5	4.6	5.9	7.3	8.7	9.2
District of Columbia	4.8	4.8	5.4	6.1	6.0	6.1	6.1	4.4	6.7	6.0
Florida	1.1	2.1	3.2	4.3	5.6	6.2	6.4	6.8	7.7	9.1
Georgia	0.9	1.7	2.5	3.4	4.1	4.3	4.7	5.1	6.2	7.3
Kentucky	1.7	1.9	2.8	3.0	3.4	3.2	3.5	3.6	4.5	5.0
Louisiana	1.8	3.0	3.4	4.1	4.8	5.5	5.5	5.1	6.1	7.5
Maryland	0.5	1.0	1.4	1.9	2.1	2.4	3.0	3.5	3.7	4.2
Mississippi	0.6	1.2	1.6	2.0	2.6	2.9	3.2	3.3	3.6	3.6
North Carolina	1.2	2.0	3.0	4.0	4.4	5.0	5.5	6.8	8.7	9.7
Oklahoma	1.3	1.9	2.6	3.3	4.1	5.1	6.2	7.3	8.2	9.0
South Carolina	1.0	1.4	1.8	2.5	3.0	3.8	4.5	5.4	6.3	6.3
Tennessee	0.9	1.3	2.0	2.3	2.5	2.5	2.6	2.9	3.3	3.0
Texas	1.0	1.8	2.6	3.3	4.0	4.4	5.0	6.1	7.7	9.0
Virginia	0.6	0.9	1.0	1.3	1.7	2.3	2.8	3.3	3.9	3.9
West Virginia	0.6	0.7	1.0	1.4	2.0	2.7	3.5	4.5	5.3	5.2
West	0.6	1.2	1.6	1.9	2.2	2.3	2.2	2.2	2.5	2.2
Alaska	1.3	1.9	2.8	3.4	4.3	6.0	7.8	10.1	12.7	14.9
Arizona	2.3	3.4	5.0	6.0	6.9	7.9	7.5	8.6	9.6	11.2
California	0.9	1.5	2.0	2.7	3.3	3.8	3.9	4.1	4.8	4.8
Colorado	0.7	1.2	1.5	2.0	2.7	3.6	4.7	5.9	7.1	8.3
Hawaii	1.9	3.1	4.3	6.0	8.4	10.6	13.1	15.4	17.9	21.0
Idaho	0.9	2.0	3.0	3.8	4.6	4.9	5.0	4.9	5.0	4.8
Montana	1.1	1.9	2.9	4.2	5.7	7.8	10.1	12.6	15.3	17.8
Nevada	1.3	2.9	4.7	6.6	8.5	10.4	12.2	14.5	17.1	20.4
New Mexico	1.3	2.1	2.6	3.5	4.8	6.6	8.5	10.4	11.2	12.6
Oregon	0.8	1.2	1.4	1.4	2.1	2.5	2.7	3.2	3.7	4.2
Utah	1.6	1.9	2.2	3.0	3.6	4.8	5.9	7.3	7.9	7.5
Washington	0.5	0.8	1.1	1.4	1.8	2.3	2.7	3.0	2.8	3.2
Wyoming	1.0	1.6	2.9	4.5	6.8	9.1	10.8	13.6	15.7	18.3

NOTE: Mean absolute percentage error (MAPE) is the average value over past projections of the absolute values of errors expressed in percentage terms. National MAPEs for prekindergarten–8 enrollments were calculated using the last 29 editions of *Projections of Education Statistics*, and state MAPEs were calculated using the last 17 editions of *Projections of Education Statistics*. Calculations were made using unrounded numbers. Some data have been revised from previously published figures.
SOURCE: U.S. Department of Education, National Center for Education Statistics, *Projections of Education Statistics*, various issues. (This table was prepared February 2013.)

Table A-9. Mean absolute percentage errors (MAPEs) for projected grades 9–12 enrollment in public schools, by lead time, region, and state: 2013

Region and state	Lead time (years)									
	1	2	3	4	5	6	7	8	9	10
1	2	3	4	5	6	7	8	9	10	11
United States	0.4	0.7	0.9	1.1	1.2	1.4	1.8	2.1	2.3	2.5
Northeast	0.9	1.0	1.1	1.2	1.3	1.3	1.1	1.2	1.2	1.8
Connecticut	0.7	1.0	1.0	1.2	1.9	2.6	3.5	4.4	5.9	7.6
Maine	1.8	3.1	3.8	4.9	5.8	6.6	7.4	8.4	9.3	8.5
Massachusetts	0.6	1.0	1.5	1.8	2.3	2.7	2.8	2.4	2.5	2.6
New Hampshire	0.6	1.1	1.5	1.8	2.0	2.4	2.9	4.0	4.7	5.0
New Jersey	0.7	1.4	2.1	2.3	2.8	4.0	5.1	6.1	7.5	8.5
New York	1.5	1.6	1.9	2.1	2.4	2.8	2.6	3.0	3.5	3.5
Pennsylvania	1.8	2.3	2.3	2.2	2.4	2.4	2.6	2.6	2.1	3.5
Rhode Island	0.9	1.6	2.4	3.2	3.8	4.3	4.4	4.4	4.1	4.6
Vermont	1.0	2.5	3.0	3.6	3.9	4.2	4.2	4.4	4.3	3.6
Midwest	0.5	0.8	1.0	1.2	1.3	1.4	1.8	2.1	2.2	2.3
Illinois	0.8	1.1	1.3	1.5	1.8	2.4	2.8	3.3	3.5	3.9
Indiana	0.5	1.0	1.5	1.9	2.3	2.8	3.4	4.0	4.4	4.7
Iowa	0.8	1.0	1.3	1.2	1.6	1.7	1.8	1.8	2.1	2.1
Kansas	1.2	1.8	2.3	2.6	2.4	2.1	1.8	1.7	1.6	1.0
Michigan	1.6	2.6	3.2	3.5	4.2	5.0	6.4	7.9	9.6	9.9
Minnesota	0.6	1.0	1.2	1.4	1.7	2.0	2.3	2.8	3.0	3.3
Missouri	0.4	0.8	1.0	1.4	1.6	1.7	1.8	1.8	2.0	2.3
Nebraska	0.4	0.8	1.2	1.4	1.7	2.1	2.5	3.1	3.3	3.2
North Dakota	0.7	1.3	1.7	2.1	2.6	3.3	4.4	5.9	7.0	7.5
Ohio	1.1	1.8	2.3	2.5	2.7	3.2	3.7	3.8	3.6	3.2
South Dakota	1.7	3.2	4.7	5.9	7.2	8.1	9.3	10.2	10.6	11.1
Wisconsin	0.8	1.3	1.5	1.8	2.0	2.2	2.4	2.3	2.1	2.3
South	0.4	0.9	1.4	1.5	1.8	2.1	2.4	2.7	3.2	3.6
Alabama	0.9	1.4	1.9	2.4	2.9	3.8	4.6	5.3	6.0	6.1
Arkansas	0.5	0.9	1.3	1.4	1.8	2.2	2.5	3.0	3.2	3.5
Delaware	1.3	1.6	2.0	2.5	2.8	3.4	4.2	4.6	5.7	6.7
District of Columbia	7.5	8.2	11.3	13.8	15.6	16.5	14.7	15.1	17.0	16.9
Florida	0.8	1.2	1.6	1.7	2.0	3.2	4.2	5.0	5.5	6.6
Georgia	0.5	1.0	1.3	1.4	1.9	2.5	3.1	3.9	4.7	5.2
Kentucky	1.6	2.0	2.1	2.1	2.2	3.5	4.2	4.5	5.3	4.8
Louisiana	3.0	4.2	5.6	7.3	8.7	9.6	8.3	8.2	10.2	11.7
Maryland	0.6	0.9	1.4	1.7	1.6	1.5	1.5	1.8	2.1	2.0
Mississippi	0.6	1.3	2.0	2.4	2.8	3.2	3.6	4.2	4.4	4.2
North Carolina	1.0	1.5	1.6	1.8	2.2	2.6	3.1	3.3	3.9	4.8
Oklahoma	0.5	0.9	1.3	1.7	2.1	2.6	2.9	3.5	3.9	4.4
South Carolina	0.8	1.5	2.1	2.6	3.0	3.3	3.3	3.8	4.4	5.5
Tennessee	2.1	2.2	3.0	4.0	4.6	5.5	6.0	6.5	6.2	5.7
Texas	0.6	1.2	1.7	2.1	2.5	3.1	3.9	4.7	5.6	6.6
Virginia	0.5	1.0	1.6	2.1	2.6	3.0	3.2	3.4	3.8	4.0
West Virginia	0.7	1.0	1.2	1.7	2.2	3.0	3.7	4.5	4.9	5.0
West	0.5	0.8	1.1	1.4	1.6	1.8	2.1	2.3	2.0	1.6
Alaska	1.1	2.3	3.1	3.4	3.5	3.4	3.6	3.8	3.7	3.9
Arizona	4.1	6.0	8.1	9.2	9.9	10.0	8.6	8.4	9.6	12.0
California	0.5	1.0	1.4	1.8	2.1	2.4	2.6	2.8	2.4	2.2
Colorado	0.7	1.3	1.9	2.4	2.5	2.9	3.0	2.7	3.0	3.7
Hawaii	1.9	2.5	3.3	4.0	4.4	5.1	5.8	6.7	6.5	8.0
Idaho	0.7	1.0	1.5	2.1	2.7	3.2	3.8	4.3	4.2	3.8
Montana	0.6	1.0	1.4	1.9	2.5	3.2	3.7	4.1	3.5	3.3
Nevada	1.2	2.3	2.8	3.2	3.8	4.4	5.2	7.4	8.5	8.7
New Mexico	2.7	4.6	5.9	7.1	8.7	9.6	10.8	12.0	12.6	13.8
Oregon	1.1	1.8	2.4	2.9	3.1	3.8	4.3	4.9	4.8	4.9
Utah	2.1	2.0	1.8	3.4	2.8	3.5	4.7	4.7	5.7	6.2
Washington	0.6	0.9	1.2	1.8	2.2	2.6	3.3	3.6	4.2	4.2
Wyoming	0.8	1.3	2.1	3.2	4.3	5.6	6.9	8.1	8.6	8.5

NOTE: Mean absolute percentage error (MAPE) is the average value over past projections of the absolute values of errors expressed in percentage terms. National MAPEs for public 9–12 enrollments were calculated using the last 29 editions of *Projections of Education Statistics,* and state MAPEs were calculated using the last 17 editions of *Projections of* *Education Statistics.* Calculations were made using unrounded numbers. Some data have been revised from previously published figures.
SOURCE: U.S. Department of Education, National Center for Education Statistics, *Projections of Education Statistics,* various issues. (This table was prepared February 2013.)

A.2. HIGH SCHOOL GRADUATES

Projections in this edition

This edition of *Projections of Education Statistics* presents projected trends in the number of high school graduates from 2010–11 to 2022–23. These projections were made using three models:

» The *National High School Graduates Model* was used to project the number of public high school graduates, the number of private high school graduates, and the total number of high school graduates for the nation.

» The *State Public High School Graduates Model* was used to project the number of public high school graduates for individual states and regions.

» The *National Public High School Graduates by Race/Ethnicity Model* was used to project the number of public high school graduates for the nation by race/ethnicity.

Overview of approach

All the high school graduates models first calculated the number of high school graduates as a percentage of grade 12 enrollment based on historical data. Single exponential smoothing was used to project this percentage. The projected percentage was then applied to projections of grade 12 enrollment.

Assumptions underlying this approach

The percentage of 12th-graders who graduate was assumed to remain constant at levels consistent with the most recent rates. This methodology assumes that past trends in factors affecting graduation rates, such as dropouts, migration, and public or private transfers, will continue over the forecast period. No specific assumptions were made regarding the dropout rate, retention rate, or the rate at which alternative credentials are awarded. The combined effect of these proportions is reflected implicitly in the graduate proportion. In addition to student behaviors, the projected number of graduates could be affected by changes in graduation requirements, but this is not considered in the projections in this report.

For more details on the steps used for projections of high school graduates, see "Procedures used in all three high school graduates models," below.

Procedures used in all three high school graduates models

The following steps were used to project the numbers of high school graduates:

Step 1. *For each year in the historic period, express the number of high school graduates as a percentage of grade 12 enrollment.* This value represents the approximate percentage of 12th graders who graduate. For information about the specific historical data and analysis periods used for the National High School Graduates Model, the State Public High School Graduates Model, and the National Public High School Graduates by Race/Ethnicity Model, see the description of the appropriate model, later in this section of appendix A.

Step 2. *Project the percentage of 12th-graders who graduate from step 1.* This percentage was projected using single exponential smoothing with a smoothing constant chosen to minimize the sum of squared forecast errors. Because single exponential smoothing produces a single forecast for all years in the forecast period, the same projected percentage of grade 12 enrollment was used for each year in the forecast period.

Step 3. *Calculate projections of the numbers of high school graduates.* For each year in the forecast period, the projected percentage from step 2 was applied to projections of grade 12 enrollment to yield projections of high school graduates.

National High School Graduates Model

This model was used to project the number of public high school graduates, the number of private high school graduates, and the total number of high school graduates for the nation. Public and private high school graduates were projected separately. The public and private projections were then summed to yield projections of the total number of high school graduates for the nation.

For details of the procedures used to develop the projections, see "Procedures used in all three high school graduates models," above.

Data used in the National High School Graduates Model

Public school data on graduates and grade 12 enrollment. Data on public school 12th-grade enrollments and high school graduates from the NCES *Statistics of Public Elementary and Secondary School Systems* for 1972–73 to 1980–81 and the NCES Common Core of Data (CCD) for 1981–82 to 2009–10 were used to develop national projections of public high school graduates.

Private school data on graduates and grade 12 enrollment. Data on private school 12th-grade enrollments for 1989–90 through 2010–11 and high school graduates for 1988–89 through 2009–10 were used to develop national projections of private high school graduates. The data were from the biennial NCES Private School Universe Survey (PSS) from 1989–90 to 2011–12 with data for 12th grade enrollment the same as the year of the survey and the data for high school graduates for the preceding year (i.e. the 2011–12 PSS presents high school graduates for 2010–11). Since the PSS is collected in the fall of odd-numbered years, data for missing years were estimated using data from the PSS. For 12th grade enrollment, estimates for missing years were linear interpolations of the prior year's and succeeding year's actual values. For high school graduates, estimates for the missing years were the interpolations of the high school graduates to estimated 12th grade enrollment percentages for the prior and succeeding years multiplied by the estimated enrollments for the current year.

Public and private school enrollment projections for grade 12. Projections of grade 12 enrollment in public schools and in private schools were used to develop projections of public high school graduates and private high school graduates, respectively. The grade 12 enrollment projections were made using the grade progression method. For more information, see Section A.1. Elementary and Secondary Enrollment, earlier in this appendix.

Accuracy of national high school graduates projections

Mean absolute percentage errors (MAPEs) for projections of graduates from public high schools were calculated using the last 22 editions of *Projections of Education Statistics*, while MAPEs for projections of graduates from private high schools were calculated using the last 11 editions. Table B, below, shows MAPEs for both public and private school graduation projections.

Table B.   Mean absolute percentage errors (MAPEs) of projections of high school graduates, by lead time and control of school: 2013

Statistic	Lead time (years)									
	1	2	3	4	5	6	7	8	9	10
Public high school graduates	1.0	1.1	1.6	1.8	1.7	2.1	2.8	3.8	4.4	4.6
Private high school graduates	0.7	1.2	1.6	2.8	4.1	5.2	3.3	5.6	4.6	4.9

NOTE: MAPEs for public high school graduates were calculated from the past 22 editions of *Projections of Education Statistics*. MAPEs for private high school graduates were calculated from the past 11 editions. Calculations were made using unrounded numbers. Some data have been revised from previously published figures.
SOURCE: U.S. Department of Education, National Center for Education Statistics, *Projections of Education Statistics*, various issues. (This table was prepared February 2013.)

For more information about MAPEs, see Section A.0. Introduction, earlier in appendix A.

State Public High School Graduates Model

This edition of *Projections of Education Statistics* contains projections of public high school graduates from 2010–11 to 2022–23 for each of the 50 states and the District of Columbia, as well as for each region of the country. The state projections of high school graduates were produced in two stages:

» first, an initial set of projections for each state was produced; and

» second, these initial projections were adjusted to sum to the national public school totals produced by the National High School Graduates Model.

For each region, the high school graduate projections equaled the sum of high school graduate projections for the states within that region.

Initial set of state projections

The same steps used to produce the national projections of high school graduates were used to produce an initial set of projections for each state and the District of Columbia. A separate smoothing constant, chosen to minimize the sum of squared forecast errors, was used to calculate the projected percentage of 12th grade enrollment for each jurisdiction.

For details on the steps used to develop the initial sets of projections, see "Procedures used in all three high school graduate models," earlier in this section of appendix A.

Adjustments to the state projections

The initial projections of state public high school graduates were adjusted to sum to the national projections of public high school graduates shown in table 12 on page 47. This was done through the use of ratio adjustments in which all the states' high school graduate projections were multiplied by the ratio of the national public high school graduate projection to the sum of the state public high school graduate projections.

Data used in the State Public High School Graduates Model

Public school data on graduates and grade 12 enrollment at the state level. State-level data on public school 12th-grade enrollments and high school graduates from the NCES *Statistics of Public Elementary and Secondary School Systems, 1980–81* and the NCES Common Core of Data (CCD) for 1981–82 to 2009–10 were used to develop these projections.

Public school projections for grade 12 enrollment at the state level. State-level projections of grade 12 enrollment in public schools were used to develop the state-level projections of public high school graduates. The grade 12 enrollment projections were made using the grade progression method. For more information, see Section A.1. Elementary and Secondary Enrollment, earlier in this appendix.

Accuracy of state public high school graduate projections

Mean absolute percentage errors (MAPEs) for projections of the number of public high school graduates by state were calculated using the last 17 editions of *Projections of Education Statistics*. Table A-10 on page 98 shows MAPEs for the number of high school graduates by state.

National Public High School Graduates by Race/Ethnicity Model

The projections of public high school graduates by race/ethnicity were produced in two stages:

» first, an initial set of projections for each racial/ethnic group was produced; and

» second, these initial projections were adjusted to sum to the national public school totals produced by the National High School Graduates Model.

Initial set of projections by race/ethnicity

The same steps used to produce the national projections of high school graduates were used to produce an initial set of projections for each of the following five racial/ethnic groups: White, Black, Hispanic, Asian/Pacific Islander, and American Indian/Alaska Native. For example, the number of White public high school graduates was projected as a percentage of White grade 12 enrollment in public schools. A separate smoothing constant, chosen to minimize the sum of squared forecast errors, was used to calculate the projected percentage of 12th-grade enrollment for each racial/ethnic group.

Adjustments to the projections by race/ethnicity

The projections of public high school graduates by race/ethnicity were adjusted to sum to the national projections of public high school graduates shown in table 12 on page 47. This was done through the use of ratio adjustments in which all high school graduate projections by race/ethnicity were multiplied by the ratio of the national high school graduate projection to the sum of the high school projections by race/ethnicity.

Data and imputations used in the Public High School Graduates by Race/Ethnicity Model

Public school data on graduates and grade 12 enrollment by race/ethnicity. Data on public high school graduates and grade 12 enrollment by race/ethnicity from the NCES Common Core of Data (CCD) for 1994–95 to 2008–09 were used to develop these projections. (Data on public high school graduates by race/ethnicity for 2009–10 were not available when these projections were produced.) In those instances where states did not report their high school graduate data by race/ethnicity, the state-level data had to be examined and some imputations made. For example, in 1994, Arizona did not report high school graduate data by race/ethnicity. It did, however, report grade 12 enrollment numbers by race/ethnicity for that year. So, to impute the high school graduate numbers by race/ethnicity for that year, Arizona's total number of high school graduates for 1994 was multiplied by the state's 1994 racial/ethnic distribution for grade 12 enrollment. In 2008–09 and 2009–10, jurisdictions could classify high school graduates by an additional racial/ethnic group—two or more races. As only a limited number of states used this reporting category, those numbers were proportioned among the other five racial/ethnic groups by each of the five ethnic groups' shares of total number of high school graduates, excluding those of two or more races. When a sufficient number of states use this racial/ethnic group, projections will be developed for this group.

Public enrollment projections for grade 12 by race/ethnicity. Projections of grade 12 enrollment in public schools by race/ethnicity were used to develop the projections of public high school graduates by race/ethnicity. The grade 12 enrollment projections were made using the grade progression method. For more information, see Section A.1. Elementary and Secondary Enrollment, earlier in this appendix.

Accuracy of enrollment projections by race/ethnicity

Because this is the fourth edition of *Projections of Education Statistics* to include projections of public high school graduates by race/ethnicity, the difference between the projections and actual data for a reasonable sample of time points cannot yet be determined.

Table A-10. Mean absolute percentage errors (MAPEs) for the projected number of high school graduates in public schools, by lead time, region, and state: 2013

Region and state	Lead time (years)									
	1	2	3	4	5	6	7	8	9	10
1	2	3	4	5	6	7	8	9	10	11
United States	**1.0**	**1.1**	**1.6**	**1.8**	**1.7**	**2.1**	**2.8**	**3.8**	**4.4**	**4.6**
Northeast	1.3	1.7	1.7	1.8	2.1	2.6	2.8	3.3	4.4	4.6
Connecticut	2.6	2.3	2.1	2.8	3.1	3.4	4.0	3.6	4.9	4.5
Maine	2.8	4.3	4.4	5.4	5.7	6.1	7.1	8.2	10.2	11.1
Massachusetts	0.9	1.4	2.2	2.6	2.7	2.7	2.9	2.2	2.1	1.7
New Hampshire	1.2	2.2	2.5	2.7	3.2	4.1	4.8	5.8	6.2	5.4
New Jersey	2.3	4.0	4.8	4.7	4.9	6.1	7.0	8.2	8.9	10.2
New York	1.9	3.2	3.4	4.3	4.8	5.5	6.4	7.3	8.2	8.3
Pennsylvania	1.7	2.8	3.0	2.4	1.5	2.0	2.3	2.9	3.4	3.6
Rhode Island	1.4	1.3	2.0	1.9	2.2	3.2	4.8	5.6	5.5	4.9
Vermont	2.1	2.3	3.7	4.6	6.4	6.6	7.0	8.0	9.4	9.5
Midwest	1.1	0.8	1.5	1.5	2.0	2.4	2.2	2.5	3.0	3.0
Illinois	2.9	2.2	3.3	4.0	4.1	3.6	5.7	4.3	5.3	7.1
Indiana	1.7	2.1	1.7	1.8	1.9	2.3	3.1	3.8	4.1	3.9
Iowa	1.5	1.4	2.0	1.9	2.8	2.8	2.6	2.8	2.2	2.3
Kansas	1.3	1.7	2.4	2.4	3.2	4.1	4.7	5.0	5.7	5.3
Michigan	3.4	4.3	5.1	6.1	6.3	6.3	7.9	9.4	9.5	9.0
Minnesota	2.3	1.4	1.5	1.7	2.1	2.2	2.8	3.5	4.0	4.5
Missouri	1.0	1.5	2.6	2.8	3.0	3.9	4.4	5.0	6.1	5.7
Nebraska	1.8	2.4	2.6	2.3	2.5	2.7	2.3	2.2	1.8	1.7
North Dakota	1.3	1.9	2.1	2.2	2.3	2.5	3.3	3.7	4.7	6.3
Ohio	2.3	1.5	2.7	2.9	3.3	3.3	2.9	3.7	4.2	5.3
South Dakota	2.4	3.1	3.2	5.3	8.4	9.3	10.6	12.0	14.4	16.2
Wisconsin	1.3	1.6	2.7	2.8	3.1	3.9	4.0	4.8	5.4	5.1
South	1.3	1.6	2.6	2.4	2.5	3.3	3.9	5.1	5.9	6.7
Alabama	3.4	3.2	2.6	4.6	4.8	5.6	6.2	6.0	7.0	7.3
Arkansas	1.5	1.7	2.2	2.7	2.9	2.6	2.4	2.8	2.4	2.9
Delaware	2.1	2.9	3.7	4.8	3.4	4.4	4.9	5.9	6.4	7.2
District of Columbia	6.9	7.2	11.2	12.5	14.1	15.3	16.3	19.2	17.9	19.7
Florida	2.0	4.1	5.3	3.7	3.9	4.3	5.9	7.7	8.7	8.5
Georgia	2.2	3.1	3.9	5.4	6.9	7.9	8.5	8.7	9.0	8.4
Kentucky	2.3	3.6	3.5	4.4	5.2	6.2	6.9	6.9	5.9	6.1
Louisiana	1.8	2.7	4.3	6.0	6.3	3.5	3.3	3.6	4.0	5.8
Maryland	1.4	1.2	1.9	1.4	1.6	1.6	2.3	2.8	2.9	4.2
Mississippi	1.3	1.7	2.2	2.4	3.1	3.6	3.6	4.0	4.1	3.2
North Carolina	2.1	2.3	3.9	3.7	4.1	4.5	4.8	5.7	6.2	8.3
Oklahoma	1.4	1.5	1.8	1.6	2.1	2.7	3.2	3.2	3.2	3.4
South Carolina	1.8	3.5	3.0	4.5	5.2	6.2	6.6	7.0	7.1	7.5
Tennessee	4.8	7.1	9.2	11.5	13.9	15.3	15.3	15.0	13.6	11.7
Texas	2.7	3.7	4.9	5.6	5.6	6.9	8.1	10.2	11.9	13.7
Virginia	1.5	2.2	2.9	3.7	4.0	4.1	3.9	3.7	4.2	4.8
West Virginia	0.7	1.1	1.8	1.9	2.1	3.1	3.5	4.8	5.1	5.1
West	1.9	2.2	2.6	3.1	2.6	2.8	2.2	2.3	3.2	3.0
Alaska	2.7	2.3	2.8	4.2	4.2	5.4	6.1	6.3	6.4	6.1
Arizona	8.7	9.2	11.7	13.6	11.8	11.3	13.4	9.5	10.3	12.3
California	2.7	2.6	3.1	3.8	4.0	4.4	4.4	3.8	5.0	5.0
Colorado	1.8	2.2	2.5	1.7	2.1	2.1	2.4	3.1	3.8	3.8
Hawaii	3.7	4.2	5.1	6.1	9.0	9.8	12.2	13.5	15.6	17.0
Idaho	1.1	1.4	1.3	1.6	2.1	2.8	3.3	4.1	5.2	5.4
Montana	0.9	0.9	1.4	1.2	2.3	3.5	4.6	6.3	7.7	8.9
Nevada	4.9	6.6	8.8	9.5	8.6	10.0	10.1	10.6	11.5	12.6
New Mexico	3.3	2.7	4.4	4.0	5.6	5.6	6.3	7.4	9.6	9.5
Oregon	2.0	2.3	3.0	4.3	5.2	5.3	5.6	6.5	7.2	6.6
Utah	5.2	6.4	5.2	5.3	5.2	4.6	3.9	4.1	3.7	2.3
Washington	2.0	2.1	2.9	2.3	2.3	3.2	3.3	3.5	4.7	4.3
Wyoming	1.7	2.2	2.4	2.8	4.0	5.4	7.1	8.1	9.5	10.3

NOTE: Mean absolute percentage error (MAPE) is the average value over past projections of the absolute values of errors expressed in percentage terms. National MAPEs for public high school graduates were calculated using the last 22 editions of *Projections of Education Statistics,* and state MAPEs were calculated using the last 17 editions of *Projections of Education Statistics.* Calculations were made using unrounded numbers. Some data have been revised from previously published figures.
SOURCE: U.S. Department of Education, National Center for Education Statistics, *Projections of Education Statistics,* various issues. (This table was prepared February 2013.)

A.3. ELEMENTARY AND SECONDARY TEACHERS

Projections in this edition

This edition of *Projections of Education Statistics* presents projected trends in elementary and secondary teachers, pupil/teacher ratios, and new teacher hires from 2012 to 2022. These projections were made using two models:

» The *Elementary and Secondary Teacher Model* was used to project the number of public school teachers, the number of private school teachers, and the total number of teachers for the nation. It was also used to project pupil/teacher ratios for public schools, private schools, and all elementary and secondary schools.

» The *New Teacher Hires Model* was used to project the number of new teacher hires in public schools, private schools, and all schools.

Overview of approach

Approach for numbers of teachers and pupil/teacher ratios

Public schools. Multiple linear regression was used to produce initial projections of public school pupil/teacher ratios separately for elementary and secondary schools. The initial projections of elementary pupil/teacher ratios and secondary pupil/teacher ratios were applied to enrollment projections to project the numbers of elementary teachers and secondary teachers, which were summed to get the total number of public school teachers. Final projections of the overall public school pupil/teacher ratios were produced by dividing total projected public school enrollment by the total projected number of teachers.

Assumptions underlying this method

This method assumes that past relationships between the public school pupil/teacher ratio (the dependent variable) and the independent variables used in the regression analysis will continue throughout the forecast period. For more information about the independent variables, see "Elementary and Secondary Teacher Model," later in this section of appendix A.

Private schools. Private school pupil/teacher ratios were projected by applying each year's projected annual percentage change in the overall public school pupil/teacher ratio to the previous year's private school pupil/teacher ratio. The projected private school pupil/teacher ratios were then applied to projected enrollments at private schools to produce projected numbers of private school teachers.

Assumptions underlying this method

This method assumes that the future pattern in the trend of private school pupil/teacher ratios will be the same as that for public school pupil/teacher ratios. The reader is cautioned that a number of factors could alter the assumption of consistent patterns of change in ratios over the forecast period.

Approach for new teacher hires

The following numbers were projected separately for public schools and for private schools:

» *The number of teachers needed to fill openings when there is an increase in the size of the teaching workforce from one year to the next and the decrease in the number of replacement teachers needed if there is a decrease in the size of the teaching workforce from one year to the next.* This number was estimated based on continuation rates of teachers by their age.

» *The number of teachers needed to fill openings due to an increase in the size of the teaching workforce from one year to the next.* This number was estimated by subtracting the projected number of teachers in one year from the projected number of teachers in the next year.

These two numbers were summed to yield the total number of "new teacher hires" for each control of school—that is, teachers who will be hired in a given year, but who did not teach in that control the previous year. A teacher who moves from one control to the other control (i.e. from a public to private school or from a private to a public school) is considered a new teacher hire, but a teacher who moves from one school to another school in the same control is not considered a new teacher hire.

Elementary and Secondary Teacher Model

Projections for public schools were produced first. Projections for private schools were produced based partially on input from the public school projections. Finally, the public and private school projections were combined into total elementary and secondary school projections (not shown in the steps below).

Steps used to project numbers of teachers and pupil/teacher ratios

Public school teachers. The following steps were used for the public school projections:

Step 1. Produce projections of pupil/teacher ratios for public elementary schools and public secondary schools separately. Two separate equations were used—one for elementary schools and one for secondary schools. The equations for elementary and secondary schools included an AR(1) term for correcting for autocorrelation and the following independent variables:

> » *Independent variables for public elementary school pupil/teacher ratios*—(1) average teacher wage relative to the overall economy-level wage, and (2) level of education revenue from state sources in constant dollars per public elementary student.

> » *Independent variables for public secondary school pupil/teacher ratios*—(1) level of education revenue from state sources in constant dollars per public secondary student, and (2) the number of students enrolled in public secondary schools relative to the secondary school–age population.

To estimate the models, they were first transformed into nonlinear models and then the coefficients were estimated simultaneously by applying a Marquardt nonlinear least squares algorithm to the transformed equation.

For details on the equations, model statistics, and data used to project public school pupil/teacher ratios, see "Data and equations used for projections of teachers and pupil/teacher ratios," below.

Step 2. Produce projections of the number of teachers for public elementary schools and public secondary schools separately. The projections of the public elementary pupil/teacher ratio and public secondary pupil/teacher ratio were applied to projections of enrollments in elementary schools and secondary schools, respectively, to produce projections of public elementary teachers and public secondary teachers.

Step 3. Produce projections of the total number of teachers for public elementary and secondary schools combined. The projections of public elementary teachers and public secondary teachers were added together to produce the projections of the total number of public elementary and secondary teachers.

Step 4. Produce projections of the pupil/teacher ratio for public elementary and secondary schools combined. The projections of the total number of public elementary and secondary teachers were divided by projections of total enrollment in public elementary and secondary schools to produce projections of the overall pupil/teacher ratio in public elementary and secondary schools.

Private school teachers. The following steps were used for the private school projections:

Step 1. Produce projections of the private school pupil/teacher ratio. First, the projection of the private school pupil/teacher ratio for 2012 was calculated by multiplying the private school pupil/teacher ratio for 2011 (the last year of actual data) by the percentage change from 2010 to 2011 in the public school pupil/teacher ratio. The same method was used to calculate the projections of the private school pupil/teacher ratio for 2012 through 2022. That is, each year's projected annual percentage change in the public school pupil/teacher ratio was applied to the previous year's private school pupil/teacher ratio.

Step 2. Produce projections of the number of private school teachers. The projected pupil/teacher ratios were applied to projected private school enrollments to produce projections of private school teachers from 2012 through 2022.

For information about the private school teacher and enrollment data used for the private school projections, see "Data and equations used for projections of teachers and pupil/teacher ratios," below.

Data and equations used for projections of teachers and pupil/teacher ratios

Public school data used in these projections were by organizational level (i.e., school level), not by grade level. Thus, secondary school enrollment is not the same as enrollment in grades 9 through 12 because some jurisdictions count some grade 7 and 8 enrollment as secondary. For example, some jurisdictions may have 6-year high schools with grades 7 through 12.

Data used to estimate the equation for public elementary school pupil/teacher ratios. The following data were used to estimate the equation:

> » To compute the historical elementary school pupil/teacher ratios—Data on 1973–74 to 1980–81 enrollments in public elementary schools came from the NCES *Statistics of Public Elementary and Secondary Day Schools* and data on 1981–82 to 2011–12 enrollment came from the NCES Common Core of Data (CCD). The proportion of public school teachers who taught in elementary schools was taken from the National Education Association and then applied to the total number of public school teachers from the CCD to produce the number of teachers in elementary schools.

» For 1973–74 and 1975–76, the education revenue from state sources data came from *Statistics of State School Systems*, published by NCES. For 1974–75 and 1976–77, the education revenue from state sources data came from *Revenues and Expenditures for Public Elementary and Secondary Education*, also published by NCES. For 1977–78 through 2009–10, these data came from the NCES Common Core of Data (CCD).

Estimated equation and model statistics for public elementary school pupil/teacher ratios. For the estimated equation and model statistics, see table A-11 on page 104. In the public elementary pupil/teacher ratio equation, the independent variables affect the dependent variable in the expected way:

» As the average teacher wage relative to the overall economy-level wage increases, the pupil/teacher ratio increases; and

» As the level of education revenue from state sources in constant dollars per public elementary student increases, the pupil/teacher ratio decreases.

Data used to project public elementary school pupil/teacher ratios. The estimated equation was run using projected values for teacher salaries and education revenues from state sources from 2011–12 through 2022–23. For more information, see Section A.0. Introduction, earlier in this appendix and Section A.4 Expenditures for Public Elementary and Secondary Education later in this appendix.

Data used to estimate the equation for public secondary school pupil/teacher ratios. The following data were used to estimate the equation:

» To compute the historical secondary school pupil/teacher ratios—Data on 1973–74 to 1980–81 enrollments in public elementary schools came from the NCES *Statistics of Public Elementary and Secondary Day Schools* and data on 1981–82 to 2011–12 enrollment came from the NCES Common Core of Data (CCD). The proportion of public school teachers who taught in secondary schools was taken from the National Education Association and then applied to the total number of public school teachers from the CCD to produce the number of teachers in secondary schools.

» For 1973–74 and 1975–76, the education revenue from state sources data came from *Statistics of State School Systems*, published by NCES. For 1974–75 and 1976–77, the education revenue from state sources data came from *Revenues and Expenditures for Public Elementary and Secondary Education*, also published by NCES. For 1977–78 through 2009–10, these data came from the NCES Common Core of Data (CCD).

» To compute the historical secondary school enrollment rate—Data on the secondary school-age population from 1973–74 to 2011–12 came from the U.S. Census Bureau. Data on enrollments in public secondary schools during the same period came from the CCD, as noted above.

Estimated equation and model statistics for public secondary school pupil/teacher ratios. For the estimated equation and model statistics, see table A-11 on page 104. In the public secondary pupil/teacher ratio equation, the independent variables affect the dependent variable in the expected way:

» As enrollment rates (number of enrolled students relative to the school-age population) increase, the pupil/teacher ratio increases; and

» As the level of education revenue from state sources in constant dollars per public secondary student increases, the pupil/teacher ratio decreases.

Data used to project public secondary school pupil/teacher ratios. The estimated equation was run using projections for education revenues, public secondary enrollments, and secondary school–age populations from 2011–12 through 2022–23. Secondary enrollment projections were derived from the enrollment projections described in Section A.1. Elementary and Secondary Enrollment. Population projections were from the Census Bureau's 2012 National Population Projections by age and sex (December 2012), ratio-adjusted to line up with the most recent historical estimates.

Private school teacher and enrollment data. Private school data for 1989–90, 1991–92, 1993–94, 1995–96, 1997–98, 1999–2000, 2001–02, 2003–04, 2005–06, 2007–08, 2009–10, and 2011–12 came from the biennial NCES Private School Universe Survey (PSS). Since the PSS is collected in the fall of odd-numbered years, data for years without a PSS collection were estimated using data from the PSS.

Private school enrollment projections. Private school enrollments from 2011 to 2022 came from the projections described in Section A.1. Elementary and Secondary Enrollment, earlier in this appendix.

Accuracy of projections of numbers of teachers

Mean absolute percentage errors (MAPEs) for projections of public school teachers were calculated using the last 22 editions of *Projections of Education Statistics*. Table C, below, shows MAPEs for projections of the numbers of public school teachers. There was a change in the methodology for projecting private school teachers beginning with *Projections of Education Statistics to 2017*, and therefore there are too few years of data to present the MAPEs for private school teachers.

Table C. Mean absolute percentage errors (MAPEs) of projections of number of public elementary and secondary school teachers, by lead time: 2013

Statistic	Lead time (years)									
	1	2	3	4	5	6	7	8	9	10
Public elementary and secondary teachers	0.8	1.6	1.8	2.3	3.0	3.7	4.4	4.8	4.7	5.2

NOTE: MAPEs for teachers were calculated from the past 22 editions of *Projections of Education Statistics* containing teacher projections. Calculations were made using unrounded numbers. Some data have been revised from previously published figures. Number of teachers reported in full-time equivalents.
SOURCE: U.S. Department of Education, National Center for Education Statistics, *Projections of Education Statistics*, various issues. (This table was prepared March 2013.)

For more information about MAPEs, see Section A.0. Introduction, earlier in this appendix.

New Teacher Hires Model

The New Teacher Hires Model was estimated separately for public and private school teachers. The model produces projections of the number of teachers who were not teaching in the previous year, but who will be hired in a given year.

About new teacher hires

A teacher is considered to be a new teacher hire for a control of school (public or private) for a given year if the teacher teaches in that control that year but had not taught in that control in the previous year. Included among new teachers hires are: (1) teachers who are new to the profession; (2) teachers who had taught previously but had not been teaching the previous year; and (3) teachers who had been teaching in one control the previous year but have moved to the other control. Concerning the last category, if a teacher moves from one public school to a different public school, that teacher would not be counted as a new teacher hire for the purposes of this model. On the other hand, if a teacher moves from a public school to a private school, that teacher would be counted as a private school new teacher hire, since the teacher did not teach in a private school in the previous year.

The New Teacher Hires Model measures the demand for teacher hires. Due to difficulties in defining and measuring the pool of potential teachers, no attempt was made to measure the supply of new teacher candidates.

Steps used to project numbers of new teacher hires

The steps outlined below provide a general summary of how the New Teacher Hires Model was used to produce projections of the need for new teacher hires.

For more information about the New Teacher Hires Model, see Hussar (1999).

First, the series of steps outlined below was used to produce projections of public school new teacher hires. Then, the same steps were used to produce projections of private school new hires. Finally, the public and private new teacher hires were combined to produce projections of total new teacher hires.

Step 1. *Estimate the age distribution of full-time-equivalent (FTE) teachers in 2007.* For this estimate, the age distribution of the headcount of school teachers (including both full-time and part-time teachers) in 2007 was applied to the national number of FTE teachers in the same year.

Step 2. *Estimate the number of new FTE teacher hires needed to replace those who left teaching between 2007 and 2008.* In this step

- » Age-specific continuation rates for 2004 were applied to the FTE count of teachers by age for 2007, resulting in estimates of the number of FTE teachers who remained in teaching in 2008 by individual age.

- » The FTE teachers who remained in teaching by individual age were summed across all ages to produce an estimate of the total number of FTE teachers who remained teaching in 2008.

- » The total number of remaining FTE teachers in 2008 was subtracted from the total FTE teacher count for 2007 to produce the estimated number of FTE teachers who left teaching.

Step 3. *Estimate the number of new FTE teacher hires needed due to the overall increase in the teacher workforce between 2007 and 2008.* The total number of FTE teachers in 2007 was subtracted from the total number of FTE teachers in 2008 to determine the overall increase in the teaching workforce between 2007 and 2008.

Step 4. *Estimate the total number of new FTE teacher hires needed in 2008.* The number of FTE teachers who left teaching from step 2 was added to the estimated net change in the number of FTE teachers from step 3 to estimate the total number of new FTE teacher hires needed in 2008.

Step 5. *Estimate the FTE count of teachers by age for 2008.* In this step

» The age distribution for the headcount of newly hired teachers in 2007 was applied to the estimated total number of new FTE teacher hires in 2008, resulting in the estimated number of new FTE teacher hires by age.

» For each individual age, the estimated number of new FTE teacher hires was added to the estimated number of remaining FTE teachers (from step 2, first bullet) to produce the estimated FTE count of teachers by age for 2008.

Step 6. *Repeat steps 2 to 5 for each year from 2009 through 2022.*

» In step 2

- For public school teachers ages 22 through 66 and private school teachers ages 21 through 65, projections of age-specific continuation rates were used. A separate smoothing constant, chosen to minimize the sum of squared forecast errors, was used to calculate the projected progression rate for each age. (For a general description of the exponential smoothing technique, see Section A.0. Introduction, earlier in this appendix.)

- For all other ages, the age-specific continuation rates for 2008 (the last year of actual data) were used.

» In step 3, projections of the numbers of FTE teachers were used for all years in which there were no actual teacher numbers. The projections of FTE teachers are described under "Elementary and Secondary Teacher Model," earlier in this section of appendix A.

Assumptions underlying this method

A number of assumptions are made in order to make these projections. They include that (1) the age distribution of FTE teachers in 2007 was similar to that of full-time and part-time teachers in that year (step 1); (2) the age-specific continuation rates for FTE teachers for each year from 2008 through 2022 are similar to either the projections produced using single exponential smoothing or the values for 2008, depending on the age of the teachers (step 2); (3) the age distribution for newly hired FTE teachers from 2008 through 2022 is similar to that of newly hired full-time and part-time teachers in 2007 (step 3); (4) the actual numbers of FTE teachers for each year from 2008 through 2022 are similar to projections of FTE teachers shown in table 16 on page 53; and (5) no economic or political changes further affect the size of the teaching force.

Data used for projections of new teacher hires

Data on numbers of public school teachers. Numbers of FTE teachers for 2008 through 2011 came from the NCES Common Core of Data (CCD).

Data on numbers of private school teachers. Private school data on the numbers of FTE teachers in 2003–04, 2005–06, 2007–08, 2009–10, and 2011–12 came from the biennial NCES Private School Universe Survey (PSS). Since the PSS is collected in the fall of odd-numbered years, data for years without a PSS collection were estimated using data from the PSS.

Data on the age distribution of public and private school teachers. Data on the age distribution of full-time and part-time public and private school teachers came from the 2007–08 NCES Schools and Staffing Survey (SASS). These data and their standard errors are shown in table A-12 on page 104.

Data on the age distribution of public and private new teacher hires. Data on the age distribution of newly hired full-time and part-time public and private school teachers came from the 2007–08 NCES Schools and Staffing Survey (SASS). These data and their standard errors are shown in table A-13 on page 104.

Data on and projections of age-specific continuation rates of public and private school teachers. The 2008 continuation rates came from the 2008–09 NCES Teacher Follow-Up Survey (TFS). Data from the 1994–95, 2000–01, and 2004-05 TFS were also used in the projection of age-specific continuation rates. The actual data, their standard errors, and the projections are shown in table A-14 on page 105.

Projections of the numbers of public and private elementary and secondary school teachers. These projections are described under "Elementary and Secondary Teacher Model," earlier in this section of appendix A.

Accuracy of projections of new teacher hires

While this is the sixth edition of *Projections of Education Statistics* to include projections of new teacher hires, 2007 is the last year with actual numbers so there are too few years of data to present the MAPEs for new teacher hires.

Table A-11. Estimated equations and model statistics for public elementary and secondary teachers

Dependent variable	Equation[1]	R^2	Breusch-Godfrey Serial Correlation LM test statistic[2]	Time period
1	2	3	4	5
Elementary	ln(RELENRTCH) = 3.82 + .07 ln(RSALARY) - .23 ln(RSGRNTELENR) + .35 AR(1) (29.059) (3.495) (-7.647) (1.94)	0.99	9.88 (0.007)	1973 to 2011
Secondary	ln(RSCENRTCH) = 4.16 - .23 ln(RSGRNTSCENR) + .60 ln(RSCENRPU) + .51 AR(1) (47.385) (-19.125) (5.280) (3.403)	0.98	1.92 (0.384)	1973 to 2011

[1] AR(1) indicates that the model was estimated using least squares with the AR(1) process for correcting for first-order autocorrelation. To estimate the model, it was first transformed into a nonlinear model and then the coefficients were estimated simultaneously by applying a Marquardt nonlinear least squares algorithm to the transformed equation. For a general discussion of the problem of autocorrelation, and the method used to forecast in the presence of autocorrelation, see Judge, G., Hill, W., Griffiths, R., Lutkepohl, H., and Lee, T. (1985). *The Theory and Practice of Economics*. New York: John Wiley and Sons, pp. 315–318. Numbers in parentheses are *t*-statistics.

[2] The number in parentheses is the probability of the Chi-Square associated with the Breusch-Godfrey Serial Correlation LM Test. A *p* value greater that 0.05 implies that we do not reject the null hypothesis of no autocorrelation at the 5 percent significance level for a two-tailed test and 10 percent significance level for a one-tailed test (i.e., there is no autocorrelation present). For an explanation of the Breusch-Godfrey Serial Correlation LM test statistic, see Greene, W. (2000). *Econometric Analysis*. New Jersey: Prentice-Hall.
NOTE: R^2 indicates the coefficient of determination.

RELENRTCH = Ratio of public elementary school enrollment to classroom teachers (i.e., pupil/teacher ratio).
RSCENRTCH = Ratio of public secondary school enrollment to classroom teachers (i.e., pupil/teacher ratio).
RSALARY = Average annual teacher salary relative to the overall economy wage in 2000 dollars.
RSGRNTELENR = Ratio of education revenue receipts from state sources per capita to public elementary school enrollment in 2000 dollars.
RSGRNTSCENR = Ratio of education revenue receipts from state sources per capita to public secondary school enrollment in 2000 dollars.
RSCENRPU = Ln of the ratio of enrollment in public secondary schools to the 11- to 18-year-old population.
SOURCE: U.S. Department of Education, National Center for Education Statistics, Elementary and Secondary Teacher Model, 1973–2011. (This table was prepared April 2013.)

Table A-12. Percentage distribution of full-time and part-time school teachers, by age, control of school, and teaching status: School year 2007–08

Control of school and teaching status	Percent of total		Total	Age distribution												
				Less than 25 years		25–29 years		30–39 years		40–49 years		50–59 years		60–64 years		65 years or more	
1	2		3	4		5		6		7		8		9		10	
Public-actual	100.0	(†)	100.0	3.7	(0.21)	14.3	(0.51)	26.4	(0.39)	23.7	(0.47)	25.8	(0.51)	4.8	(0.24)	1.3	(0.12)
Full-time	91.8	(0.29)	100.0	3.8	(0.22)	14.6	(0.50)	26.5	(0.40)	23.6	(0.50)	25.7	(0.54)	4.7	(0.25)	1.2	(0.13)
Part-time	8.2	(0.29)	100.0	2.5	(0.46)	11.8	(1.18)	25.3	(1.56)	24.7	(1.48)	27.6	(1.33)	6.0	(0.83)	2.1	(0.34)
Private-actual	100.0	(†)	100.0	4.6	(0.34)	11.7	(0.48)	22.3	(0.91)	23.8	(0.65)	26.2	(0.87)	7.9	(0.52)	3.6	(0.41)
Full-time	78.8	(0.93)	100.0	5.0	(0.37)	13.0	(0.66)	23.0	(0.96)	23.0	(0.65)	25.0	(0.98)	8.0	(0.56)	3.0	(0.38)
Part-time	21.2	(0.93)	100.0	3.0	(0.80)	7.0	(0.90)	19.0	(1.86)	27.0	(1.90)	29.0	(1.46)	9.0	(1.57)	7.0	(1.09)

† Not applicable.
NOTE: Detail may not sum to totals because of rounding. Standard errors appear in parentheses. The 2007–08 data are the most recent data available.

SOURCE: U.S. Department of Education, National Center for Education Statistics, Schools and Staffing Survey (SASS), "Public School Teacher Questionnaire," 2007–08 and "Private School Teacher Questionnaire," 2007–08; and unpublished tabulations. (This table was prepared October 2010.)

Table A-13. Percentage distribution of full-time and part-time newly hired teachers, by age and control of school: Selected school years, 1987–88 through 2007–08

Control of school and school year	Total	Age distribution												
		Less than 25 years	25–29 years		30–39 years		40–49 years		50–59 years		60–64 years		65 years or more	
1	2	3	4		5		6		7		8		9	
Public														
1987–88	100.0	17.7 (0.79)	23.7	(1.19)	33.0	(1.43)	21.2	(0.80)	4.0	(0.51)	0.3 !	(0.11)	‡	(†)
1990–91	100.0	17.5 (1.06)	24.0	(1.35)	30.6	(1.33)	21.4	(1.28)	5.6	(0.65)	0.6	(0.18)	‡	(†)
1993–94	100.0	16.2 (0.91)	28.7	(1.15)	24.9	(1.04)	24.6	(1.16)	5.0	(0.63)	0.5	(0.13)	0.2 !	(0.09)
1999–2000	100.0	23.6 (1.28)	22.5	(0.97)	22.2	(1.10)	19.2	(0.90)	11.1	(0.88)	0.9	(0.23)	0.6 !	(0.26)
2003–04	100.0	24.4 (1.21)	19.0	(1.23)	24.6	(1.10)	16.5	(1.18)	13.3	(0.93)	1.5	(0.29)	0.7 !	(0.29)
2007–08	100.0	23.8 (1.75)	24.3	(1.79)	20.4	(1.56)	15.1	(0.94)	13.6	(1.22)	2.3	(0.39)	0.5 !	(0.22)
Private														
1987–88	100.0	17.0 (1.27)	22.8	(1.68)	32.5	(2.17)	17.9	(1.61)	5.3	(1.09)	‡	(†)	1.8 !	(0.77)
1990–91	100.0	15.8 (1.47)	26.3	(1.83)	29.1	(1.86)	21.1	(1.67)	5.6	(0.88)	1.1 !	(0.40)	1.0 !	(0.42)
1993–94	100.0	19.3 (1.13)	24.4	(1.19)	24.9	(1.49)	22.6	(1.18)	7.3	(0.85)	0.9	(0.20)	0.6 !	(0.23)
1999–2000	100.0	18.5 (0.89)	17.2	(0.87)	24.1	(1.24)	22.1	(1.19)	14.0	(1.01)	2.6	(0.39)	1.5	(0.38)
2003–04	100.0	17.1 (1.59)	16.0	(2.13)	23.0	(2.19)	22.8	(3.32)	15.3	(1.77)	3.6	(0.83)	2.1	(0.58)
2007–08	100.0	14.3 (1.26)	18.2	(1.36)	23.2	(1.97)	23.6	(1.92)	14.4	(1.49)	4.2	(0.84)	2.1 !	(0.69)

† Not applicable.
! Interpret with caution. The coefficient of variation (CV) for this estimate is 30 percent or greater.
‡ Reporting standards not met. The coefficient of variation (CV) for this estimate is 50 percent or greater.

NOTE: Detail may not sum to totals because of rounding. Standard errors appear in parentheses. The 2007–08 data are the most recent data available.
SOURCE: U.S. Department of Education, National Center for Education Statistics, Schools and Staffing Survey (SASS), "Public School Teacher Questionnaire," 1987–88 through 2007–08 and "Private School Teacher Questionnaire," 1987–88 through 2007–08; and unpublished tabulations. (This table was prepared October 2010.)

Table A-14. Actual and projected continuation rates of full-time and part-time school teachers, by age and control of school: Selected school years, 1993–94 to 1994–95 through 2022–23 to 2023–24

Control of school and school year	Total		Less than 25 years		25–29 years		30–39 years		40–49 years		50–59 years		60–64 years		65 years or more	
1	2		3		4		5		6		7		8		9	
Public actual																
1993–94 to 1994–95	93.4	(0.36)	96.2	(1.09)	90.0	(1.22)	93.3	(1.03)	96.1	(0.54)	93.7	(0.77)	69.5	(4.79)	65.9	(8.81)
1999–2000 to 2000–01	92.4	(0.38)	95.8	(0.98)	89.3	(7.38)	93.2	(2.76)	94.5	(0.61)	92.9	(4.58)	76.8 !	(29.18)	(‡)	(†)
2003–04 to 2004–05	91.4	(0.55)	94.9	(1.79)	90.1	(1.71)	92.6	(0.93)	94.5	(0.78)	90.8	(0.81)	77.2	(3.00)	70.3	(9.40)
2007–08 to 2008–09	91.8	(0.45)	92.2	(1.95)	89.0	(2.33)	92.4	(1.29)	95.1	(1.06)	92.3	(1.23)	82.8	(3.97)	88.9	(4.26)
Public projected																
2008–09 to 2009–10	90.7	(†)	88.9	(†)	89.0	(†)	92.6	(†)	94.1	(†)	91.4	(†)	76.5	(†)	65.0	(†)
2009–10 to 2010–11	90.6	(†)	89.1	(†)	89.0	(†)	92.6	(†)	93.9	(†)	91.4	(†)	76.4	(†)	64.6	(†)
2010–11 to 2011–12	90.6	(†)	89.8	(†)	89.0	(†)	92.6	(†)	94.0	(†)	91.4	(†)	76.2	(†)	63.6	(†)
2011–12 to 2012–13	90.5	(†)	88.4	(†)	89.0	(†)	92.6	(†)	94.1	(†)	91.4	(†)	76.1	(†)	62.7	(†)
2012–13 to 2013–14	90.5	(†)	88.7	(†)	89.0	(†)	92.6	(†)	94.1	(†)	91.4	(†)	76.1	(†)	63.3	(†)
2013–14 to 2014–15	90.5	(†)	88.9	(†)	89.0	(†)	92.6	(†)	94.1	(†)	91.5	(†)	76.0	(†)	62.9	(†)
2014–15 to 2015–16	90.5	(†)	88.9	(†)	89.0	(†)	92.6	(†)	94.0	(†)	91.5	(†)	75.8	(†)	64.4	(†)
2015–16 to 2016–17	90.6	(†)	88.7	(†)	89.0	(†)	92.6	(†)	94.1	(†)	91.5	(†)	75.8	(†)	64.1	(†)
2016–17 to 2017–18	90.6	(†)	88.9	(†)	89.1	(†)	92.6	(†)	94.2	(†)	91.6	(†)	75.9	(†)	63.8	(†)
2017–18 to 2018–19	90.6	(†)	89.0	(†)	89.0	(†)	92.6	(†)	94.1	(†)	91.6	(†)	75.9	(†)	63.8	(†)
2018–19 to 2019–20	90.6	(†)	89.0	(†)	89.0	(†)	92.6	(†)	94.1	(†)	91.6	(†)	75.9	(†)	63.9	(†)
2019–20 to 2020–21	90.7	(†)	89.0	(†)	89.0	(†)	92.6	(†)	94.1	(†)	91.6	(†)	75.9	(†)	63.7	(†)
2020–21 to 2021–22	90.7	(†)	88.9	(†)	89.0	(†)	92.5	(†)	94.0	(†)	91.6	(†)	76.0	(†)	63.4	(†)
2021–22 to 2022–23	90.7	(†)	89.0	(†)	89.0	(†)	92.5	(†)	94.1	(†)	91.6	(†)	76.0	(†)	63.4	(†)
2022–23 to 2023–24	90.7	(†)	89.0	(†)	89.0	(†)	92.5	(†)	94.1	(†)	91.6	(†)	76.0	(†)	63.3	(†)
Private actual																
1993–94 to 1994–95	88.1	(0.74)	80.0	(4.42)	86.9	(1.64)	85.1	(1.70)	91.3	(1.14)	91.8	(1.52)	86.9	(2.74)	58.1	(8.67)
1999–2000 to 2000–01	83.0	(0.72)	61.7	(4.90)	72.2	(2.76)	80.2	(1.57)	86.1	(1.47)	92.3	(1.00)	78.8	(4.79)	75.2	(5.17)
2003–04 to 2004–05	83.3	(2.06)	75.4	(5.97)	71.7	(3.62)	82.2	(2.30)	86.8	(2.28)	89.2	(9.17)	80.1	(4.15)	79.5	(6.07)
2007–08 to 2008–09	82.2	(1.69)	77.7	(8.33)	71.7	(6.44)	79.1	(3.43)	86.1	(2.92)	86.8	(2.17)	85.2	(4.21)	77.3	(8.23)
Private projected																
2008–09 to 2009–10	82.3	(†)	68.5	(†)	73.1	(†)	80.5	(†)	86.2	(†)	87.7	(†)	80.7	(†)	78.4	(†)
2009–10 to 2010–11	82.1	(†)	68.2	(†)	73.2	(†)	80.5	(†)	86.2	(†)	87.7	(†)	79.9	(†)	74.6	(†)
2010–11 to 2011–12	82.2	(†)	68.1	(†)	73.4	(†)	80.4	(†)	86.1	(†)	87.8	(†)	79.4	(†)	76.7	(†)
2011–12 to 2012–13	82.2	(†)	68.0	(†)	73.3	(†)	80.3	(†)	86.2	(†)	87.8	(†)	80.1	(†)	74.9	(†)
2012–13 to 2013–14	82.2	(†)	68.1	(†)	73.3	(†)	80.3	(†)	86.1	(†)	87.7	(†)	80.4	(†)	75.3	(†)
2013–14 to 2014–15	82.3	(†)	68.0	(†)	73.2	(†)	80.3	(†)	86.3	(†)	87.8	(†)	80.0	(†)	77.0	(†)
2014–15 to 2015–16	82.3	(†)	68.0	(†)	73.2	(†)	80.3	(†)	86.2	(†)	87.8	(†)	79.8	(†)	76.4	(†)
2015–16 to 2016–17	82.2	(†)	67.9	(†)	73.1	(†)	80.3	(†)	86.3	(†)	87.6	(†)	80.3	(†)	75.7	(†)
2016–17 to 2017–18	82.3	(†)	67.9	(†)	73.1	(†)	80.4	(†)	86.2	(†)	87.8	(†)	80.4	(†)	76.2	(†)
2017–18 to 2018–19	82.2	(†)	67.9	(†)	73.1	(†)	80.4	(†)	86.3	(†)	87.8	(†)	80.2	(†)	76.0	(†)
2018–19 to 2019–20	82.2	(†)	68.0	(†)	73.1	(†)	80.4	(†)	86.3	(†)	87.7	(†)	80.3	(†)	75.6	(†)
2019–20 to 2020–21	82.2	(†)	67.9	(†)	73.1	(†)	80.4	(†)	86.3	(†)	87.7	(†)	80.0	(†)	76.0	(†)
2020–21 to 2021–22	82.2	(†)	67.9	(†)	73.1	(†)	80.3	(†)	86.3	(†)	87.7	(†)	80.1	(†)	76.1	(†)
2021–22 to 2022–23	82.2	(†)	68.0	(†)	73.1	(†)	80.3	(†)	86.3	(†)	87.7	(†)	80.3	(†)	75.7	(†)
2022–23 to 2023–24	82.1	(†)	68.0	(†)	73.1	(†)	80.3	(†)	86.2	(†)	87.7	(†)	80.2	(†)	75.6	(†)

† Not applicable.
! Interpret with caution. The coefficient of variation (CV) for this estimate is 30 percent or greater.
‡ Reporting standards not met. The coefficient of variation (CV) for this estimate is 50 percent or greater.
NOTE: The continuation rate for teachers for each control of school (public schools and private schools) is the percentage of teachers in that control who continued teaching in the same control from one year to the next. Standard errors appear in parentheses. The 2008–09 data are the most recent data available.
SOURCE: U.S. Department of Education, National Center for Education Statistics, Teacher Follow-up Survey (TFS), "Public School Teacher Questionnaire," 1994–95 through 2008–09 and "Private School Teacher Questionnaire," 1994–95 through 2008–09; and unpublished tabulations. (This table was prepared April 2013.)

A.4. EXPENDITURES FOR PUBLIC ELEMENTARY AND SECONDARY EDUCATION

Projections in this edition

This edition of *Projections of Education Statistics* presents projections of total current expenditures for public elementary and secondary education, current expenditures per pupil in fall enrollment, and current expenditures per pupil in average daily attendance for 2010–11 through 2022–23.

As the source of the elementary and secondary private school data, the NCES Private School Universe Survey, does not collect data for current expenditures, there are no projections for private school current expenditures.

Overview of approach

Theoretical and empirical background

The Public Elementary and Secondary Education Current Expenditure Model used in this report is based on the theoretical and empirical literature on the demand for local public services such as education.[1] Specifically, it is based on a type of model that has been called a median voter model. In brief, a median voter model posits that spending for each public good in the community (in this case, spending for education) reflects the preferences of the "median voter" in the community. This individual is identified as the voter in the community with the median income and median property value. The amount of spending in the community reflects the price of education facing the voter with the median income, as well as his income and tastes. There are competing models in which the level of spending reflects the choices of others in the community, such as government officials.

In a median voter model, the demand for education expenditures is typically linked to four different types of independent variables: (1) measures of the income of the median voter; (2) measures of intergovernmental aid for education going indirectly to the median voter; (3) measures of the price to the median voter of providing one more dollar of education expenditures per pupil; and (4) any other variables that may affect one's tastes for education. The Public Elementary and Secondary Education Current Expenditure Model contains independent variables of the first two types. It uses multiple linear regression analysis to define the relationships between these independent variables and current expenditures (the dependent variable).

Elementary and Secondary Education Current Expenditure Model

Projections for current expenditures per pupil in fall enrollment were produced first. These projections were then used in calculating total expenditures and expenditures per pupil in average daily attendance.

Steps used to project current expenditures for public elementary and secondary education

Step 1. *Produce projections of education revenue from state sources.* The equation for education revenue included an AR(1) term for correcting for autocorrelation and the following independent variables:

» disposable income per capita in constant dollars; and

» the ratio of fall enrollment to the population.

To estimate the model, it was first transformed into a nonlinear model and then the coefficients were estimated simultaneously by applying a Marquardt nonlinear least squares algorithm to the transformed equation.

Step 2. *Produce projections of current expenditures per pupil in fall enrollment.* The equation for current expenditures per pupil for fall enrollment included an AR(1) term for correcting for autocorrelation and the following independent variables:

» disposable income per capita in constant dollars; and

» education revenue from state sources per capita in constant dollars. This variable was projected in step 1.

---

[1] For a discussion of the theory together with a review of some of the older literature, see Inman (1979). More recent empirical work includes Gamkhar and Oates (1996) and Mitias and Turnbull (2001).

To estimate the models, they were first transformed into nonlinear models and then the coefficients were estimated simultaneously by applying a Marquardt nonlinear least squares algorithm to the transformed equation.

For details on the equations used in steps 1 and 2, the data used to estimate these equations, and their results, see "Data and equations used for projections of current expenditures for public elementary and secondary education," below.

Step 3. *Produce projections of total current expenditures.* Projections of total current expenditures were made by multiplying the projections for current expenditures per pupil in fall enrollment by projections for fall enrollment.

Step 4. *Produce projections of current expenditures per pupil in average daily attendance.* The projections for total current expenditures were divided by projections for average daily attendance to produce projections of current expenditures per pupil in average daily attendance.

All the projections were developed in 1982–84 dollars and then placed in 2011–12 dollars using the projections of the Consumer Price Index. Current-dollar projections were produced by multiplying the constant-dollar projections by projections for the Consumer Price Index. The Consumer Price Index and the other economic variables used in calculating the projections presented in this report were placed in school year terms rather than calendar year terms.

Data and equations used for projections of current expenditures for public elementary and secondary education

Data used to estimate the equations for revenue from state sources and current expenditures per pupil. The following data for the period from 1973–74 to 2009–10 were used to estimate the equations:

» Current expenditures and revenues from state sources—For 1973–74 and 1975–76, the current expenditures data came from *Statistics of State School Systems*, published by NCES. For 1974–75 and 1976–77, the current expenditures data came from *Revenues and Expenditures for Public Elementary and Secondary Education*, also published by NCES. For 1977–78 through 2009–10, these data came from the NCES Common Core of Data (CCD) and unpublished data. For most years, the sources for the past values of revenue from state sources were identical to the sources for current expenditures.

» Disposable personal income per capita—Disposable personal income from the Bureau of Economic Analysis were divided by population data from the U.S. Census Bureau.

» The ratio of fall enrollment to population data—Fall enrollment data from the CCD were divided by population data from the U.S. Census Bureau.

Estimated equations and model statistics for revenue from state sources and current expenditures per pupil. For the results of the equations, see table A-15 on page 109. In each equation, the independent variables affect the dependent variable in the expected way. In the revenues from state sources equation:

» All other things being equal, as disposable income per capita increases so does local governments' education revenue from state sources per capita; and

» As enrollment increases relative to the population, so does the local governments' education revenue from state sources per capita.

» In the current expenditures per pupil equation: All other things being equal, as disposable income per capita increases, so does current expenditures per pupil; and

» As local governments' education revenue from state sources per capita increases, so does current expenditures per pupil.

Projections for economic variables. Projections for economic variables, including disposable income and the Consumer Price Index, were from the "U.S. Monthly Model: January 2013 Short-Term Projections" from the economic consulting firm, IHS Global Insight (see supplemental table B-6). The values of all the variables from IHS Global Insight were placed in school-year terms. The school-year numbers were calculated by taking the average of the last two quarters of one year and the first two quarters of the next year.

Projections for fall enrollment. The projections for fall enrollment are those presented in section 1 of this publication. The methodology for these projections is presented in Section A.1. Elementary and Secondary Enrollment, earlier in this appendix.

Projections for population. Population estimates for 1973 to 2011 and population projections for 2012 to 2022 from the U.S. Census Bureau were used to develop the public school current expenditure projections. The set of population projections used in this year's *Projections of Education Statistics* are the Census Bureau's 2012 National Population Projections (December 2012).

Historical data for average daily attendance. For 1973–74 and 1975–76, these data came from *Statistics of State School Systems*, published by NCES. For 1974–75 and 1976–77, the current expenditures data came from *Revenues and Expenditures for Public Elementary and Secondary Education*, also published by NCES. For 1977–78 through 2009–10, these data came from the CCD and unpublished NCES data.

Projections for average daily attendance. These projections were made by multiplying the projections for enrollment by the average value of the ratios of average daily attendance to enrollment from 1993–94 to 2009–10; this average value was approximately 0.94.

Accuracy of projections

Mean absolute percentage errors (MAPEs) for projections of current expenditures for public elementary and secondary education were calculated using the last 22 editions of *Projections of Education Statistics*. Table D, below, shows the MAPEs for projections of current expenditures.

Table D. Mean absolute percentage errors (MAPEs) of projections for total and per pupil current expenditures for public elementary and secondary education, by lead time: 2013

Statistic	Lead time (years)									
	1	2	3	4	5	6	7	8	9	10
Total current expenditures	1.3	2.1	2.1	2.0	2.6	3.4	4.0	4.0	3.9	3.9
Current expenditures per pupil in fall enrollment	1.3	2.0	2.1	2.0	2.9	3.6	4.4	4.6	5.0	4.9

NOTE: Expenditures were in constant dollars based on the Consumer Price Index for all urban consumers, Bureau of Labor Statistics, U.S. Department of Labor. MAPEs for current expenditures were calculated using projections from the last 22 editions of *Projections of Education Statistics* containing current expenditure projections. Calculations were made using unrounded numbers. Some data have been revised from previously published figures.
SOURCE: U.S. Department of Education, National Center for Education Statistics, *Projections of Education Statistics*, various issues. (This table was prepared February 2013.)

For more information about MAPEs, see Section A.0. Introduction, earlier in this appendix.

Table A-15. Estimated equations and model statistics for current expenditures per pupil in fall enrollment for public elementary and secondary schools, and education revenue from state sources per capita

Dependent variable	Equation[1]	R^2	Breusch-Godfrey Serial Correlation LM test statistic[2]	Time period
1	2	3	4	5
Current expenditures per pupil..................................	$\ln(CUREXP) = $ 4.00 + 0.40ln(PCI) + 0.15ln(SGRANT) + 0.99AR(1) (1.775) (2.137) (1.837) (48.558)	0.997	8.07 (0.02)	1973–74 to 2009–10
Education revenue from state sources per capita...	$\ln(SGRNT) = $ 1.99 + 1.09ln(PCI) + 0.84ln(ENRPOP) + 0.63AR(1) (0.124) (15.781) (3.571) (4.721)	0.987	1.45 (0.48)	1973–74 to 2009–10

[1]AR(1) indicates that the model was estimated using least squares with the AR(1) process for correcting for first-order autocorrelation. To estimate the model, it was first transformed into a nonlinear model and then the coefficients were estimated simultaneously by applying a Marquardt nonlinear least squares algorithm to the transformed equation. For a general discussion of the problem of autocorrelation, and the method used to forecast in the presence of autocorrelation, see Judge, G., Hill, W., Griffiths, R., Lutkepohl, H., and Lee, T. (1985). *The Theory and Practice of Econometrics*. New York: John Wiley and Sons, pp. 315–318. Numbers in parentheses are *t*-statistics.

[2]The number in parentheses is the probability of the Chi-Square associated with the Breusch-Godfrey Serial Correlation LM Test. A *p* value greater that 0.05 implies that we do not reject the null hypothesis of no autocorrelation at the 5 percent significance level for a two-tailed test and 10 percent significance level for a one-tailed test (i.e., there is no autocorrelation present). For an explanation of the Breusch-Godfrey Serial Correlation LM test statistic, see Greene, W. (2000). *Economic Analysis*. New Jersey: Prentice-Hall.

NOTE: R^2 indicates the coefficient of determination.

CUREXP = Current expenditures of public elementary and secondary schools per pupil in fall enrollment in constant 1982–84 dollars.

SGRANT = Local governments' education revenue from state sources, per capita, in constant 1982–84 dollars.

PCI = Disposable income per capita in constant 2000 chained dollars.

ENRPOP = Ratio of fall enrollment to the population.

SOURCE: U.S. Department of Education, National Center for Education Statistics, Elementary and Secondary School Current Expenditures Model, 1973–74 through 2009–10; and Revenue Receipts from State Sources Model, 1973–74 through 2009–10. (This table was prepared March 2013.)

A.5. ENROLLMENT IN POSTSECONDARY DEGREE-GRANTING INSTITUTIONS

Projections in this edition

This edition of *Projections of Education Statistics* presents projections of enrollment in postsecondary degree-granting institutions for fall 2012 through fall 2022. Three different models were used to produce these enrollment projections:

» The *Enrollment in Degree-Granting Institutions Model* produced projections of enrollments by attendance status, level of student, level of institution, control of institution, sex, and age. It also produced projections of full-time-equivalent enrollments by level of student, level of institution, and control of institution.

» The *Enrollment in Degree-Granting Institutions by Race/Ethnicity Model* produced projections of enrollments by race/ethnicity.

» The *First-Time Freshmen Model* produced projections of enrollments of first-time freshmen by sex.

Overview of approach

Basic features of the three degree-granting enrollment models

The Enrollment in Degree-Granting Institutions Model is the primary model for projecting enrollment in postsecondary degree-granting institutions. For this model, enrollment rates by attendance status and sex are projected for various age categories using either the pooled seemingly unrelated regression method or the pooled seemingly unrelated regression method with a first-order autocorrelation correction. These rates are applied to projections of populations of the same sex and age to produce projections of enrollment by attendance status, sex, and age. To project enrollments by level of student, level of institution, and control of institution, rates for these characteristics are projected using single exponential smoothing and applied to enrollment projections previously produced by the model.

The Enrollment in Degree-Granting Institutions by Race/Ethnicity Model takes an approach similar to that of the Enrollment in Degree-Granting Institutions Model. Enrollment rates by attendance status, sex, and race/ethnicity are projected for the age categories using either the pooled seemingly unrelated regression method or the pooled seemingly unrelated regression method with a first-order autocorrelation correction. The resulting rates are iteratively corrected to ensure consistency with those projected by the Enrollment in Degree-Granting Institutions Model. The adjusted rates are then applied to projections of populations of the same sex, age, and race/ethnicity.

The First-Time Freshmen Enrollment in Degree-Granting Institutions Model uses single exponential smoothing to project the ratio of freshmen enrollment to undergraduate enrollment separately for males and for females. It then applies the projected ratios to the projections of undergraduate enrollment by sex that were produced by the Enrollment in Degree-Granting Institutions Model.

The Enrollment in Degree-Granting Institutions Model

The Enrollment in Degree-Granting Institutions Model produces projections of enrollment counts by six levels of detail, as well as projections of full-time-equivalent enrollments by level of student, level of institution, and control of institution.

Steps used in the Enrollment in Degree-Granting Institutions Model

Step 1. Adjust age-specific enrollment counts from the U.S. Census Bureau to make them agree with the more highly aggregated NCES enrollment counts that do not include age. The Enrollment in Degree-Granting Institutions Model projects enrollments by six levels of detail: attendance status, level of student, level of institution, control of institution, sex, and age. While NCES does produce enrollment counts by the first five levels of detail, it does not produce data by the sixth level of detail, age, every year. However, the U.S. Census Bureau does produce age-specific enrollment counts.

In step 1, the age distributions from the Census Bureau counts for 1980 to 2011 were applied to the NCES counts to produce a set of enrollment data that breaks enrollments down by age while being consistent with NCES counts. Specifically, the most detailed level of Census Bureau data (by attendance status, level of student, level of institution, control of institution, sex, and age) was iteratively changed using proportions based on the more highly aggregated NCES enrollment numbers to ensure that all sums across this most detailed level of Census enrollment data equaled the more highly aggregated NCES enrollment totals that did not include age.

Step 2. *Calculate enrollment rates by attendance status, sex, and age category.* The enrollment data were broken up into 14 age categories, with separate age categories for individual ages 14 through 24 as well as for the age groups 25 to 29, 30 to 34, and 35 and over. For each of the 14 age categories, 4 enrollment rates were calculated—part-time male, full-time male, part-time female, and full-time female—resulting in a total of 56 enrollment rates. Each of the 56 enrollment rates was calculated by dividing the enrollment count for that combination of attendance status, sex, and age category by the total population for the corresponding combination of sex and age category. For each combination of attendance and sex, the enrollment rate for the oldest age category was calculated by dividing the enrollment count for those 35 and over by the total population for those 35 to 44.

Step 3. *Produce projections of enrollment rates by attendance status, sex, and age category.* Enrollment rates for most of the age groups were projected using multiple linear regression. However, because enrollment in postsecondary degree-granting institutions is negligible for ages 14, 15, and 16, these ages were not included in the multiple linear regression models. Instead, projections for individual ages 14, 15, and 16 were produced by double exponential smoothing.

The following 11 age categories were modeled: individual ages 17 through 24 and age groups 25 to 29, 30 to 34, and 35 and over. For each of these age categories, enrollment rates by attendance status and sex were produced using four pooled time-series models—one for each combination of attendance status and sex. Each model was pooled across age categories. Each equation contained two independent variables, which were measures of

- » disposable income; and
- » the unemployment rate.

Either the pooled seemingly unrelated regression method or the pooled seemingly unrelated regression method with a first-order autocorrelation correction was used to estimate each equation.

For more details on the equations used in step 3, the data used to estimate these equations, and their results, see tables A-16 through A-18 on pages 116–118.

Step 4. *Produce projections of enrollments by attendance status, sex, and age category.* For each combination of attendance status, sex, and age category, enrollment projections were produced by multiplying the projected enrollment rate for that combination by projections of the total population with the corresponding combination of sex and age category.

Step 5. *Add two additional levels of detail—level of student and level of institution—to the projected enrollments by attendance status, sex, and age category.* For this step, the 14 age categories used in the previous steps were collapsed into the following 8 categories: ages 14 to 16, 17, 18 and 19, 20 and 21, 22 to 24, 25 to 29, 30 to 34, and 35 and over. Step 5 can be broken into three parts:

First, the historic data were used to calculate the percentage distribution of enrollment by level of student and level of institution for each combination of attendance status, sex, and age category. Because it was assumed that there was no enrollment in 2-year institutions at the postbaccalaureate level, three combinations of student level and institution type were used: undergraduates at 4-year institutions, undergraduates at 2-year institutions, and postbaccalaureate students at 4-year institutions.

Second, for each combination of attendance status, sex, and age category, the percentage distribution by level of student and level of institution was projected using single exponential smoothing. A separate smoothing constant, chosen to minimize the sum of squared forecast errors, was used in each case. The percentages were then adjusted so the sum of the categories by attendance status, level of student, level of institution, sex, and age category would equal 100 percent.

For the projected percentage distributions from step 5 and the actual 2011 distributions, see tables A-19 and A-20 on pages 119.

Third, the projected distributions by level of student and type of institution were applied to the projected enrollments by attendance status, sex, and age category from step 4 to obtain the enrollment projections by attendance status, level of student, level of institution, sex, and age category.

Step 6. *Add the sixth level of detail—control of institutions—to the projected enrollments in postsecondary degree-granting institutions.* In this step, the data on enrollment by age category were not used. Control of institutions was added in the following manner:

First, the historic data were used to calculate the percentage of enrollment in public institutions for each combination of attendance status, level of student, level of institution, and sex.

Second, the percentages of enrollment in public institutions were projected using single exponential smoothing. A separate smoothing constant, chosen to minimize the sum of squared forecast errors, was used for each percentage.

For the projected percentages from step 6 and the actual 2011 percentages, see table A-21 on page 120.

Third, the projected percentages were applied to the projected enrollments in each corresponding enrollment combination to obtain projections for public institutions by attendance status, level of student, level of institution, and sex.

Fourth, the projected enrollments for public institutions were subtracted from the total to produce the projected enrollments for private institutions.

Step 7. *Produce projections of full-time-equivalent enrollment by level of student, level of institution, and control of institution.* Full-time-equivalent enrollment represents total full-time and part-time enrollment as if it were enrollment on a full-time basis. It equals the sum of full-time enrollment plus the full-time-equivalent of part-time enrollment. Full-time-equivalent enrollment projections were produced in the following manner:

First, for each combination of level of student, level of institution, and control of institution, the historic data were used to calculate the full-time-equivalent of part-time enrollment as a percentage of part-time enrollment.

Second, for each combination of level of student, level of institution, and control of institution, the full-time equivalent of part-time enrollment as a percentage of part-time enrollment was projected using single exponential smoothing. A separate smoothing constant, chosen to minimize the sum of squared forecast errors, was used for each percentage.

Third, for each combination of level of student, level of institution, and control of institution, the projected percentages were applied to the projections of part-time enrollment to project the full-time equivalent of the part-time enrollment.

Fourth, the projections of full-time equivalents of part-time enrollment were added to projections of full-time enrollment to obtain projections of full-time-equivalent enrollment.

Data and equation results for the Enrollment in Degree-Granting Institutions Model

Enrollment data for postsecondary degree-granting institutions. Enrollment data for 1981 to 2011 by attendance status, level of student, level of institution, control of institution, and sex came from the NCES Integrated Postsecondary Education Data System (IPEDS). These are universe counts. The U.S. Census Bureau was the source for enrollment estimates for 1981 to 2011 by the characteristics listed above, as well as age of student.

Population data and projections. Population counts for 1980 to 2011 came from the U.S. Census Bureau. Population projections for 2012 to 2022 are the Census Bureau's 2012 National Population Projections of the population by sex and age (December 2012), ratio-adjusted to line up with the most recent historical estimates. For more information, see Section A.0. Introduction, earlier in this appendix.

Projections for economic variables. The economic variables used in developing these projections were from the "U.S. Monthly Model: January 2013 Short-Term Projections" from the economic consulting firm, IHS Global Insight.

Data and results for the equations. The following details for the equations are shown on pages 116–120:

» Table A-16 shows enrollment rates by sex, attendance status, and age for fall 2011 and projected enrollment rates for fall 2017 and fall 2022.

» Table A-17 shows the estimated equations and model statistics used to project enrollments for men by attendance status, and table A-18 shows the estimated equations and model statistics used to project enrollment rates for women by attendance status. The particular equations shown were selected on the basis of their statistical properties, such as coefficients of determination (R^2s), the *t*-statistics of the coefficients, the Durbin-Watson statistic, the Breusch-Godfrey Serial Correlation LM test statistic, and residual plots.

» Table A-19 shows actual and projected percentage distributions of full-time students, and table A-20 shows actual and projected percentage distributions of part-time students.

» Table A-21 shows actual and projected data for enrollment in public degree-granting institutions as a percentage of total enrollment by sex, attendance status, student level, and level of institution.

Accuracy of projections for the Enrollment in Degree-Granting Institutions Model

Mean absolute percentage errors (MAPEs) for enrollment in degree-granting institutions were calculated using the last 15 editions of *Projections of Education Statistics*. Table E, below, shows MAPEs for key projections of the Enrollment in Degree-Granting Institutions Model.

Table E. Mean absolute percentage errors (MAPEs) of projected enrollment in postsecondary degree-granting institutions, by lead time, sex, and level of institution: 2013

Statistic	Lead time (years)									
	1	2	3	4	5	6	7	8	9	10
Total enrollment	**1.6**	**2.5**	**3.8**	**5.0**	**5.8**	**6.5**	**7.8**	**9.4**	**11.5**	**13.1**
Men	1.7	2.9	4.3	5.7	6.6	7.4	8.5	9.8	11.8	13.3
Women	1.7	2.5	3.9	4.7	5.1	5.7	7.3	9.0	11.2	12.9
4-year institutions	1.7	3.0	4.3	5.7	6.6	7.3	8.9	10.6	13.1	14.8
2-year institutions	2.3	3.1	4.2	4.9	5.2	5.1	5.9	7.1	8.7	10.1

NOTE: MAPEs for degree-granting institution enrollments were calculated using the last 15 editions of *Projections of Education Statistics*. Calculations were made using unrounded numbers. Some data have been revised from previously published figures.
SOURCE: U.S. Department of Education, National Center for Education Statistics, *Projections of Education Statistics*, various issues. (This table was prepared February 2013.)

For more information about MAPEs, see Section A.0. Introduction, earlier in this appendix.

The Enrollment in Degree-Granting Institutions by Race/Ethnicity Model

The Enrollment in Degree-Granting Institutions by Race/Ethnicity Model projects enrollments in degree-granting institutions by attendance status, sex, age, and race/ethnicity. The following groups are projected in this model:

- » White;
- » Black;
- » Hispanic;
- » Asian/Pacific Islander;
- » American Indian/Alaska Native; and
- » nonresident alien.

See the glossary for definitions of the five racial/ethnic categories and the nonresident alien category. (The race/ethnicity of nonresident aliens is unknown, but they are considered a separate group for purposes of this analysis.)

Steps used in the Degree-Granting Institutions by Race/Ethnicity Model

Step 1. *Adjust U.S. Census Bureau enrollment counts by attendance status, sex, age, and race/ethnicity to make them sum to NCES enrollment counts by attendance status, sex, and race/ethnicity.* For 1981 to 2011, the most detailed levels of Census Bureau enrollment data (by enrollment status, sex, age, and race/ethnicity) were iteratively changed using proportions that were based on the more highly aggregated NCES enrollment numbers to ensure that the sums across these most detailed levels of enrollment data equaled the more highly aggregated NCES enrollment numbers that did not include age.

Step 2. *Calculate enrollment rates by attendance status, sex, age category, and race/ethnicity.* The enrollment data were broken up into 14 age categories, with separate age categories for individual ages 14 through 24 as well as for the age groups 25 to 29, 30 to 34, and 35 and over. For each of the 14 age categories, enrollment rates were calculated for each combination of attendance status, sex, and the six racial/ethnic groups, resulting in a total of 336 enrollment rates. Each of the 336 enrollment rates was calculated by dividing the enrollment count for that combination of attendance status, sex, age category, and race/ethnicity by the total population for the corresponding combination of sex, age category, and race/ethnicity. For each combination of attendance status, sex and racial/ethnic group, the enrollment rate for the oldest age category was calculated by dividing the enrollment count for those 35 and over by the total population for those 35 to 44.

Step 3. *Produce projections of enrollment rates by attendance status, sex, age category, and race/ethnicity.* Enrollment rates for most of the age groups and racial/ethnic groups were projected using multiple linear regression. However, there were several exceptions:

» Due to negligible enrollments for ages 14, 15, and 16, these ages were not included in the multiple linear regression models. Instead, projections of enrollment rates for individual ages 14, 15, and 16 were produced by single exponential smoothing.

» Due to the relatively large fluctuations in the historical enrollment rates resulting from small sample sizes, American Indian/Alaska Native enrollments were projected using single exponential smoothing.

» Since there were no applicable population counts to compute enrollment rates for nonresident aliens, their enrollments were projected using patterns in recent historical growth.

Four racial/ethnic groups were modeled: White, Black, Hispanic, and Asian/Pacific Islander. Eleven age categories were modeled: individual ages 17 through 24 and age groups 25 to 29, 30 to 34, and 35 to 44. For each of the age categories, projected enrollment rates by attendance status, sex, and race/ethnicity were produced using 16 pooled time-series models—one for each combination of attendance status, sex, and the four racial/ethnic groups. Each equation included variables measuring

» recent trends;

» economic conditions (such as disposable income); and

» demographic changes.

For more information on the equations used to project enrollment rates for the combinations of attendance status, sex, and race/ethnicity, see tables A-22 through A-29, under "Data and equations used for the Enrollment in Degree-Granting Institutions by Race/Ethnicity Model," below.

The final set of projected rates by attendance status, sex, age, and race/ethnicity were controlled to enrollment rates by attendance status, sex, and age produced by the Enrollment in Degree-Granting Institutions Model to ensure consistency across models.

Step 4. *Produce projections of enrollments by attendance status, sex, age category, and race/ethnicity.* For each combination of attendance status, sex, age category, and race/ethnicity, enrollment projections were produced by multiplying the projected enrollment rate for that combination by projections of the total population with the corresponding combination of sex, age category, and race/ethnicity.

Data and equations used for the Enrollment in Degree-Granting Institutions by Race/Ethnicity Model

Enrollment data for degree-granting institutions by race/ethnicity. Enrollment data for 1981 to 2011 by attendance status, sex, and race/ethnicity came from the NCES Integrated Postsecondary Education Data System (IPEDS). These are universe counts. The U.S. Census Bureau, Current Population Survey was the source for enrollment estimates for 1981 to 2011 by the characteristics listed above, as well as age of student.

Population data and projections by race/ethnicity. Population counts for 1981 to 2011 came from the U.S. Census Bureau, Population Estimates series. Population projections for 2012 to 2022 are the Census Bureau's 2012 National Population Projections of the population by sex, age and race/ethnicity (December 2012), ratio-adjusted to line up with most recent historical estimates.

Projections for economic variables. The economic variables used in developing these projections were from the "U.S. Monthly Model: January 2013 Short-Term Projections" from the economic consulting firm, IHS Global Insight.

Estimated equations and model statistics. Tables A-22 through A-29 show the estimated equations and model statistics used to project enrollment rates for the various combinations of attendance status, sex, and race/ethnicity.

Accuracy of projections for the Degree-Granting Institutions by Race/Ethnicity Model

Mean absolute percentage errors (MAPEs) for enrollment in degree-granting institutions by race/ethnicity were calculated using the last seven editions of *Projections of Education Statistics*. Table F, below, shows MAPEs for key projections of the Enrollment in Degree-Granting Institutions by Race/Ethnicity Model.

Table F. **Mean absolute percentage errors (MAPEs) of projected enrollment in postsecondary degree-granting institutions, by lead time and race/ethnicity: 2013**

Statistic	Lead time (years)									
	1	2	3	4	5	6	7	8	9	10
Total enrollment	**1.6**	**2.5**	**3.8**	**5.0**	**5.8**	**6.5**	**7.8**	**9.4**	**11.5**	**13.1**
White	1.0	2.4	3.7	5.1	6.4	5.8	5.2	—	—	—
Black	4.1	8.8	12.7	16.4	19.3	19.9	20.0	—	—	—
Hispanic	3.8	8.6	13.3	16.9	20.0	22.1	24.0	—	—	—
Asian/Pacific Islander	2.3	5.0	5.5	5.5	4.8	2.5	2.9	—	—	—
American Indian/Alaska Native	5.5	4.1	5.1	6.8	4.7	8.2	11.9	—	—	—
Nonresident alien	2.9	4.8	6.6	9.5	11.7	9.0	3.9	—	—	—

— Not available.
NOTE: MAPEs for total postsecondary degree-granting institution enrollments were calculated using the last 15 editions of *Projections of Education Statistics*, and MAPEs for degree-granting institution enrollments were calculated using the last seven editions of *Projections of Education Statistics*. Calculations were made using unrounded numbers. Some data have been revised from previously published figures.
SOURCE: U.S. Department of Education, National Center for Education Statistics, *Projections of Education Statistics*, various issues. (This table was prepared February 2013.)

The First-Time Freshmen Enrollment in Degree-Granting Institutions Model

The First-Time Freshmen Enrollment in Degree-Granting Institutions Model produced projections of first-time freshmen enrollment in degree-granting institutions by sex.

Steps used in the First-Time Freshmen Enrollment in Degree-Granting Institutions Model

The projections were produced in the following manner:

Step 1. Calculate the ratio of first-time freshmen enrollment to undergraduate enrollment. For 1975 to 2011, the ratio of first-time freshmen enrollment to undergraduate enrollment was calculated for males and females.

Step 2. Project the ratio of first-time freshmen enrollment to undergraduate enrollment. The percentages of undergraduate enrollment for both males and females were projected using single exponential smoothing. A separate smoothing constant, chosen to minimize the sum of squared forecast errors, was used for each percentage.

Step 3. Apply the projected ratio to projected undergraduate enrollment. The projected ratios were applied to projections of undergraduate enrollment by sex from the Enrollment in Degree-Granting Institutions Model to yield projections of first-time freshmen enrollment.

Assumptions underlying this method

This method assumes that the future pattern in the trend of first-time freshmen enrollment will be the same as that for undergraduate enrollment.

Data used in the First-Time Freshmen Enrollment in Degree-Granting Institutions Model

Undergraduate and freshmen enrollment data for degree-granting institutions. Undergraduate and freshmen enrollment data by sex for 1975 to 2011 came from the NCES Integrated Postsecondary Education Data System (IPEDS).

Projections of undergraduate enrollment. Projections of undergraduate enrollment by sex came from the Enrollment in Degree-Granting Institutions Model, discussed earlier in this section of appendix A.

Accuracy of projections for the First-Time Freshmen Enrollment Model

Because this is the fifth edition of *Projections of Education Statistics* to include projections of first-time freshmen, there are too few years of data to present the MAPEs.

Table A-16. Actual and projected numbers for enrollment rates of all students at postsecondary degree-granting institutions, by sex, attendance status, and age: Fall 2011, fall 2017, and fall 2022

Sex, attendance status, and age	Actual 2011	Projected	
		2017	2022
1	2	3	4
Men			
Full-time			
16 years old	0.6	0.5	0.5
17 years old	2.5	2.7	2.7
18 years old	29.0	29.7	30.4
19 years old	38.3	39.7	40.4
20 years old	35.8	36.9	37.6
21 years old	33.1	34.2	34.9
22 years old	22.2	23.1	23.6
23 years old	16.3	17.1	17.5
24 years old	13.9	14.6	14.9
25 to 29 years old	6.6	6.9	7.1
30 to 34 years old	2.8	2.9	3.0
35 to 44 years old	1.9	2.0	2.1
Part-time			
16 years old	0.1	0.2	0.2
17 years old	1.0	1.0	1.0
18 years old	6.4	6.5	6.5
19 years old	9.8	9.8	9.8
20 years old	10.1	10.1	10.1
21 years old	10.9	10.8	10.9
22 years old	9.8	9.9	10.0
23 years old	8.4	8.4	8.5
24 years old	6.6	6.7	6.7
25 to 29 years old	6.2	6.3	6.4
30 to 34 years old	3.5	3.6	3.6
35 to 44 years old	3.7	3.8	3.8
Women			
Full-time			
16 years old	0.5	0.5	0.5
17 years old	3.6	4.1	4.4
18 years old	41.2	43.9	45.0
19 years old	47.3	49.7	50.7
20 years old	44.1	46.4	47.4
21 years old	39.3	41.5	42.5
22 years old	26.6	28.5	29.4
23 years old	21.6	23.2	24.0
24 years old	13.7	14.9	15.5
25 to 29 years old	8.0	8.8	9.2
30 to 34 years old	4.4	4.8	5.0
35 to 44 years old	3.5	3.8	4.0
Part-time			
16 years old	0.2	0.2	0.2
17 years old	0.4	0.5	0.5
18 years old	7.0	7.5	7.7
19 years old	11.6	12.3	12.6
20 years old	10.6	11.3	11.6
21 years old	11.3	12.1	12.4
22 years old	10.8	11.7	12.1
23 years old	12.4	13.6	14.1
24 years old	11.0	12.2	12.7
25 to 29 years old	8.9	9.9	10.3
30 to 34 years old	5.7	6.3	6.6
35 to 44 years old	7.9	8.7	9.1

SOURCE: U.S. Department of Education, National Center for Education Statistics, Integrated Postsecondary Education Data System, Spring 2011; Enrollment in Degree-Granting Institutions Model, 1980–2011; and U.S. Department of Commerce, Census Bureau, Current Population Reports, "Social and Economic Characteristics of Students," 2011. (This table was prepared February 2013.)

Table A-17. Estimated equations and model statistics for full-time and part-time enrollment rates of men at postsecondary degree-granting institutions

Independent variable	Coefficient	Standard error	t-statistic	R^2	D.W. statistic
1	2	3	4	5	6
Full-time					
Intercept term for 17-year-olds..............................	-7.65	0.335	-22.84	1.00	1.89*
Intercept term for 18-year-olds..............................	-4.79	0.315	-15.20		
Intercept term for 19-year-olds..............................	-4.36	0.279	-15.61		
Intercept term for 20-year-olds..............................	-4.41	0.282	-15.65		
Intercept term for 21-year-olds..............................	-4.56	0.281	-16.22		
Intercept term for 22-year-olds..............................	-5.00	0.285	-17.58		
Intercept term for 23-year-olds..............................	-5.49	0.282	-19.47		
Intercept term for 24-year-olds..............................	-5.81	0.302	-19.26		
Intercept term for 25- to 29-year-olds	-6.51	0.290	-22.44		
Intercept term for 30- to 34-year-olds	-7.47	0.318	-23.51		
Intercept term for 35- to 44-year-olds	-7.92	0.331	-23.95		
Log of three-period weighted average of per capita disposable income in 2000 dollars, using the present period and the previous two periods.....	0.71	0.047	14.98		
Log age-specific unemployment rate for men	0.22	0.023	9.45		
Autocorrelation coefficient for 17-year-olds..............	0.88	0.044	19.96		
Autocorrelation coefficient for 18-year-olds..............	0.90	0.043	21.01		
Autocorrelation coefficient for 19-year-olds..............	0.45	0.135	3.34		
Autocorrelation coefficient for 20-year-olds..............	0.64	0.113	5.62		
Autocorrelation coefficient for 21-year-olds..............	0.59	0.130	4.53		
Autocorrelation coefficient for 22-year-olds..............	0.77	0.105	7.33		
Autocorrelation coefficient for 23-year-olds..............	0.65	0.119	5.49		
Autocorrelation coefficient for 24-year-olds..............	0.86	0.097	8.92		
Autocorrelation coefficient for 25- to 29-year-olds ...	0.80	0.089	9.05		
Autocorrelation coefficient for 30- to 34-year-olds ...	0.90	0.066	13.58		
Autocorrelation coefficient for 35- to 44-year-olds ...	0.89	0.069	12.92		
Part-time					
Intercept term for 17-year-olds..............................	-8.06	0.351	-22.94	0.98	1.83*
Intercept term for 18-year-olds..............................	-5.70	0.306	-18.61		
Intercept term for 19-year-olds..............................	-5.11	0.404	-12.64		
Intercept term for 20-year-olds..............................	-5.14	0.321	-16.03		
Intercept term for 21-year-olds..............................	-5.24	0.311	-16.87		
Intercept term for 22-year-olds..............................	-5.46	0.308	-17.71		
Intercept term for 23-year-olds..............................	-5.50	0.301	-18.30		
Intercept term for 24-year-olds..............................	-5.56	0.302	-18.45		
Intercept term for 25- to 29-year-olds	-5.95	0.316	-18.82		
Intercept term for 30- to 34-year-olds	-6.47	0.313	-20.66		
Intercept term for 35- to 44-year-olds	-6.38	0.303	-21.02		
Log of three-period weighted average of per capita disposable income in 2000 dollars, using the present period and the previous two periods.....	0.47	0.049	9.52		
Log unemployment rate	0.17	0.022	8.02		
Autocorrelation coefficient for 17-year-olds..............	0.69	0.108	6.40		
Autocorrelation coefficient for 18-year-olds..............	0.67	0.092	7.30		
Autocorrelation coefficient for 19-year-olds..............	0.91	0.058	15.66		
Autocorrelation coefficient for 20-year-olds..............	0.82	0.087	9.39		
Autocorrelation coefficient for 21-year-olds..............	0.77	0.092	8.32		
Autocorrelation coefficient for 22-year-olds..............	0.68	0.110	6.19		
Autocorrelation coefficient for 23-year-olds..............	0.42	0.100	4.19		
Autocorrelation coefficient for 24-year-olds..............	0.51	0.111	4.58		
Autocorrelation coefficient for 25- to 29-year-olds ...	0.86	0.044	19.30		
Autocorrelation coefficient for 30- to 34-year-olds ...	0.89	0.043	20.75		
Autocorrelation coefficient for 35- to 44-year-olds ...	0.58	0.092	6.37		

* $p < .05$.
NOTE: R^2 = Coefficient of determination. D.W. statistic = Durbin-Watson statistic, a test for autocorrelation among regression residuals. For more details see Johnston, J., and Dinardo, J. (1996). *Econometric Methods*. New York: McGraw-Hill. The regression method used to estimate the full-time and part-time equations was the pooled seemingly unrelated regression method with a first-order autocorrelation correction. The time period used to estimate both equations is from 1981 to 2011, and the number of observations is 341 after the correction for autocorrelation. For additional information, see Intriligator, M.D. (1978). *Econometric Models, Techniques, & Applications*. New Jersey: Prentice-Hall, Inc., pp. 165–173.
SOURCE: U.S. Department of Education, National Center for Education Statistics, Enrollment in Degree-Granting Institutions Model, 1980–2011. (This table was prepared February 2013.)

Table A-18. Estimated equations and model statistics for full-time and part-time enrollment rates of women at postsecondary degree-granting institutions

Independent variable	Coefficient	Standard error	t-statistic	R^2	D.W. statistic
1	2	3	4	5	6
Full-time					
Intercept term for 17-year-olds............................	-9.65	0.158	-61.21	1.00	1.22~
Intercept term for 18-year-olds............................	-6.84	0.139	-49.35		
Intercept term for 19-year-olds............................	-6.70	0.134	-50.21		
Intercept term for 20-year-olds............................	-6.78	0.135	-50.20		
Intercept term for 21-year-olds............................	-7.00	0.135	-51.75		
Intercept term for 22-year-olds............................	-7.65	0.137	-55.94		
Intercept term for 23-year-olds............................	-8.13	0.139	-58.53		
Intercept term for 24-year-olds............................	-8.52	0.139	-61.10		
Intercept term for 25- to 29-year-olds	-9.07	0.143	-63.62		
Intercept term for 30- to 34-year-olds	-9.77	0.141	-69.39		
Intercept term for 35- to 44-year-olds	-9.99	0.141	-70.73		
Log of three-period weighted average of per capita disposable income in 2000 dollars, using the present period and the previous two periods.....	1.21	0.025	49.35		
Log age-specific unemployment rate for women	0.35	0.033	10.84		
Part-time					
Intercept term for 17-year-olds............................	-11.79	0.572	-20.63	0.99	1.86*
Intercept term for 18-year-olds............................	-8.98	0.345	-26.03		
Intercept term for 19-year-olds............................	-8.41	0.331	-25.43		
Intercept term for 20-year-olds............................	-8.58	0.325	-26.36		
Intercept term for 21-year-olds............................	-8.59	0.323	-26.64		
Intercept term for 22-year-olds............................	-8.77	0.323	-27.18		
Intercept term for 23-year-olds............................	-8.83	0.324	-27.24		
Intercept term for 24-year-olds............................	-8.90	0.327	-27.21		
Intercept term for 25- to 29-year-olds	-9.31	0.331	-28.18		
Intercept term for 30- to 34-year-olds	-9.77	0.334	-29.25		
Intercept term for 35- to 44-year-olds	-9.43	0.340	-27.77		
Log of three-period weighted average of per capita disposable income in 2000 dollars, using the present period and the previous two periods.....	1.07	0.052	20.62		
Log unemployment rate	0.18	0.023	7.96		
Autocorrelation coefficient for 17-year-olds.............	0.86	0.064	13.38		
Autocorrelation coefficient for 18-year-olds.............	0.79	0.075	10.65		
Autocorrelation coefficient for 19-year-olds.............	0.78	0.073	10.69		
Autocorrelation coefficient for 20-year-olds.............	0.61	0.106	5.72		
Autocorrelation coefficient for 21-year-olds.............	0.40	0.121	3.32		
Autocorrelation coefficient for 22-year-olds.............	0.46	0.099	4.58		
Autocorrelation coefficient for 23-year-olds.............	0.50	0.077	6.54		
Autocorrelation coefficient for 24-year-olds.............	0.75	0.059	12.68		
Autocorrelation coefficient for 25- to 29-year-olds ...	0.87	0.037	23.79		
Autocorrelation coefficient for 30- to 34-year-olds ...	0.89	0.025	36.21		
Autocorrelation coefficient for 35- to 44-year-olds ...	0.89	0.027	33.11		

* $p < .05$.
~ Inconclusive
NOTE: R^2 = Coefficient of determination. D.W. statistic = Durbin-Watson statistic, a test for autocorrelation among regression residuals. For more details see Johnston, J., and Dinardo, J. (1996). *Econometric Methods*. New York: McGraw-Hill. The regression method used to estimate the full-time and part-time equations was the pooled seemingly unrelated regression method with a first-order autocorrelation correction. The time period used to estimate both equations is from 1981 to 2011, and the number of observations is 341 after the correction for autocorrelation. For additional information, see Intriligator, M.D. (1978). *Econometric Models, Techniques, & Applications*. New Jersey: Prentice-Hall, Inc., pp. 165–173.
SOURCE: U.S. Department of Education, National Center for Education Statistics, Enrollment in Degree-Granting Institutions Model, 1980–2011. (This table was prepared February 2013.)

Table A-19. Actual and projected percentages of full-time students at postsecondary degree-granting institutions, by sex, age group, student level, and level of institution: Fall 2011, and fall 2012 through fall 2022

Age group, student level, and institution level	Men		Women	
	Actual 2011	Projected 2012 through 2022	Actual 2011	Projected 2012 through 2022
1	2	3	4	5
18 and 19 years old				
Undergraduate, 4-year institutions...........................	66.8	65.7	70.7	70.6
Undergraduate, 2-year institutions...........................	33.7	33.9	28.9	29.0
Postbaccalaureate, 4-year institutions	#	0.4	0.3	0.3
20 and 21 years old				
Undergraduate, 4-year institutions...........................	78.0	77.2	77.5	77.8
Undergraduate, 2-year institutions...........................	21.6	21.3	20.4	20.2
Postbaccalaureate, 4-year institutions	0.4	1.5	2.1	2.0
22 to 24 years old				
Undergraduate, 4-year institutions...........................	63.5	63.6	61.0	60.8
Undergraduate, 2-year institutions...........................	16.7	16.8	17.3	17.3
Postbaccalaureate, 4-year institutions	19.8	19.6	21.8	22.0
25 to 29 years old				
Undergraduate, 4-year institutions...........................	41.0	41.6	40.5	40.5
Undergraduate, 2-year institutions...........................	20.1	19.7	25.6	25.6
Postbaccalaureate, 4-year institutions	38.9	38.7	33.9	33.9
30 to 34 years old				
Undergraduate, 4-year institutions...........................	44.4	44.4	49.2	49.2
Undergraduate, 2-year institutions...........................	23.1	23.1	28.3	28.3
Postbaccalaureate, 4-year institutions	32.4	32.4	22.5	22.5
35 years and over				
Undergraduate, 4-year institutions...........................	47.7	48.0	41.6	41.8
Undergraduate, 2-year institutions...........................	22.0	22.2	31.6	31.8
Postbaccalaureate, 4-year institutions	30.3	29.8	26.8	26.4

Rounds to zero.
NOTE: Detail may not sum to totals because of rounding.
SOURCE: U.S. Department of Education, National Center for Education Statistics, Integrated Postsecondary Education Data System, Spring 2012; Enrollment in Degree-Granting Institutions Model, 1980–2011; and U.S. Department of Commerce, Census Bureau, Current Population Reports, "Social and Economic Characteristics of Students," 2011. (This table was prepared February 2013.)

Table A-20. Actual and projected percentages of part-time students at postsecondary degree-granting institutions, by sex, age group, student level, and level of institution: Fall 2011, and fall 2012 through fall 2022

Age, student level, and level of institution	Men		Women	
	Actual 2011	Projected 2012 through 2022	Actual 2011	Projected 2012 through 2022
1	2	3	4	5
18 and 19 years old				
Undergraduate, 4-year institutions...........................	23.2	23.2	22.1	22.1
Undergraduate, 2-year institutions...........................	75.0	75.9	78.8	77.5
Postbaccalaureate, 4-year institutions	1.8	0.9	#	0.4
20 and 21 years old				
Undergraduate, 4-year institutions...........................	25.0	25.1	26.6	26.5
Undergraduate, 2-year institutions...........................	73.8	74.2	73.5	72.5
Postbaccalaureate, 4-year institutions	1.2	0.8	#	1.0
22 to 24 years old				
Undergraduate, 4-year institutions...........................	32.0	31.9	34.5	34.4
Undergraduate, 2-year institutions...........................	59.5	59.0	54.5	54.2
Postbaccalaureate, 4-year institutions	8.6	9.1	11.0	11.3
25 to 29 years old				
Undergraduate, 4-year institutions...........................	30.7	30.7	35.6	35.6
Undergraduate, 2-year institutions...........................	50.6	50.6	44.3	44.3
Postbaccalaureate, 4-year institutions	18.7	18.7	20.1	20.1
30 to 34 years old				
Undergraduate, 4-year institutions...........................	38.4	38.4	32.8	32.8
Undergraduate, 2-year institutions...........................	40.8	40.8	44.8	44.9
Postbaccalaureate, 4-year institutions	20.9	20.9	22.4	22.4
35 years and over				
Undergraduate, 4-year institutions...........................	29.8	30.1	25.3	25.4
Undergraduate, 2-year institutions...........................	40.6	41.4	49.5	49.5
Postbaccalaureate, 4-year institutions	29.5	28.5	25.2	25.1

Rounds to zero.
NOTE: Detail may not sum to totals because of rounding.
SOURCE: U.S. Department of Education, National Center for Education Statistics, Integrated Postsecondary Education Data System, Spring 2012; Enrollment in Degree-Granting Institutions Model, 1981–2011; and U.S. Department of Commerce, Census Bureau, Current Population Reports, "Social and Economic Characteristics of Students," 2011. (This table was prepared February 2013.)

Table A-21. Actual and projected enrollment in public postsecondary degree-granting institutions as a percentage of total postsecondary enrollment, by sex, attendance status, student level, and level of institution: Fall 2011, and fall 2012 through fall 2022

Attendance status, student level, and level of institution	Men		Women	
	Actual 2011	Projected 2012 through 2022	Actual 2011	Projected 2012 through 2022
Full-time, undergraduate, 4-year institutions...............	64.9	64.9	60.4	60.4
Part-time, undergraduate, 4-year institutions...............	66.2	66.2	62.1	62.1
Full-time, undergraduate, 2-year institutions...............	90.6	90.6	85.7	85.7
Part-time, undergraduate, 2-year institutions...............	99.2	99.2	98.4	98.5
Full-time, postbaccalaureate, 4-year institutions	48.8	48.8	45.4	45.4
Part-time, postbaccalaureate, 4-year institutions........	50.9	50.9	50.2	50.2

SOURCE: U.S. Department of Education, National Center for Education Statistics, Integrated Postsecondary Education Data System, Spring 2012; and Enrollment in Degree-Granting Institutions Model, 1980–2011. (This table was prepared February 2013.)

Table A-22. Estimated equations and model statistics for full-time and part-time enrollment rates of White men at postsecondary degree-granting institutions

Independent variable	Coefficient	Standard error	t-statistic	R^2	D.W. statistic
1	2	3	4	5	6
Full-time					
Intercept term for 17-year-olds...............................	-9.59	0.198	-48.44	1.00	1.44~
Intercept term for 18-year-olds...............................	-6.57	0.182	-36.12		
Intercept term for 19-year-olds...............................	-6.32	0.178	-35.54		
Intercept term for 20-year-olds...............................	-6.50	0.179	-36.40		
Intercept term for 21-year-olds...............................	-6.64	0.179	-37.19		
Intercept term for 22-year-olds...............................	-7.14	0.179	-39.98		
Intercept term for 23-year-olds...............................	-7.69	0.178	-43.10		
Intercept term for 24-year-olds...............................	-8.09	0.181	-44.74		
Intercept term for 25- to 29-year-olds	-8.95	0.179	-49.92		
Intercept term for 30- to 34-year-olds	-9.99	0.182	-54.87		
Intercept term for 35- to 44-year-olds	-10.61	0.183	-58.07		
Log of White per capita disposable income in current dollars	0.31	0.009	33.41		
Part-time					
Intercept term for 17-year-olds...............................	-4.88	0.153	-31.88	0.94	1.45~
Intercept term for 18-year-olds...............................	-1.57	0.091	-17.34		
Intercept term for 19-year-olds...............................	-1.17	0.103	-11.28		
Intercept term for 20-year-olds...............................	-1.14	0.092	-12.50		
Intercept term for 21-year-olds...............................	-1.16	0.095	-12.28		
Intercept term for 22-year-olds...............................	-1.37	0.091	-15.13		
Intercept term for 23-year-olds...............................	-1.41	0.087	-16.14		
Intercept term for 24-year-olds...............................	-1.42	0.087	-16.41		
Intercept term for 25- to 29-year-olds	-1.75	0.087	-20.17		
Intercept term for 30- to 34-year-olds	-2.20	0.089	-24.73		
Intercept term for 35- to 44-year-olds	-2.24	0.085	-26.23		
Log of real total private compensation employment cost index	1.36	0.111	12.17		

~ Inconclusive.

NOTE: R^2 = Coefficient of determination. D.W. statistic = Durbin-Watson statistic, a test for autocorrelation among regression residuals. For more details see Johnston, J., and Dinardo, J. (1996). *Econometric Methods*. New York: McGraw-Hill. The regression method used to estimate the full-time and part-time equations was the pooled seemingly unrelated regression method. The time period used to estimate the equations is from 1980 to 2011. The number of observations is 352. For additional information, see Intriligator, M.D. (1978). *Econometric Models, Techniques, & Applications*. New Jersey: Prentice-Hall, Inc., pp. 165–173. Race categories exclude persons of Hispanic ethnicity.

SOURCE: U.S. Department of Education, National Center for Education Statistics, Enrollment in Degree-Granting Institutions by Race/Ethnicity Model, 1980–2011. (This table was prepared February 2013.)

Table A-23. Estimated equations and model statistics for full-time and part-time enrollment rates of White women at postsecondary degree-granting institutions

Independent variable	Coefficient	Standard error	t-statistic	R^2	D.W. statistic
1	2	3	4	5	6
Full-time					
Intercept term for 17-year-olds..................................	-14.24	0.248	-57.45	0.99	1.41~
Intercept term for 18-year-olds..................................	-11.27	0.231	-48.82		
Intercept term for 19-year-olds..................................	-11.13	0.228	-48.90		
Intercept term for 20-year-olds..................................	-11.37	0.228	-49.92		
Intercept term for 21-year-olds..................................	-11.62	0.228	-50.95		
Intercept term for 22-year-olds..................................	-12.35	0.229	-53.97		
Intercept term for 23-year-olds..................................	-12.91	0.230	-56.03		
Intercept term for 24-year-olds..................................	-13.31	0.230	-57.77		
Intercept term for 25- to 29-year-olds	-14.11	0.229	-61.49		
Intercept term for 30- to 34-year-olds	-14.83	0.229	-64.85		
Intercept term for 35- to 44-year-olds	-15.01	0.229	-65.52		
Log of White per capita disposable income in current dollars	0.57	0.012	48.63		
Part-time					
Intercept term for 17-year-olds..................................	-9.55	0.352	-27.11	0.79	1.52~
Intercept term for 18-year-olds..................................	-6.17	0.302	-20.41		
Intercept term for 19-year-olds..................................	-5.72	0.304	-18.80		
Intercept term for 20-year-olds..................................	-5.80	0.304	-19.10		
Intercept term for 21-year-olds..................................	-5.88	0.302	-19.45		
Intercept term for 22-year-olds..................................	-6.08	0.301	-20.18		
Intercept term for 23-year-olds..................................	-6.12	0.302	-20.29		
Intercept term for 24-year-olds..................................	-6.16	0.301	-20.48		
Intercept term for 25- to 29-year-olds	-6.47	0.300	-21.58		
Intercept term for 30- to 34-year-olds	-6.81	0.301	-22.60		
Intercept term for 35- to 44-year-olds	-6.49	0.300	-21.63		
Log of real total private compensation employment cost index	0.20	0.015	13.13		

~ Inconclusive.
NOTE: R^2 = Coefficient of determination. D.W. statistic = Durbin-Watson statistic, a test for autocorrelation among regression residuals. For more details see Johnston, J., and Dinardo, J. (1996). *Econometric Methods.* New York: McGraw-Hill. The regression method used to estimate the full-time and part-time equations was the pooled seemingly unrelated regression method. The time period used to estimate the equations is from 1980 to 2011. The number of observations is 352. For additional information, see Intriligator, M.D. (1978). *Econometric Models, Techniques, & Applications.* New Jersey: Prentice-Hall, Inc., pp. 165–173. Race categories exclude persons of Hispanic ethnicity.
SOURCE: U.S. Department of Education, National Center for Education Statistics, Enrollment in Degree-Granting Institutions by Race/Ethnicity Model, 1980–2011. (This table was prepared February 2013.)

Table A-24. Estimated equations and model statistics for full-time and part-time enrollment rates of Black men at postsecondary degree-granting institutions

Independent variable	Coefficient	Standard error	t-statistic	R^2	D.W. statistic
1	2	3	4	5	6
Full-time					
Intercept term for 17-year-olds..............................	-10.97	0.673	-16.29	0.96	1.84*
Intercept term for 18-year-olds..............................	-8.66	0.668	-12.96		
Intercept term for 19-year-olds..............................	-8.39	0.668	-12.58		
Intercept term for 20-year-olds..............................	-8.48	0.668	-12.69		
Intercept term for 21-year-olds..............................	-8.72	0.669	-13.05		
Intercept term for 22-year-olds..............................	-8.92	0.669	-13.34		
Intercept term for 23-year-olds..............................	-9.39	0.671	-13.98		
Intercept term for 24-year-olds..............................	-9.67	0.669	-14.44		
Intercept term for 25- to 29-year-olds	-10.45	0.670	-15.61		
Intercept term for 30- to 34-year-olds	-11.23	0.672	-16.71		
Intercept term for 35- to 44-year-olds	-11.58	0.671	-17.25		
Log of Black per capita disposable income in current dollars	0.38	0.036	10.61		
Part-time					
Intercept term for 17-year-olds..............................	-11.46	0.577	-19.84	0.60	1.84*
Intercept term for 18-year-olds..............................	-10.57	0.593	-17.83		
Intercept term for 19-year-olds..............................	-9.76	0.581	-16.79		
Intercept term for 20-year-olds..............................	-9.69	0.581	-16.70		
Intercept term for 21-year-olds..............................	-9.71	0.575	-16.89		
Intercept term for 22-year-olds..............................	-9.74	0.583	-16.72		
Intercept term for 23-year-olds..............................	-9.96	0.586	-16.99		
Intercept term for 24-year-olds..............................	-9.96	0.587	-16.98		
Intercept term for 25- to 29-year-olds	-10.06	0.574	-17.51		
Intercept term for 30- to 34-year-olds	-10.32	0.573	-18.01		
Intercept term for 35- to 44-year-olds	-10.36	0.571	-18.14		
Log of Black per capita disposable income in current dollars	0.37	0.031	11.97		

* $p < .05$.
NOTE: R^2 = Coefficient of determination. D.W. statistic = Durbin-Watson statistic, a test for autocorrelation among regression residuals. For more details see Johnston, J., and Dinardo, J. (1996). *Econometric Methods*. New York: McGraw-Hill. The regression method used to estimate the full-time and part-time equations was the pooled seemingly unrelated regression method. The time period used to estimate the equations is from 1980 to 2011. The number of observations is 352. For additional information, see Intriligator, M.D. (1978). *Econometric Models, Techniques, & Applications*. New Jersey: Prentice-Hall, Inc., pp. 165–173. Race categories exclude persons of Hispanic ethnicity.
SOURCE: U.S. Department of Education, National Center for Education Statistics, Enrollment in Degree-Granting Institutions by Race/Ethnicity Model, 1980–2011. (This table was prepared February 2013.)

Table A-25. Estimated equations and model statistics for full-time and part-time enrollment rates of Black women at postsecondary degree-granting institutions

Independent variable	Coefficient	Standard error	t-statistic	R^2	D.W. statistic
1	2	3	4	5	6
Full-time					
Intercept term for 17-year-olds..................................	-15.78	0.644	-24.51	0.97	1.77*
Intercept term for 18-year-olds..................................	-13.56	0.639	-21.23		
Intercept term for 19-year-olds..................................	-13.37	0.638	-20.97		
Intercept term for 20-year-olds..................................	-13.61	0.638	-21.32		
Intercept term for 21-year-olds..................................	-13.78	0.638	-21.62		
Intercept term for 22-year-olds..................................	-14.22	0.638	-22.30		
Intercept term for 23-year-olds..................................	-14.50	0.639	-22.71		
Intercept term for 24-year-olds..................................	-14.86	0.639	-23.26		
Intercept term for 25- to 29-year-olds	-15.63	0.640	-24.44		
Intercept term for 30- to 34-year-olds	-16.10	0.639	-25.21		
Intercept term for 35- to 44-year-olds	-16.45	0.640	-25.70		
Log of Black per capita disposable income in current dollars	0.68	0.034	19.84		
Part-time					
Intercept term for 17-year-olds..................................	-14.74	0.617	-23.91	0.61	1.75*
Intercept term for 18-year-olds..................................	-13.19	0.610	-21.62		
Intercept term for 19-year-olds..................................	-12.76	0.610	-20.92		
Intercept term for 20-year-olds..................................	-12.78	0.609	-20.98		
Intercept term for 21-year-olds..................................	-12.71	0.609	-20.87		
Intercept term for 22-year-olds..................................	-12.71	0.608	-20.90		
Intercept term for 23-year-olds..................................	-12.71	0.608	-20.91		
Intercept term for 24-year-olds..................................	-12.85	0.609	-21.10		
Intercept term for 25- to 29-year-olds	-13.04	0.604	-21.59		
Intercept term for 30- to 34-year-olds	-13.17	0.605	-21.78		
Intercept term for 35- to 44-year-olds	-13.01	0.604	-21.52		
Log of Black per capita disposable income in current dollars	0.56	0.033	17.09		

* $p < .05$.
NOTE: R^2 = Coefficient of determination. D.W. statistic = Durbin-Watson statistic, a test for autocorrelation among regression residuals. For more details see Johnston, J., and Dinardo, J. (1996). *Econometric Methods*. New York: McGraw-Hill. The regression method used to estimate the full-time and part-time equations was the pooled seemingly unrelated regression method. The time period used to estimate the equations is from 1980 to 2011. The number of observations is 352. For additional information, see Intriligator, M.D. (1978). *Econometric Models, Techniques, & Applications*. New Jersey: Prentice-Hall, Inc., pp. 165–173. Race categories exclude persons of Hispanic ethnicity.
SOURCE: U.S. Department of Education, National Center for Education Statistics, Enrollment in Degree-Granting Institutions by Race/Ethnicity Model, 1980–2011. (This table was prepared February 2013.)

Table A-26. Estimated equations and model statistics for full-time and part-time enrollment rates of Hispanic men at postsecondary degree-granting institutions

Independent variable	Coefficient	Standard error	t-statistic	R^2	D.W. statistic
1	2	3	4	5	6
Full-time					
Intercept term for 17-year-olds..............................	-11.62	0.803	-14.47	0.93	1.91*
Intercept term for 18-year-olds..............................	-9.59	0.798	-12.02		
Intercept term for 19-year-olds..............................	-9.37	0.798	-11.75		
Intercept term for 20-year-olds..............................	-9.57	0.798	-12.00		
Intercept term for 21-year-olds..............................	-9.80	0.799	-12.27		
Intercept term for 22-year-olds..............................	-10.25	0.798	-12.84		
Intercept term for 23-year-olds..............................	-10.57	0.799	-13.23		
Intercept term for 24-year-olds..............................	-10.73	0.798	-13.44		
Intercept term for 25- to 29-year-olds	-11.54	0.799	-14.45		
Intercept term for 30- to 34-year-olds	-12.35	0.800	-15.44		
Intercept term for 35- to 44-year-olds	-12.84	0.802	-16.00		
Log of Hispanic per capita disposable income in current dollars	0.42	0.044	9.62		
Part-time					
Intercept term for 17-year-olds..............................	-11.03	0.564	-19.58	0.68	1.73*
Intercept term for 18-year-olds..............................	-9.44	0.561	-16.82		
Intercept term for 19-year-olds..............................	-9.12	0.566	-16.12		
Intercept term for 20-year-olds..............................	-9.02	0.561	-16.07		
Intercept term for 21-year-olds..............................	-9.06	0.560	-16.16		
Intercept term for 22-year-olds..............................	-9.43	0.559	-16.86		
Intercept term for 23-year-olds..............................	-9.40	0.566	-16.61		
Intercept term for 24-year-olds..............................	-9.54	0.561	-17.01		
Intercept term for 25- to 29-year-olds	-9.81	0.554	-17.72		
Intercept term for 30- to 34-year-olds	-10.29	0.555	-18.53		
Intercept term for 35- to 44-year-olds	-10.32	0.554	-18.65		
Log of Hispanic per capita disposable income in current dollars	0.35	0.030	11.64		

* $p < .05$.
NOTE: R^2 = Coefficient of determination. D.W. statistic = Durbin-Watson statistic, a test for autocorrelation among regression residuals. For more details see Johnston, J., and Dinardo, J. (1996). *Econometric Methods*. New York: McGraw-Hill. The regression method used to estimate the full-time and part-time equations was the pooled seemingly unrelated regression method. The time period used to estimate the equations is from 1980 to 2011. The number of observations is 352. For additional information, see Intriligator, M.D. (1978). *Econometric Models, Techniques, & Applications*. New Jersey: Prentice-Hall, Inc., pp. 165–173.
SOURCE: U.S. Department of Education, National Center for Education Statistics, Enrollment in Degree-Granting Institutions by Race/Ethnicity Model, 1980–2011. (This table was prepared February 2013.)

Table A-27. Estimated equations and model statistics for full-time and part-time enrollment rates of Hispanic women at postsecondary degree-granting institutions

Independent variable	Coefficient	Standard error	t-statistic	R^2	D.W. statistic
1	2	3	4	5	6
Full-time					
Intercept term for 17-year-olds.................................	-18.52	0.711	-26.06	0.94	1.83*
Intercept term for 18-year-olds.................................	-15.98	0.699	-22.86		
Intercept term for 19-year-olds.................................	-15.87	0.698	-22.75		
Intercept term for 20-year-olds.................................	-16.21	0.698	-23.22		
Intercept term for 21-year-olds.................................	-16.32	0.699	-23.34		
Intercept term for 22-year-olds.................................	-16.91	0.700	-24.14		
Intercept term for 23-year-olds.................................	-17.19	0.699	-24.57		
Intercept term for 24-year-olds.................................	-17.68	0.703	-25.16		
Intercept term for 25- to 29-year-olds	-18.30	0.698	-26.23		
Intercept term for 30- to 34-year-olds	-19.00	0.700	-27.16		
Intercept term for 35- to 44-year-olds	-19.30	0.701	-27.54		
Log of Hispanic per capita disposable income in current dollars	0.80	0.038	21.05		
Part-time					
Intercept term for 17-year-olds.................................	-15.52	0.556	-27.93	0.69	1.89*
Intercept term for 18-year-olds.................................	-13.37	0.546	-24.49		
Intercept term for 19-year-olds.................................	-12.97	0.543	-23.90		
Intercept term for 20-year-olds.................................	-13.27	0.548	-24.24		
Intercept term for 21-year-olds.................................	-13.12	0.547	-23.97		
Intercept term for 22-year-olds.................................	-13.43	0.548	-24.49		
Intercept term for 23-year-olds.................................	-13.30	0.544	-24.45		
Intercept term for 24-year-olds.................................	-13.56	0.546	-24.83		
Intercept term for 25- to 29-year-olds	-13.86	0.539	-25.74		
Intercept term for 30- to 34-year-olds	-14.24	0.538	-26.45		
Intercept term for 35- to 44-year-olds	-14.11	0.538	-26.23		
Log of Hispanic per capita disposable income in current dollars	0.59	0.029	20.20		

* $p < .05$.
NOTE: R^2 = Coefficient of determination. D.W. statistic = Durbin-Watson statistic, a test for autocorrelation among regression residuals. For more details see Johnston, J., and Dinardo, J. (1996). *Econometric Methods*. New York: McGraw-Hill. The regression method used to estimate the full-time and part-time equations was the pooled seemingly unrelated regression method. The time period used to estimate the equations is from 1980 to 2011. The number of observations is 352. For additional information, see Intriligator, M.D. (1978). *Econometric Models, Techniques, & Applications*. New Jersey: Prentice-Hall, Inc., pp. 165–173.
SOURCE: U.S. Department of Education, National Center for Education Statistics, Enrollment in Degree-Granting Institutions by Race/Ethnicity Model, 1980–2011. (This table was prepared February 2013.)

Table A-28. Estimated equations and model statistics for full-time and part-time enrollment rates of Asian/Pacific Islander men at postsecondary degree-granting institutions

Independent variable	Coefficient	Standard error	t-statistic	R^2	D.W. statistic
1	2	3	4	5	6
Full-time					
Intercept term for 17-year-olds..............................	-5.76	0.591	-14.87	0.94	1.92*
Intercept term for 18-year-olds..............................	-2.97	0.577	-10.11		
Intercept term for 19-year-olds..............................	-2.75	0.578	-9.69		
Intercept term for 20-year-olds..............................	-2.86	0.577	-9.94		
Intercept term for 21-year-olds..............................	-2.86	0.577	-9.87		
Intercept term for 22-year-olds..............................	-3.22	0.578	-10.48		
Intercept term for 23-year-olds..............................	-3.47	0.578	-10.88		
Intercept term for 24-year-olds..............................	-3.84	0.580	-11.46		
Intercept term for 25- to 29-year-olds	-4.67	0.577	-13.19		
Intercept term for 30- to 34-year-olds	-5.65	0.578	-14.98		
Intercept term for 35- to 44-year-olds	-6.45	0.577	-16.47		
Log of Asian/Pacific Islander per capita disposable income in current dollars....................................	0.15	0.029	5.16		
Log unemployment rate for Asian/Pacific Islanders .	0.12	0.048	2.50		
Part-time					
Intercept term for 17-year-olds..............................	-2.05	0.737	-2.78	0.68	1.91*
Intercept term for 18-year-olds..............................	-1.04	0.747	-1.40		
Intercept term for 19-year-olds..............................	-0.32	0.731	-0.44		
Intercept term for 20-year-olds..............................	-0.39	0.740	-0.53		
Intercept term for 21-year-olds..............................	-0.50	0.742	-0.68		
Intercept term for 22-year-olds..............................	-0.49	0.748	-0.66		
Intercept term for 23-year-olds..............................	-0.51	0.734	-0.69		
Intercept term for 24-year-olds..............................	-0.69	0.732	-0.95		
Intercept term for 25- to 29-year-olds	-1.09	0.722	-1.51		
Intercept term for 30- to 34-year-olds	-1.68	0.723	-2.32		
Intercept term for 35- to 44-year-olds	-2.05	0.722	-2.84		
Log of Asian/Pacific Islander level of educational attainment per household	0.08	0.046	1.73		

* $p < .05$.
NOTE: R^2 = Coefficient of determination. D.W. statistic = Durbin-Watson statistic, a test for autocorrelation among regression residuals. For more details see Johnston, J., and Dinardo, J. (1996). *Econometric Methods.* New York: McGraw-Hill. The regression method used to estimate the full-time and part-time equations was the pooled seemingly unrelated regression method. The time period used to estimate the part-time equation is from 1989 to 2011 with the number of observations equal to 253. The time period used to estimate the part-

time equation is from 1980 to 2011 with the number of observations equal to 352. For additional information, see Intriligator, M.D. (1978). *Econometric Models, Techniques, & Applications.* New Jersey: Prentice-Hall, Inc., pp. 165–173. Race categories exclude persons of Hispanic ethnicity.
SOURCE: U.S. Department of Education, National Center for Education Statistics, Enrollment in Degree-Granting Institutions by Race/Ethnicity Model, 1980–2011. (This table was prepared February 2013.)

Table A-29. Estimated equations and model statistics for full-time and part-time enrollment rates of Asian/Pacific Islander women at postsecondary degree-granting institutions

Independent variable	Coefficient	Standard error	t-statistic	R^2	D.W. statistic
1	2	3	4	5	6
Full-time					
Intercept term for 17-year-olds...............................	-9.15	0.620	-14.76	0.97	2.00*
Intercept term for 18-year-olds...............................	-6.83	0.611	-11.18		
Intercept term for 19-year-olds...............................	-6.34	0.615	-10.31		
Intercept term for 20-year-olds...............................	-6.60	0.612	-10.78		
Intercept term for 21-year-olds...............................	-6.65	0.611	-10.89		
Intercept term for 22-year-olds...............................	-7.15	0.613	-11.66		
Intercept term for 23-year-olds...............................	-7.49	0.612	-12.25		
Intercept term for 24-year-olds...............................	-8.05	0.621	-12.96		
Intercept term for 25- to 29-year-olds	-8.94	0.609	-14.67		
Intercept term for 30- to 34-year-olds	-10.17	0.613	-16.59		
Intercept term for 35- to 44-year-olds	-10.72	0.614	-17.45		
Log of Asian/Pacific Islander per capita disposable income in current dollars..................................	0.35	0.032	10.95		
Part-time					
Intercept term for 17-year-olds...............................	-6.89	0.625	-11.01	0.76	1.97*
Intercept term for 18-year-olds...............................	-5.06	0.619	-8.17		
Intercept term for 19-year-olds...............................	-4.44	0.647	-6.86		
Intercept term for 20-year-olds...............................	-4.85	0.635	-7.64		
Intercept term for 21-year-olds...............................	-4.23	0.624	-6.77		
Intercept term for 22-year-olds...............................	-4.54	0.626	-7.24		
Intercept term for 23-year-olds...............................	-4.71	0.620	-7.60		
Intercept term for 24-year-olds...............................	-4.87	0.629	-7.75		
Intercept term for 25- to 29-year-olds	-5.38	0.609	-8.84		
Intercept term for 30- to 34-year-olds	-6.04	0.611	-9.89		
Intercept term for 35- to 44-year-olds	-5.88	0.607	-9.69		
Log of Asian/Pacific Islander per capita disposable income in current dollars..................................	0.16	0.031	5.03		

* $p < .05$.
NOTE: R^2 = Coefficient of determination. D.W. statistic = Durbin-Watson statistic, a test for autocorrelation among regression residuals. For more details see Johnston, J., and Dinardo, J. (1996). *Econometric Methods*. New York: McGraw-Hill. The regression method used to estimate the full-time and part-time equations was the pooled seemingly unrelated regression method. The time period used to estimate the equations is from 1989 to 2011.

The number of observations is 253. For additional information, see Intriligator, M.D. (1978). *Econometric Models, Techniques, & Applications*. New Jersey: Prentice-Hall, Inc., pp. 165–173. Race categories exclude persons of Hispanic ethnicity.
SOURCE: U.S. Department of Education, National Center for Education Statistics, Enrollment in Degree-Granting Institutions by Race/Ethnicity Model, 1980–2011. (This table was prepared February 2013.)

A.6. POSTSECONDARY DEGREES CONFERRED

Projections in this edition

This edition of *Projections of Education Statistics* presents projections of postsecondary degrees conferred by level of degree and sex of recipient for 2011–12 through 2022–23.

Overview of approach

Basic approach

Projections of associate's, bachelor's, master's, and doctor's degrees for men and women were produced using forecasting equations that relate degrees conferred to full-time enrollment in degree-granting institutions by sex, student level (undergraduate or postbaccalaureate), and institution level (2-year or 4-year).

Degrees Conferred Model

Procedures used to project degrees

For all degree levels, projections of degrees conferred were made separately for men and for women. The projections for men and women were then summed to get projections of the total number of degrees.

Multiple linear regression was used to project associate's, bachelor's, master's, and doctor's degrees based on enrollment variables for men and women. The enrollment variables used for the different levels of degrees are briefly described below.

For details and results of the regression analyses used to project associate's, bachelor's, master's, and doctor's degrees, see table A-30, under "Data and equations used to project degrees," later in this section.

Associate's degrees. *Projections were based on full-time undergraduate enrollment in 2-year institutions by sex.* Men's projections of associate's degrees were based on current full-time enrollment and full-time enrollment lagged 2 years. Women's projections of associate's degrees were based on current full-time enrollment and full-time enrollment lagged 1 and 2 years.

Bachelor's degrees. *Projections were based on full-time undergraduate enrollment in 4-year institutions by sex.* For men and for women, bachelor's degree projections were based on current full-time enrollment and full-time enrollment lagged 2 years.

Master's degrees. *Projections were based on full-time postbaccalaureate enrollment by sex.* Men's projections of master's degrees were based on current full-time enrollment and full-time enrollment lagged 1 year. Women's projections of master's degrees were based on current full-time enrollment.

Doctor's degrees. *Projections were based on full-time postbaccalaureate enrollment by sex.* For men and for women, doctor's degree projections were based on current full-time postbaccalaureate enrollment and full-time postbaccalaureate enrollment lagged 1 and 2 years.

Data and equations used to project degrees

Enrollment data and projections for degree-granting institutions. Historical enrollment data by sex, level of student, and level of institution came from the NCES Integrated Postsecondary Education Data System (IPEDS). For the time period used for each level of degree, see table A-30 on page 130. The enrollment projections used are those produced for this edition of *Projections of Education Statistics*. For more information about the enrollment projections, see Section A.5. Enrollment in Postsecondary Degree-Granting Institutions, earlier in this appendix.

Data on degrees awarded at all levels. Historical data by level of degree and sex of recipient came from the NCES Integrated Postsecondary Education Data System (IPEDS). All degrees were projected using data for 1980–81 to 2010–11.

Estimated equations and model statistics. For details on the equations used to project associate's, bachelor's, master's, and doctor's degrees, see table A-30 on page 130. The equations shown were selected on the basis of their statistical properties, such as coefficients of determination (R^2s), the *t*-statistics of the coefficients, the Durbin-Watson statistic, the Breusch-Godfrey Serial Correlation LM test statistic, and residual plots.

Accuracy of projections

No MAPEs were calculated for degrees conferred because, for associate's and bachelor' degrees, the current models for producing the projections have been used for only four other editions of *Projections of Education Statistics,* and for master's and doctor's degrees as currently defined, the current models have only been used for one other edition.

For more information about MAPEs, see Section A.0. Introduction, earlier in this appendix.

Table A-30. Estimated equations and model statistics for degrees conferred, by degree level and sex

Dependent variable	Equation[1]	R^2	Breusch-Godfrey Serial Correlation LM test statistic[2]	Time period
1	2	3	4	5
Associate's degrees, men	DASSOCM = 2,587 + 101DUGFT2M + 77DUGFT2ML2 (2.3) (5.2) (3.6)	0.54	3.89 (0.143)	1980–81 to 2010–11
Associate's degrees, women	DLOGASSOCW = #† + 0.9DLOGUGFT2WS3 + .5MA(1) (8.01) (3.83)	0.81	4.12 (0.122)	1980–81 to 2010–11
Bachelor's degrees, men	DBACHM = 215 + 61DUGFT4M + 150DUGFT4ML2 (0.20) (3.2) (7.2)	0.72	0.60 (0.743)	1980–81 to 2010–11
Bachelor's degrees, women	DBACHW = 2808 + 47DUGFT4W + 150DUGFT4WL2 (2.3) (2.3) (3.5)	0.61	1.40 (0.479)	1980–81 to 2010–11
Master's degrees, men	PCHMASTM = #† + 0.6PCHPBFTM + 0.5PCHPBFTML1 (3.91) (3.21)	0.66	0.80 (0.669)	1980–81 to 2010–11
Master's degrees, women	PCHMASTW = #† + 0.4PCHPBFTW + 0.6AR(1) (2.06) (4.35)	0.56	3.43 (0.180)	1980–81 to 2010–11
Doctor's degrees, men	DDOCM = -372 + 57DPBFTML1 + 61DPBFTML2 (-1.5) (2.4) (2.5)	0.48	1.25 (0.536)	1980–81 to 2010–11
Doctor's degrees, women	DDOCW = 495 + 29DPBFTWL1 + 40DPBFTWL2 (1.6) (2.2) (2.8)	0.47	0.25 (0.884)	1980–81 to 2010–11

† Not applicable.
# Rounds to zero.
[1]AR(1) indicates that the model was estimated to account for first-order autocorrelation. To estimate the model, it was first transformed into a nonlinear model and then the coefficients were estimated simultaneously by applying a Marquardt nonlinear least squares algorithm to the transformed equation. MA(1) indicates that the model was estimated to incorporate moving average of the residual into model fit. For a general discussion of the problem of autocorrelation, and the method used to forecast in the presence of autocorrelation, see Judge, G., Hill, W., Griffiths, R., Lutkepohl, H., and Lee, T. (1985). *The Theory and Practice of Econometrics.* New York: John Wiley and Sons, pp. 315–318. Numbers in parentheses are *t*-statistics.
[2]The number in parentheses is the probability of the Chi-Square associated with the Breusch-Godfrey Serial Correlation LM Test. A *p* value greater that 0.05 implies that we do not reject the null hypothesis of no autocorrelation at the 5 percent significance level for a two-tailed test or 10 percent significance level for a one-tailed test (i.e., there is no autocorrelation present). For an explanation of the Breusch-Godfrey Serial Correlation LM test statistic, see Greene, W. (2000). *Econometric Analysis.* New Jersey: Prentice-Hall.
NOTE: R^2 is the coefficient of determination.
DASSOCM = First difference of associate's degrees awarded to men.
DLOGASSOCW = First difference of the log of associate's degrees awarded to women.
DBACHM = First difference of bachelor's degrees awarded to men.
DBACHW = First difference of bachelor's degrees awarded to women.
PCHMASTM = Percentage change in master's degrees awarded to men.
PCHMASTW = Percentage change in master's degrees awarded to women.

DDOCM = First difference of doctor's degrees awarded to men.
DDOCW = First difference of doctor's degrees awarded to women.
DUGFT2M = First difference of full-time male undergraduate enrollment in 2-year institutions.
DUGFT2ML2 = First difference of full-time male undergraduate enrollment in 2-year institutions, lagged two periods.
DLOGUGFT2WS3= First difference of the sum of the full-time female undergraduate enrollment in 2-year institutions over the present year and the previous 2 years.
DUGFT4M = First difference of full-time male undergraduate enrollment in 4-year institutions.
DUGFT4ML2 = First difference of full-time male undergraduate enrollment in 4-year institutions, lagged two periods.
DUGFT4W = First difference of full-time female undergraduate enrollment in 4-year institutions.
DUGFT4WL2 = First difference of full-time female undergraduate enrollment in 4-year institutions, lagged two periods.
PCHPBFTM = Percentage change in full-time male postbaccalaureate enrollment.
PCHPBFTML1 = Percentage change in full-time male postbaccalaureate enrollment, lagged 1 year.
PCHPBFTW = Percentage change in full-time female postbaccalaureate enrollment.
DPBFTML1 = First difference of full-time male postbaccalaureate enrollment, lagged 1 year.
DPBFTML2 = First difference of full-time male postbaccalaureate enrollment, lagged 2 years.
DPBFTWL1 = First difference of full-time female postbaccalaureate enrollment, lagged 1 year.
DPBFTWL2 = First difference of full-time female postbaccalaureate enrollment, lagged 2 years.
SOURCE: U.S. Department of Education, National Center for Education Statistics, Degrees Conferred Model, 1980–81 through 2010–11. (This table was prepared March 2013.)

Appendix B
Supplementary Tables

Table B-1. Annual number of births: 1946 through 2011

Calendar year	Number of births, in thousands	Calendar year	Number of births, in thousands
1	2	1	2
1946	3,426	1979	3,494
1947	3,834	1980	3,612
1948	3,655	1981	3,629
1949	3,667	1982	3,681
1950	3,645	1983	3,639
1951	3,845	1984	3,669
1952	3,933	1985	3,761
1953	3,989	1986	3,757
1954	4,102	1987	3,809
1955	4,128	1988	3,910
1956	4,244	1989	4,041
1957	4,332	1990	4,158
1958	4,279	1991	4,111
1959	4,313	1992	4,065
1960	4,307	1993	4,000
1961	4,317	1994	3,953
1962	4,213	1995	3,900
1963	4,142	1996	3,891
1964	4,070	1997	3,881
1965	3,801	1998	3,942
1966	3,642	1999	3,959
1967	3,555	2000	4,059
1968	3,535	2001	4,026
1969	3,626	2002	4,022
1970	3,739	2003	4,090
1971	3,556	2004	4,112
1972	3,258	2005	4,138
1973	3,137	2006	4,266
1974	3,160	2007	4,317
1975	3,144	2008	4,248
1976	3,168	2009	4,131
1977	3,327	2010	3,999
1978	3,333	2011	3,954

NOTE: Some data have been revised from previously published figures.
SOURCE: U.S. Department of Health and Human Services, National Center for Health Statistics (NCHS), *National Vital Statistics Reports*, various years. (This table was prepared January 2013.)

Table B-2. Actual and projected prekindergarten- and kindergarten-age populations, by age: 1997 through 2022

[In thousands]

Year (July 1)	3- to 5-year-olds	3-year-olds	4-year-olds	5-year-olds
1	2	3	4	5
Actual				
1997....................................	12,019	3,894	4,021	4,104
1998....................................	11,880	3,862	3,979	4,040
1999....................................	11,768	3,827	3,946	3,996
2000....................................	11,691	3,821	3,902	3,968
2001....................................	11,540	3,803	3,827	3,910
2002....................................	11,454	3,804	3,813	3,837
2003....................................	11,501	3,861	3,817	3,824
2004....................................	11,714	4,008	3,877	3,830
2005....................................	11,866	3,943	4,030	3,893
2006....................................	11,987	3,966	3,971	4,051
2007....................................	11,996	4,004	3,998	3,993
2008....................................	12,058	3,992	4,041	4,024
2009....................................	12,129	4,026	4,033	4,070
2010....................................	12,280	4,134	4,076	4,070
2011....................................	12,313	4,102	4,122	4,088
Projected				
2012....................................	12,228	3,983	4,113	4,133
2013....................................	12,098	3,991	3,990	4,117
2014....................................	12,026	4,029	4,000	3,998
2015....................................	12,273	4,227	4,038	4,008
2016....................................	12,541	4,258	4,237	4,046
2017....................................	12,800	4,287	4,268	4,245
2018....................................	12,886	4,313	4,297	4,277
2019....................................	12,966	4,336	4,323	4,306
2020....................................	13,039	4,358	4,348	4,332
2021....................................	13,105	4,378	4,370	4,357
2022....................................	13,166	4,396	4,390	4,380

NOTE: Some data have been revised from previously published figures. Detail may not sum to totals because of rounding. As the Census Bureau projections were not updated to reflect the most recent 2012 Census Bureau population estimates, the Census Bureau age-specific population projections for each year were adjusted by multiplying the ratio of the total Census Bureau estimate for 2012 to the total Census Bureau projection for 2012.

SOURCE: U.S. Department of Commerce, Census Bureau, Population Estimates, retrieved December 19, 2012, from http://www.census.gov/popest/data/index.html; and Population Projections, retrieved December 12, 2012, from http://www.census.gov/population/projections/data/national/2012/downloadablefiles.html. (This table was prepared February 2013.)

Table B-3. Actual and projected school-age populations, by selected ages: 1997 through 2022

[In thousands]

Year (July 1)	5-year-olds	6-year-olds	5- to 13-year-olds	14- to 17-year-olds
1	2	3	4	5
Actual				
1997	4,104	4,127	35,915	15,769
1998	4,040	4,112	36,454	15,829
1999	3,996	4,045	36,804	16,007
2000	3,968	4,004	37,054	16,144
2001	3,910	3,973	37,093	16,280
2002	3,837	3,913	37,001	16,506
2003	3,824	3,838	36,814	16,694
2004	3,830	3,822	36,458	17,054
2005	3,893	3,828	36,248	17,358
2006	4,051	3,891	36,269	17,549
2007	3,993	4,046	36,296	17,597
2008	4,024	3,988	36,438	17,395
2009	4,070	4,018	36,657	17,232
2010	4,070	4,068	36,932	17,063
2011	4,088	4,075	36,910	16,862
Projected				
2012	4,133	4,098	36,995	16,707
2013	4,117	4,135	36,983	16,579
2014	3,998	4,124	36,830	16,644
2015	4,008	4,005	36,745	16,676
2016	4,046	4,015	36,793	16,618
2017	4,245	4,055	37,016	16,577
2018	4,277	4,253	37,235	16,498
2019	4,306	4,285	37,485	16,473
2020	4,332	4,315	37,741	16,564
2021	4,357	4,342	37,980	16,673
2022	4,380	4,366	38,252	16,735

NOTE: Some data have been revised from previously published figures. As the Census Bureau projections were not updated to reflect the most recent 2012 Census Bureau population estimates, the Census Bureau age-specific population projections for each year were adjusted by multiplying the ratio of the total Census Bureau estimate for 2012 to the total Census Bureau projection for 2012.

SOURCE:U.S. Department of Commerce, Census Bureau, Population Estimates, retrieved December 19, 2012, from http://www.census.gov/popest/data/index.html; and Population Projections, retrieved December 12, 2012, from http://www.census.gov/population/projections/data/national/2012/downloadablefiles.html. (This table was prepared February 2013.)

Table B-4. Actual and projected college-age populations, by selected ages: 1997 through 2022

[In thousands]

Year (July 1)	18-year-olds	18- to 24-year-olds	25- to 29-year-olds	30- to 34-year-olds	35- to 44-year-olds
1	2	3	4	5	6
Actual					
1997	3,780	25,574	19,960	21,494	44,282
1998	3,984	26,155	19,863	20,999	44,802
1999	3,993	26,780	19,632	20,647	45,130
2000	4,080	27,315	19,280	20,524	45,169
2001	4,103	27,993	18,819	20,652	45,052
2002	4,084	28,481	18,691	20,658	44,641
2003	4,202	28,917	18,772	20,472	44,154
2004	4,214	29,302	19,107	20,160	43,800
2005	4,225	29,442	19,535	19,724	43,506
2006	4,301	29,603	20,110	19,285	43,244
2007	4,395	29,808	20,543	19,171	42,796
2008	4,588	30,194	20,903	19,305	42,192
2009	4,535	30,530	21,078	19,645	41,488
2010	4,487	30,708	21,153	20,094	40,981
2011	4,396	31,065	21,280	20,511	40,628
Projected					
2012	4,352	31,318	21,360	20,889	40,483
2013	4,273	31,412	21,573	21,275	40,444
2014	4,195	31,308	21,940	21,498	40,392
2015	4,176	30,983	22,367	21,602	40,400
2016	4,178	30,635	22,846	21,768	40,398
2017	4,188	30,356	23,272	21,884	40,697
2018	4,267	30,256	23,511	22,088	41,192
2019	4,215	30,151	23,582	22,474	41,701
2020	4,126	30,029	23,381	22,919	42,244
2021	4,154	30,011	23,078	23,417	42,893
2022	4,195	30,053	22,816	23,862	43,430

NOTE: Some data have been revised from previously published figures. As the Census Bureau projections were not updated to reflect the most recent 2012 Census Bureau population estimates, the Census Bureau age-specific population projections for each year were adjusted by multiplying the ratio of the total Census Bureau estimate for 2012 to the total Census Bureau projection for 2012.

SOURCE:U.S. Department of Commerce, Census Bureau, Population Estimates, retrieved December 19, 2012, from http://www.census.gov/popest/data/index.html; and Population Projections, retrieved December 12, 2012, from http://www.census.gov/population/projections/data/national/2012/downloadablefiles.html. (This table was prepared February 2013.)

Table B-5. Actual and projected fall enrollment in public elementary and secondary schools, change in fall enrollment from previous year, resident population, and fall enrollment as a ratio of the population: School years 1997–98 through 2022–23

School year	Fall enrollment (in thousands)	Change in fall enrollment from previous year (in thousands)	Resident population (in millions)	Fall enrollment as a ratio of the population
1	2	3	4	5
Actual				
1997–98	46,127	516	272.9	0.169
1998–99	46,539	412	276.1	0.169
1999–2000	46,857	319	279.3	0.168
2000–01	47,204	346	282.2	0.167
2001–02	47,672	468	285.0	0.167
2002–03	48,183	511	287.6	0.168
2003–04	48,540	357	290.1	0.167
2004–05	48,795	255	292.8	0.167
2005–06	49,113	318	295.5	0.166
2006–07	49,316	203	298.4	0.165
2007–08	49,293	-23	301.2	0.164
2008–09	49,266	-27	304.1	0.162
2009–10	49,361	95	306.8	0.161
2010–11	49,484	123	309.3	0.160
2011–12	49,522	37	311.6	0.159
Projected				
2012–13	49,636	115	313.9	0.158
2013–14	49,785	148	316.6	0.157
2014–15	50,018	233	319.0	0.157
2015–16	50,328	310	321.5	0.157
2016–17	50,654	326	324.0	0.156
2017–18	50,999	346	326.5	0.156
2018–19	51,336	336	329.0	0.156
2019–20	51,707	372	331.5	0.156
2020–21	52,124	416	334.1	0.156
2021–22	52,534	410	336.6	0.156
2022–23	52,952	418	339.1	0.156

NOTE: Resident population includes civilian population and armed forces personnel residing within the United States: it excludes armed forces personnel overseas. Calculations were made using unrounded numbers. Some data have been revised from previously published figures. Detail may not sum to totals because of rounding. As the Census Bureau projections were not updated to reflect the most recent 2011 Census Bureau population estimates, the Census Bureau age-specific population projections for each year were adjusted by multiplying the ratio of the total Census Bureau estimate for 2011 to the total Census Bureau projection for 2011.

SOURCE: U.S. Department of Commerce, Census Bureau, Population Estimates, retrieved December 19, 2012, from http://www.census.gov/popest/data/index.html; and Population Projections, retrieved December 12, 2012, from http://www.census.gov/population/projections/data/national/2012/downloadablefiles.html. U.S. Department of Education, National Center for Education Statistics, Common Core of Data (CCD), "State Nonfiscal Survey of Public Elementary/Secondary Education," 1995–96 through 2011–12; and Elementary and Secondary Enrollment Model, 1972–2011. (This table was prepared February 2013.)

Table B-6. Actual and projected macroeconomic measures of the economy: School years 1997–98 through 2022–23

School year	Disposable income per capita in constant 2011–12 dollars[1]	Education revenue receipts from state sources per capita in constant 2011–12 dollars[2]	Consumer Price Index[3]
1	2	3	4
Actual			
1997–98	$30,833	$813	0.711
1998–99	31,879	848	0.723
1999–2000	32,741	889	0.744
2000–01	33,588	919	0.769
2001–02	34,377	925	0.783
2002–03	34,682	930	0.800
2003–04	35,642	915	0.818
2004–05	36,172	925	0.842
2005–06	36,716	936	0.874
2006–07	37,641	984	0.897
2007–08	38,297	1,007	0.930
2008–09	37,686	963	0.943
2009–10	36,868	887	0.953
2010–11	37,565	893	0.971
2011–12[4]	37,414	894	1.000
Projected			
2012–13	37,569	900	1.016
2013–14	37,996	911	1.033
2014–15	38,925	934	1.049
2015–16	39,887	959	1.066
2016–17	40,731	980	1.087
2017–18	41,462	997	1.107
2018–19	42,094	1,012	1.129
2019–20	42,761	1,028	1.151
2020–21	43,360	1,043	1.174
2021–22	43,938	1,057	1.197
2022–23	44,324	1,066	1.214

[1]Based on the price deflator for personal consumption expenditures, Bureau of Labor Statistics, U.S. Department of Labor.
[2]Based on the Consumer Price Index for all urban consumers, Bureau of Labor Statistics, U.S. Department of Labor.
[3]Consumer Price Index adjusted to a school-year basis (July through June).
[4]Education revenue receipts from state sources per capita is a projection.

NOTE: Calculations were made using unrounded numbers. Some data have been revised from previously published figures.
SOURCE: U.S. Department of Education, National Center for Education Statistics, Common Core of Data (CCD), "National Public Education Financial Survey," 1997–98 through 2009–10; Revenue Receipts From State Sources Model, 1971–72 through 2010–11; and IHS Global Insight, "U.S. Monthly Model: January 2013 Short-Term-Projections." (This table was prepared February 2013.)

This page intentionally left blank.

Appendix C
Data Sources

SOURCES AND COMPARABILITY OF DATA

The information in this report was obtained from many sources, including federal and state agencies, private research organizations, and professional associations. The data were collected by many methods, including surveys of a universe (such as all colleges) or of a sample, and compilations of administrative records. Care should be used when comparing data from different sources. Differences in procedures, such as timing, phrasing of questions, and interviewer training, mean that the results from the different sources are not strictly comparable. More extensive documentation of one survey's procedures than of another's does not imply more problems with the data, only that more information is available on the survey.

ACCURACY OF DATA

The accuracy of any statistic is determined by the joint effects of "sampling" and "nonsampling" errors. Estimates based on a sample will differ from the figures that would have been obtained if a complete census had been taken using the same survey instruments, instructions, and procedures. Besides sampling errors, both of the surveys, universe and sample, are subject to errors of design, reporting, and processing, and errors due to nonresponse. To the extent possible, these nonsampling errors are kept to a minimum by methods built into the survey procedures. In general, however, the effects of nonsampling errors are more difficult to gauge than those produced by sampling variability.

SAMPLING ERRORS

The standard error is the primary measure of the sampling variability of an estimate. Standard errors can be used to produce confidence intervals. For example, from table A-12, an estimated 91.8 percent of public school teachers reported that they worked full time in 2007–08. This figure has an estimated standard error of 0.29 percent. Therefore, the estimated 95 percent confidence interval for this statistic is approximately 91.27 to 92.41 percent (91.8 ± 1.96 (0.29)). That is, if the processes of selecting a sample, collecting the data, and constructing the confidence interval were repeated, it would be expected that in 95 out of 100 samples from the same population, the confidence interval would contain the true full-time working rate.

Analysis of standard errors can help assess how valid a comparison between two estimates might be. The *standard error of a difference* between two independent sample estimates is equal to the square root of the sum of the squared standard errors of the estimates. The standard error (se) of the difference between independent sample estimates a and b is

$$se_{a-b} = (se_a^2 + se_b^2)^{1/2}$$

Note that some of the standard errors in the original documents are approximations. That is, to derive estimates of standard errors that would be applicable to a wide variety of items and could be prepared at a moderate cost, a number of approximations were required. As a result, most of the standard errors presented provide a general order of magnitude rather than the exact standard error for any specific item.

NONSAMPLING ERRORS

Both universe and sample surveys are subject to nonsampling errors. Nonsampling errors are of two kinds—random and nonrandom. Random nonsampling errors may arise when respondents or interviewers interpret questions differently, when respondents must estimate values, or when coders, keyers, and other processors handle answers differently. Nonrandom nonsampling errors result from total nonresponse (no usable data obtained for a sampled unit), partial or item nonresponse (only a portion of a response may be usable), inability or unwillingness on the part of respondents to provide information, difficulty interpreting questions, mistakes in recording or keying data, errors of collection or processing, and overcoverage or undercoverage of the target universe. Random nonresponse errors usually, but not always, result in an understatement of sampling errors and thus an overstatement of the precision of survey estimates. Because estimating the magnitude of nonsampling errors would require special experiments or access to independent data, these magnitudes are seldom available..

To compensate for suspected nonrandom errors, adjustments of the sample estimates are often made. For example, adjustments are frequently made for nonresponse, both total and partial. Imputations are usually made separately within various groups of sample members that have similar survey characteristics. Imputation for item nonresponse is usually made by substituting for a missing item the response to that item of a respondent having characteristics similar to those of the respondent.

Although the magnitude of nonsampling errors in the data used in *Projections of Education* Statistics is frequently unknown, idiosyncrasies that have been identified are noted on the appropriate tables.

FEDERAL AGENCY SOURCES

National Center for Education Statistics (NCES)

Common Core of Data

The Common Core of Data (CCD) is NCES's primary database on public elementary and secondary education in the United States. It is a comprehensive, annual, national statistical database of all public elementary and secondary schools and school districts containing data designed to be comparable across all states. This database can be used to select samples for other NCES surveys and provide basic information and descriptive statistics on public elementary and secondary schools and schooling in general.

The CCD collects statistical information annually from approximately 100,000 public elementary and secondary schools and approximately 18,000 public school districts (including supervisory unions and regional education service agencies) in the 50 states, the District of Columbia, Department of Defense (DoD) dependents schools, the Bureau of Indian Education, Puerto Rico, American Samoa, Guam, the Northern Mariana Islands, and the U.S. Virgin Islands. Three categories of information are collected in the CCD survey: general descriptive information on schools and school districts; data on students and staff; and fiscal data. The general descriptive information includes name, address, phone number, and type of locale; the data on students and staff include selected demographic characteristics; and the fiscal data pertain to revenues and current expenditures.

The EDFacts data collection system is the primary collection tool for the CCD. NCES works collaboratively with the Department of Education's Performance Information Management Service to develop the CCD collection procedures and data definitions. Coordinators from State Education Agencies (SEAs) submit the CCD data at different levels (school, local education agency, and state) to the EDFacts collection system. Prior to submitting CCD files to EDFacts, SEAs must collect and compile information from their respective Local Education Agencies (LEAs) through established administrative records systems within their state or jurisdiction.

Once SEAs have completed their submissions, the CCD survey staff analyzes and verifies the data for quality assurance. Even though the CCD is a universe collection and thus not subject to sampling errors, nonsampling errors can occur. The two potential sources of nonsampling errors are nonresponse and inaccurate reporting. NCES attempts to minimize nonsampling errors through the use of annual training of SEA coordinators, extensive quality reviews, and survey editing procedures. In addition, each year, SEAs are given the opportunity to revise their state-level aggregates from the previous survey cycle.

The CCD survey consists of six components: The Public Elementary/Secondary School Universe Survey, the Local Education Agency (School District) Universe Survey, the State Nonfiscal Survey of Public Elementary/Secondary Education, the National Public Education Financial Survey (NPEFS), the School District Fiscal Data Survey (F-33), and the Teacher Compensation Survey.

Public Elementary/Secondary School Universe Survey

The Public Elementary/Secondary School Universe Survey includes all public schools providing education services to prekindergarten, kindergarten, grade 1–12, and ungraded students. The CCD Public Elementary/Secondary School Universe Survey includes records for each public elementary and secondary school in the 50 states, the District of Columbia, Puerto Rico, the Commonwealth of the Northern Mariana Islands, the U.S. Virgin Islands, the Bureau of Indian Education, and the DoD dependents schools (overseas and domestic).

The Public Elementary/Secondary School Universe Survey includes data for the following variables: NCES school ID number, state school ID number, name of the school, name of the agency that operates the school, mailing address, physical location address, phone number, school type, operational status, locale code, latitude, longitude, county number, county name, full-time-equivalent (FTE) classroom teacher count, low/high grade span offered, congressional district code, school level, free lunch eligible students, reduced-price lunch eligible students, total free and reduced-price lunch eligible students, and student totals and detail (by grade, by race/ethnicity, and by sex). The survey also contains flags indicating whether a school is Title I eligible, schoolwide Title I eligible, a magnet school, a charter school, a shared-time school, or a BIE school; which grades are offered at the school; and if the school was reconstituted due to Annual Yearly Progress (AYP) reasons.

Local Education Agency (School District) Universe

The coverage of the Local Education Agency Universe Survey includes all school districts and administrative units providing education services to prekindergarten, kindergarten, grade 1–12, and ungraded students. The CCD Local Education Agency Universe Survey includes records for the 50 states, the District of Columbia, Puerto Rico, the Bureau of Indian Education, American Samoa, Guam, the Commonwealth of the Northern Mariana Islands, the U.S. Virgin Islands, and the DoD dependents schools (overseas and domestic).

The Local Education Agency Universe Survey includes the following variables: NCES agency ID number, state agency ID number, agency name, phone number, mailing address, physical location address, agency type code, supervisory union number, American National Standards Institute (ANSI) state and county code, county name, core based statistical area (CBSA) code, metropolitan/micropolitan code, metropolitan status code, district locale code, congressional district code, operational status code, BIE agency status, low/high grade span offered, agency charter status, number of schools, number of full-time-equivalent (FTE) teachers, number of ungraded students, number of PreK–12 students, number of special education/Individualized Education Program (IEP) students, number of English language learner (ELL) students, instructional staff fields, support staff fields, and a flag indicating whether student counts by race/ethnicity were reported by five or seven racial/ethnic categories.

State Nonfiscal Survey of Public Elementary/Secondary Education

The State Nonfiscal Survey of Public Elementary/Secondary Education for the 2010–11 school year provides state-level, aggregate information about students and staff in public elementary and secondary education. It includes 58 responding units: the 50 states, the District of Columbia, Puerto Rico, American Samoa, Guam, the Commonwealth of the Northern Mariana Islands, the U.S. Virgin Islands, the DoD dependents schools (overseas and domestic), and the Bureau of Indian Education. This survey covers public school student membership by grade, race/ethnicity, and state or jurisdiction and covers number of staff in public schools by category and state or jurisdiction. Beginning with the 2006–07 school year, the number of diploma recipients and other high school completers are no longer included in the State Nonfiscal Survey of Public Elementary/Secondary Education file. These data are now published in the public-use Common Core of Data State Dropout and Completion Data File.

National Public Education Financial Survey

The purpose of the National Public Education Financial Survey (NPEFS) is to provide district, state, and federal policymakers, researchers, and other interested users with descriptive information about revenues and expenditures for public elementary and secondary education. The data collected are useful to (1) chief officers of state education agencies; (2) policymakers in the executive and legislative branches of federal and state governments; (3) education policy and public policy researchers; and (4) the public, journalists, and others.

Data for NPEFS are collected from SEAs in the 50 states, the District of Columbia, Puerto Rico, and four other jurisdictions (American Samoa, Guam, the Commonwealth of the Northern Mariana Islands, and the U.S. Virgin Islands). The data file is organized by state or jurisdiction and contains revenue data by source and expenditure data by source (e.g., local, state, federal), function (the activity being supported by the expenditure), and object (the category of expenditure). The data file also contains average daily attendance data, as well as total student membership data from the CCD State Nonfiscal Survey of Public Elementary/Secondary Education.

School District Finance Survey

The purpose of the School District Finance Survey (F-33) is to provide finance data for all local education agencies (LEAs) that provide free public elementary and secondary education in the United States. National and state totals are not included (national- and state-level figures are presented, however, in the National Public Education Financial Survey [NPEFS]).

Both NCES and the Governments Division of the U.S. Census Bureau collect public school system finance data, and they collaborate in their efforts to gather these data. The Census Bureau acts as the primary collection agent and produces two data files: one for distribution and reporting by the Census Bureau and the other for distribution and reporting by NCES.

The data file for the FY 09 CCD School District Finance Survey (F-33) contains 16,563 records representing the public elementary and secondary education agencies in the 50 states and the District of Columbia. The F-33 file includes variables for revenues by source, expenditures by function, indebtedness, assets, student membership counts, as well as identification variables.

Teacher Compensation Survey

The Teacher Compensation Survey (TCS) collects total compensation, teacher status, and demographic data about individual teachers from multiple states. Twenty-three (23) states participated in the TCS for SY 2008–09.

Further information on the nonfiscal CCD data may be obtained from

Patrick Keaton
Elementary/Secondary and Library Studies Division
Elementary/Secondary Cooperative System and Institutional Studies Program
National Center for Education Statistics
1990 K Street NW
Washington, DC 20006
patrick.keaton@ed.gov
http://nces.ed.gov/ccd

Further information on the fiscal CCD data may be obtained from

Stephen Cornman
Elementary/Secondary and Library Studies Division
Elementary/Secondary Cooperative System and Institutional Studies Program
National Center for Education Statistics
1990 K Street NW
Washington, DC 20006
stephen.cornman@ed.gov
http://nces.ed.gov/ccd

INTEGRATED POSTSECONDARY EDUCATION DATA SYSTEM

The Integrated Postsecondary Education Data System (IPEDS) surveys approximately 7,500 postsecondary institutions, including universities and colleges, as well as institutions offering technical and vocational education beyond the high school level. IPEDS, an annual universe collection that began in 1986, replaced the Higher Education General Information Survey (HEGIS).

IPEDS consists of nine interrelated components that are collected over three collection periods (fall, winter, and spring) each year. These components obtain information on postsecondary institutions, student enrollment, programs offered, degrees and certificates conferred, and both the human and financial resources involved in the provision of institutionally based postsecondary education. Until 2000, these components were institutional characteristics, fall enrollment, completions, salaries, finance, and fall staff. Beginning in 2000, data were collected in the fall for institutional characteristics and completions; in the winter for employees by assigned position (EAP), salaries, and fall staff; and in the spring for enrollment, student financial aid, finances, and graduation rates. With the winter 2005–06 survey, the employees by assigned position, fall staff, and salaries components were merged into the human resources component. In 2007–08, the enrollment component was broken into two separate components: 12-month enrollment (collected in the fall) and fall enrollment (collected in the spring). In the 2011–12 IPEDS data collection year, the student financial aid component was moved to the winter data collection to aid in the timing of the net price of attendance calculations displayed on College Navigator (http://nces.ed.gov/collegenavigator).

Beginning in 2008–09, the first-professional degree category was combined with the doctor's degree category. However, some degrees formerly identified as first-professional that take more than two full-time-equivalent academic years to complete, such as those in Theology (M.Div, M.H.L./Rav), are included in the Master's degree category. Doctor's degrees were broken out into three distinct categories: research/scholarship, professional practice, and other doctor's degrees.

IPEDS race/ethnicity data collection also changed in 2008–09. The "Asian" race category is now separate from a "Native Hawaiian or Other Pacific Islander" category. Also, a "Two or more races" category was introduced.

The degree-granting institutions portion of IPEDS is a census of colleges that award associate's or higher degrees and are eligible to participate in Title IV financial aid programs. Prior to 1993, data from technical and vocational institutions were collected through a sample survey. Beginning in 1993, all data are gathered in a census of all postsecondary institutions. Beginning in 1997, the survey was restricted to institutions participating in Title IV programs.

The classification of institutions offering college and university education changed as of 1996. Prior to 1996, institutions that had courses leading to an associate's or higher degree or that had courses accepted for credit toward those degrees were considered higher education institutions. Higher education institutions were accredited by an agency or association that was recognized by the U.S. Department of Education or were recognized directly by the Secretary of Education. The newer standard includes institutions that award associate's or higher degrees and that are eligible to participate in Title IV federal financial aid programs. Tables that contain any data according to this standard are titled "degree-granting" institutions. Time-series tables may contain data from both series, and they are noted accordingly. The impact of this change on data collected in 1996 was not large. For example, tables on faculty salaries and benefits were only affected to a very small extent. Also, degrees awarded at the bachelor's level or higher were not heavily affected. The largest impact was on private 2-year college enrollment. In contrast, most of the data on public 4-year colleges were affected to a minimal extent. The impact on enrollment in public 2-year colleges was noticeable in certain states, but was relatively small at the national level. Overall, total enrollment for all institutions was about one-half of a percent higher in 1996 for degree-granting institutions than for higher education institutions.

Prior to the establishment of IPEDS in 1986, HEGIS acquired and maintained statistical data on the characteristics and operations of institutions of higher education. Implemented in 1966, HEGIS was an annual universe survey of institutions accredited at the college level by an agency recognized by the Secretary of the U.S. Department of Education. These institutions were listed in NCES's *Education Directory, Colleges and Universities*.

HEGIS surveys collected information on institutional characteristics, faculty salaries, finances, enrollment, and degrees. Since these surveys, like IPEDS, were distributed to all higher education institutions, the data presented are not subject to sampling error. However, they are subject to nonsampling error, the sources of which varied with the survey instrument.

The NCES Taskforce for IPEDS Redesign recognized that there were issues related to the consistency of data definitions as well as the accuracy, reliability, and validity of other quality measures within and across surveys. The IPEDS redesign in 2000 provided institution-specific web-based data forms. While the new system shortened data processing time and provided better data consistency, it did not address the accuracy of the data provided by institutions.

Beginning in 2003–04 with the Prior Year Data Revision System, prior-year data have been available to institutions entering current data. This allows institutions to make changes to their prior-year entries either by adjusting the data or by providing missing data. These revisions allow the evaluation of the data's accuracy by looking at the changes made.

NCES conducted a study (NCES 2005-175) of the 2002–03 data that were revised in 2003–04 to determine the accuracy of the imputations, track the institutions that submitted revised data, and analyze the revised data they submitted. When institutions made changes to their data, it was assumed that the revised data were the "true" data. The data were analyzed for the number and type of institutions making changes, the type of changes, the magnitude of the changes, and the impact on published data.

Because NCES imputes for missing data, imputation procedures were also addressed by the Redesign Taskforce. For the 2003–04 assessment, differences between revised values and values that were imputed in the original files were compared (i.e., revised value minus imputed value). These differences were then used to provide an assessment of the effectiveness of imputation procedures. The size of the differences also provides an indication of the accuracy of imputation procedures. To assess the overall impact of changes on aggregate IPEDS estimates, published tables for each component were reconstructed using the revised 2002–03 data. These reconstructed tables were then compared to the published tables to determine the magnitude of aggregate bias and the direction of this bias.

The fall 2011 and spring 2012 data collection were entirely web-based. Data were provided by "keyholders," institutional representatives appointed by campus chief executives, who were responsible for ensuring that survey data submitted by the institution were correct and complete. Because Title IV institutions are the primary focus of IPEDS and because these institutions are required to respond to the survey, response rates for Title IV institutions in the fall 2011 IPEDS collection were high. The Institutional Characteristics (IC) component response rate among all Title IV entities was 100.0 percent (all 7,479 Title IV entities responded). In addition, the response rates for the Completions and 12-Month Enrollment components were also 100.0 percent.

NCES statistical standards require that the potential for nonresponse bias for all institutions (including those in other U.S. jurisdictions) be analyzed for sectors for which the response rate is less than 85 percent. Due to response rates of 100.0 percent at the unit level for all three of the survey components, analysis for nonresponse bias was not necessary for the fall 2011 collection. However, data from four institutions that responded to the IC component contained item nonresponse. Price of attendance data collected during fall 2011 but covering prior academic years were imputed for these institutions.

Although IPEDS provides the most comprehensive data system for postsecondary education, there are 100 or more entities that collect their own information from postsecondary institutions. This raises the issue of how valid IPEDS data are when compared to education data collected by non-IPEDS sources. In the Data Quality Study, Thomson Peterson data were chosen to assess the validity of IPEDS data because Thomson Peterson is one of the largest and most comprehensive sources of postsecondary data available.

Not all IPEDS components could be compared to Thomson Peterson. Either Thomson Peterson did not collect data related to a particular IPEDS component, or the data items collected by Thomson Peterson were not comparable to the IPEDS items (i.e., the data items were defined differently). Comparisons were made for a selected number of data items in five areas—tuition and price, employees by assigned position, enrollment, student financial aid, and finance. More details on the accuracy and reliability of IPEDS data can be found in the *Integrated Postsecondary Education Data System Data Quality Study* (NCES 2005-175).

Further information on IPEDS may be obtained from

Richard Reeves
Postsecondary, Adult, and Career Education Division
Postsecondary Institutional Studies Program
National Center for Education Statistics
1990 K Street NW
Washington, DC 20006
richard.reeves@ed.gov
http://nces.ed.gov/ipeds

Fall (12-Month Enrollment)

Data on 12-month enrollment are collected for award levels ranging from postsecondary certificates of less than 1 year to doctoral degrees. The 12-month period during which data are collected is July 1 through June 30. Data are collected by race/ethnicity and gender and include unduplicated headcounts and instructional activity (contact or credit hours). These data are also used to calculate a full-time-equivalent (FTE) enrollment based on instructional activity. FTE enrollment is useful for gauging the size of the educational enterprise at the institution. Prior to the 2007–08 IPEDS data collection, the data collected in the 12-Month Enrollment component were part of the Fall Enrollment component, which is conducted during the Spring data collection period. However, to improve the timeliness of the data, a separate 12-Month Enrollment survey component was developed in 2007. These data are now collected in the fall for the previous academic year. All of the 7,380 Title IV entities eligible for the 12-Month Enrollment component of the fall 2011 data collection responded, for a response rate of 100.0 percent.

Fall (Completions)

This survey was part of the HEGIS series throughout its existence. However, the degree classification taxonomy was revised in 1970–71, 1982–83, 1991–92, 2002–03, and 2009–10. Collection of degree data has been maintained through IPEDS.

Data on associate's and other formal awards below the baccalaureate degree, by field of study, may not be comparable with figures from years prior to 1982–83. The nonresponse rate does not appear to be a significant source of nonsampling error for this survey. The unweighted response rate over the years has been high, with the response rate at 100.0 percent for fall 2011. Because of the high response rate for degree-granting institutions, nonsampling error caused by imputation is also minimal. Imputation methods and the response bias analysis for the fall 2010 Completions component are discussed in *Postsecondary Institutions and Price of Attendance in 2011–12, Degrees and Other Awards Conferred: 2010–11, and 12-Month Enrollment: 2010–11* (NCES 2012-289rev).

The *Integrated Postsecondary Education Data System Data Quality Study* (NCES 2005-175) indicated that most Title IV institutions supplying revised data on completions in 2003–04 were able to supply missing data for the prior year. The small differences between imputed data for the prior year and the revised actual data supplied by the institution indicated that the imputed values produced by NCES were acceptable.

Fall (Institutional Characteristics)

This survey collects the basic information necessary to classify institutions, including control, level, and types of programs offered, as well as information on tuition, fees, and room and board charges. Beginning in 2000, the survey collected institutional pricing data from institutions with first-time, full-time, degree/certificate-seeking undergraduate students. Unduplicated full-year enrollment counts and instructional activity are now collected in the Fall Enrollment survey. Beginning in 2008–09, student financial aid data collected includes greater detail.

The response rate for the Institutional Characteristics (IC) component among all Title IV entities was 100.0 percent (all 7,479 Title IV entities responded). Imputation methods for the fall 2011 Institutional Characteristics component are discussed in the *2011–12 Integrated Postsecondary Education Data System (IPEDS) Methodology Report* (NCES 2012-293).

The *Integrated Postsecondary Education Data System Data Quality Study* (NCES 2005-175) looked at tuition and price in Title IV institutions. Only 8 percent of institutions in 2002–03 and 2003–04 reported the same data to IPEDS and Thomson Peterson consistently across all selected data items. Differences in wordings or survey items may account for some of these inconsistencies.

Winter (Human Resources)

The IPEDS Human Resources (HR) component comprises three sections: Employees by Assigned Position (EAP), Fall Staff, and Salaries.

Employees by Assigned Position

Data gathered by the Employees by Assigned Position (EAP) section categorizes all employees by full- or part-time status, faculty status, and primary function/occupational activity. Institutions with M.D. or D.O. programs are required to report their medical school employees separately. A response to the EAP was required of all 6,858 Title IV institutions and administrative offices in the United States and other jurisdictions for winter 2008–09, and 6,845, or 99.8 percent unweighted, responded. Of the 6,970 Title IV institutions and administrative offices required to respond to the winter 2009–10 EAP, 6,964, or 99.9 percent, responded. And of the 7,256 Title IV institutions and administrative offices required to respond to the EAP for winter 2010–11, 7,252, or 99.9 percent, responded.

The primary functions/occupational activities of the EAP section are primarily instruction, instruction combined with research and/or public service, primarily research, primarily public service, executive/administrative/managerial, other professionals (support/service), graduate assistants, technical and paraprofessionals, clerical and secretarial, skilled crafts, and service/maintenance.

All full-time instructional faculty classified in the EAP full-time nonmedical school part as either (1) primarily instruction or (2) instruction combined with research and/or public service are included in the Salaries section, unless they are exempt.

Fall Staff

The section categorizes all staff on the institution's payroll as of November 1 of the collection year, by employment status (full time or part time), primary function/occupational activity, gender, and race/ethnicity. These data elements are collected from degree-granting and non-degree-granting institutions; however, additional data elements are collected from degree-granting institutions and related administrative offices with 15 or more full-time staff. These elements include faculty status, contract length/teaching period, academic rank, salary class intervals, and newly hired full-time permanent staff.

The Fall Staff section, which is required only in odd-numbered reporting years, was not required during the 2008–09 HR data collection. However, of the 6,858 Title IV institutions and administrative offices in the United States and other jurisdictions, 3,295, or 48.0 percent unweighted, did provide data in the Fall Staff section that year. During the 2009–10 HR data collection, when all 6,970 Title IV institutions and administrative offices were required to respond to the Fall Staff section, 6,964, or 99.9 percent, did so. A response to the Fall Staff section of the 2010–11 HR collection was optional, and 3,364 Title IV institutions and administrative offices responded that year (a response rate of 46.3 percent).

The study *Integrated Postsecondary Education Data System Data Quality Study* (NCES 2005-175) found that for 2003–04 employee data items, changes were made by 1.2 percent (77) of the institutions that responded. All who made changes made changes that resulted in different employee counts. For both institutional and aggregate differences, the changes had little impact on the original employee count submissions. A large number of institutions reported different staff data to IPEDS and Thomson Peterson; however, the magnitude of the differences was small—usually no more than 17 faculty members for any faculty variable.

Salaries

This section collects data for full-time instructional faculty on the institution's payroll as of November 1 of the collection year (except those in medical schools of the EAP section, as described above), by contract length/teaching period, gender, and academic rank. The reporting of data by faculty status in the Salaries section is required from 4-year degree-granting institutions and above only. Salary outlays and fringe benefits are also collected for full-time instructional staff on 9/10- and 11/12-month contracts/teaching periods. This section is applicable to degree-granting institutions unless exempt.

This institutional survey was conducted for most years from 1966–67 to 1987–88; it has been conducted annually since 1989–90, except for 2000–01. Although the survey form has changed a number of times during these years, only comparable data are presented.

Between 1966–67 and 1985–86, this survey differed from other HEGIS surveys in that imputations were not made for nonrespondents. Thus, there is some possibility that the salary averages presented in this report may differ from the results of a complete enumeration of all colleges and universities. Beginning with the surveys for 1987–88, the IPEDS data tabulation procedures included imputations for survey nonrespondents. The unweighted response rate for the 2008–09 Salaries survey section was 99.9 percent. The response rate for the 2009–10 Salaries section was 100.0 percent (4,453 of the 4,455 required institutions responded), and the response rate for 2010–11 was 99.9 percent (4,561 of the 4,565 required institutions responded). Imputation methods for the 2010–11 Salaries survey section are discussed in *Employees in Postsecondary Institutions, Fall 2010, and Salaries of Full-Time Instructional Staff, 2010–11* (NCES 2012-276).

Although data from this survey are not subject to sampling error, sources of nonsampling error may include computational errors and misclassification in reporting and processing. The electronic reporting system does allow corrections to prior-year reported or missing data, and this should help with these problems. Also, NCES reviews individual institutions' data for internal and longitudinal consistency and contacts institutions to check inconsistent data.

The *Integrated Postsecondary Education Data System Data Quality Study* (NCES 2005-175) found that only 1.3 percent of the responding Title IV institutions in 2003–04 made changes to their salaries data. The differences between the imputed data and the revised data were small and found to have little impact on the published data.

Winter (Student Financial Aid)

This component was part of the spring data collection from IPEDS data collection years 2000–01 to 2010–11, but it moved to the winter data collection starting with the 2011–12 IPEDS data collection year. This move will aid in the timing of the net price of attendance calculations displayed on College Navigator (http://nces.ed.gov/collegenavigator).

Financial aid data are collected for undergraduate students. Data are collected regarding federal grants, state and local government grants, institutional grants, and loans. The collected data include the number of students receiving each type of financial assistance and the average amount of aid received by type of aid. Beginning in 2008–09, student financial aid data collected includes greater detail on types of aid offered.

In the winter 2011–12 data collection, the Student Financial Aid component presented data on the number of full-time, first-time degree- and certificate-seeking undergraduate financial aid recipients for the 2010–11 academic year. The response rate for this component was 99.8 percent for degree-granting institutions overall.

Spring (Fall Enrollment)

This survey has been part of the HEGIS and IPEDS series since 1966. Response rates for this survey have been relatively high, generally exceeding 85 percent. Beginning in 2000, with web-based data collection, higher response rates were attained. In the spring 2012 data collection, where the Fall Enrollment component covered fall 2011, the response rate was 99.8 percent. Data collection procedures for the Fall Enrollment component of the spring 2012 data collection are presented in *Enrollment in Postsecondary Institutions, Fall 2011; Financial Statistics, Fiscal Year 2011; and Graduation Rates, Selected Cohorts, 2003–2008: First Look (Provisional Data)* (NCES 2012-174rev).

Beginning with the fall 1986 survey and the introduction of IPEDS (see above), the survey was redesigned. The survey allows (in alternating years) for the collection of age and residence data. Beginning in 2000, the survey collected instructional activity and unduplicated headcount data, which are needed to compute a standardized, full-time-equivalent (FTE) enrollment statistic for the entire academic year. As of 2007–08, the timeliness of the instructional activity data has been improved by collecting these data in the fall as part of the 12-Month-Enrollment component instead of in the spring as part of the Fall Enrollment component.

The *Integrated Postsecondary Education Data System Data Quality Study* (NCES 2005-175) showed that public institutions made the majority of changes to enrollment data during the 2004 revision period. The majority of changes were made to unduplicated headcount data, with the net differences between the original data and the revised data at about 1 percent. Part-time students in general and enrollment in private nonprofit institutions were often underestimated. The fewest changes by institutions were to Classification of Instructional Programs (CIP) code data. (The CIP is a taxonomic coding scheme that contains titles and descriptions of primarily postsecondary instructional programs.) More institutions provided enrollment data to IPEDS than to Thomson Peterson. A fairly high percentage of institutions that provided data to both provided the same data, and among those that did not, the difference in magnitude was less than 10 percent.

Spring (Finance)

This survey was part of the HEGIS series and has been continued under IPEDS. Substantial changes were made in the financial survey instruments in fiscal year (FY) 1976, FY 82, FY 87, FY 97, and FY 02. While these changes were significant, considerable effort has been made to present only comparable information on trends in this report and to note inconsistencies. The FY 76 survey instrument contained numerous revisions to earlier survey forms, which made direct comparisons of line items very difficult. Beginning in FY 82, Pell Grant data were collected in the categories of federal restricted grant and contract revenues and restricted scholarship and fellowship expenditures. Finance tables for this publication have been adjusted by subtracting the largely duplicative Pell Grant amounts from the later data to maintain comparability with pre-FY 82 data. The introduction of IPEDS in the FY 87 survey included several important changes to the survey instrument and data processing procedures. Beginning in FY 97, data for private institutions were collected using new financial concepts consistent with Financial Accounting Standards Board (FASB) reporting standards, which provide a more comprehensive view of college finance activities. The data for public institutions continued to be collected using the older survey form. The data for public and private institutions were no longer comparable and, as a result, no longer presented together in analysis tables. In FY 01, public institutions had the option of either continuing to report using Government Accounting Standards Board (GASB) standards or using the new FASB reporting standards. Beginning in FY 02, public institutions had three options: the original GASB standards, the FASB standards, or the new GASB Statement 35 standards (GASB35).

Possible sources of nonsampling error in the financial statistics include nonresponse, imputation, and misclassification. The unweighted response rate has been about 85 to 90 percent for many of the historic years; however, in more recent years, response rates have been much higher because Title IV institutions are required to respond. The 2002 IPEDS data collection was a full-scale web-based collection, which offered features that improved the quality and timeliness of the data. The ability of IPEDS to tailor online data entry forms for each institution based on characteristics such as institutional control, level of institution, and calendar system, and the institutions' ability to submit their data online, were two such features that improved response.

The response rate for the FY 2011 Finance survey component was 99.8 percent. Data collection procedures for the FY 2011 survey are discussed in *Enrollment in Postsecondary Institutions, Fall 2011; Financial Statistics, Fiscal Year 2011; and Graduation Rates, Selected Cohorts, 2003–2008: First Look (Provisional Data)* (NCES 2012-174rev). Two general methods of imputation were used in HEGIS. If prior-year data were available for a nonresponding institution, they were inflated using the Higher Education Price Index and adjusted according to changes in enrollments. If prior-year data were not available, current data were used from peer institutions selected for location (state or region), control, level, and enrollment size of institution. In most cases, estimates for nonreporting institutions in HEGIS were made using data from peer institutions.

Beginning with FY 87, IPEDS included all postsecondary institutions, but maintained comparability with earlier surveys by allowing 2- and 4-year institutions to be tabulated separately. For FY 87 through FY 91, in order to maintain comparability with the historical time series of HEGIS institutions, data were combined from two of the three different survey forms that make up IPEDS. The vast majority of the data were tabulated from form 1, which was used to collect information from public and private nonprofit 2- and 4-year colleges. Form 2, a condensed form, was used to gather data for 2-year for-profit institutions. Because of the differences in the data requested on the two forms, several assumptions were made about the form 2 reports so that their figures could be included in the degree-granting institution totals.

In IPEDS, the form 2 institutions were not asked to separate appropriations from grants and contracts, nor were they asked to separate state from local sources of funding. For the form 2 institutions, all federal revenues were assumed to be federal grants and contracts, and all state and local revenues were assumed to be restricted state grants and contracts. All other form 2 sources of revenue, except for tuition and fees and sales and services of educational activities, were included under "other." Similar adjustments were made to the expenditure accounts. The form 2 institutions reported instruction and scholarship and fellowship expenditures only. All other educational and general expenditures were allocated to academic support.

The *Integrated Postsecondary Education Data System Data Quality Study* (NCES 2005-175) found that only a small percentage (2.9 percent, or 168) of postsecondary institutions either revised 2002–03 data or submitted data for items they previously left unreported. Though relatively few institutions made changes, the changes made were relatively large—greater than 10 percent of the original data. With a few exceptions, these changes, large as they were, did not greatly affect the aggregate totals.

Again, institutions were more likely to report data to IPEDS than to Thomson Peterson, and there was a higher percentage reporting different values among those reporting to both. The magnitude of the difference was generally greater for research expenditures. It is likely that the large differences are a function of the way institutions report these data to each entity, rather than incidental reporting errors.

Spring (Graduation Rates and Graduation Rates 200 Percent)

Graduation rates data are collected for full-time, first-time degree- and certificate-seeking undergraduate students. Data included are the number of students entering the institution as full-time, first-time degree- or certificate-seeking students in a particular year (cohort), by race/ethnicity and gender; the number of students completing their program within a time period equal to 1½ times (150 percent) the normal period of time; and the number of students who transferred to other institutions.

In the spring 2012 data collection, the Graduation Rates component collected counts of full-time, first-time degree- and certificate-seeking undergraduate students entering an institution in the cohort year (4-year institutions used the cohort year 2005; less-than-4-year institutions used the cohort year 2008), and their completion status as of August 31, 2011 (150 percent of normal program completion time) at the institution initially entered. The response rate for this component was 99.8 percent.

The 200 Percent Graduation Rates component collected counts of full-time, first-time degree- and certificate-seeking undergraduate students beginning their postsecondary education in the reference period and their completion status as of August 31, 2011 (200 percent of normal program completion time) at the same institution where the students started. Four-year institutions report on bachelor's or equivalent degree-seeking students and use cohort year 2003 as the reference period, while less-than-4-year institutions report on all students in the cohort and use cohort year 2007 as the reference period. The response rate for this component was 99.8 percent.

Private School Universe Survey

The purposes of the Private School Universe Survey (PSS) data collection activities are (1) to build an accurate and complete list of private schools to serve as a sampling frame for NCES sample surveys of private schools and (2) to report data on the total number of private schools, teachers, and students in the survey universe. Begun in 1989 under the U.S. Census Bureau, the PSS has been conducted every 2 years, and data for the 1989–90, 1991–92, 1993–94, 1995–96, 1997–98, 1999–2000, 2001–02, 2003–04, 2005–06, 2007–08, 2009–10, and 2011–12 school years have been released. A *First Look* report of the 2011–12 PSS data was released in July 2013.

The PSS produces data similar to that of the CCD for public schools, and can be used for public-private comparisons. The data are useful for a variety of policy- and research-relevant issues, such as the growth of religiously affiliated schools, the number of private high school graduates, the length of the school year for various private schools, and the number of private school students and teachers.

The target population for this universe survey is all private schools in the United States that meet the PSS criteria of a private school (i.e., the private school is an institution that provides instruction for any of grades K through 12, has one or more teachers to give instruction, is not administered by a public agency, and is not operated in a private home). The survey universe is composed of schools identified from a variety of sources. The main source is a list frame initially developed for the 1989–90 PSS. The list is updated regularly by matching it with lists provided by nationwide private school associations, state departments of education, and other national guides and sources that list private schools. The other source is an area frame search in approximately 124 geographic areas, conducted by the U.S. Census Bureau.

Of the 39,325 schools included in the 2011–12 sample, 10,030 were found ineligible for the survey (NCES 2013-316). Those not responding numbered 2,312, and those responding numbered 26,983. The unweighted response rate for the 2011–12 PSS survey was 92.1 percent.

Further information on the PSS may be obtained from

Steve Broughman
Elementary/Secondary and Libraries Studies Division
Elementary/Secondary Sample Survey Studies Program
National Center for Education Statistics
1990 K Street NW
Washington, DC 20006
stephen.broughman@ed.gov
http://nces.ed.gov/surveys/pss

Schools and Staffing Survey

The Schools and Staffing Survey (SASS) is a set of linked questionnaires used to collect the information necessary for a comprehensive picture of elementary and secondary education in the United States. The abundance of data collected permits detailed analyses of the characteristics of the nation's public and private elementary and secondary schools, principals, teachers, school libraries, and school/school district policies. SASS data are collected through a mail questionnaire with telephone follow-up. SASS was first conducted for NCES by the Census Bureau during the 1987–88 school year. SASS subsequently was conducted in 1990–91, 1993–94, 1999–2000, 2003–04, 2007–08, and 2011–12. The 1990–91, 1993–94, 1999–2000, 2003–04, and 2007–08 SASS also obtained data on Bureau of Indian Education (BIE) schools (schools funded or operated by the BIE). The universe of charter schools in operation in 1998–99 was given the Charter School Questionnaire to complete as part of the 1999–2000 SASS. In subsequent SASS administrations, charter schools were not administered a separate questionnaire, but were included in the public school sample. Another change in the 2003–04 administration included a revised data collection methodology using a primary in-person contact with the school with the aim of reducing the field follow-up phase. Also, school library media centers were surveyed only in the public and BIE schools.

School library data were collected on the School and Principal Surveys of the 1990–91 Schools and Staffing Survey (SASS), and the School Library Media Centers (LMC) Survey became a component of SASS with the 1993–94 administration of the survey. Thus, the readers should refer to the section on the Schools and Staffing Survey, below, regarding data on school libraries. Since then, the LMC Survey has been conducted during the 1999–2000, 2003–04, and 2007–08 school years. During the 2007–08 administration, only the public and Bureau of Indian Education (BIE) school library media centers were surveyed. School library questions focus on facilities, services and policies, staffing, technology, information literacy, collections and expenditures, and media equipment. New or revised topics include access to online licensed databases, resource availability, and additional elements on information literacy.

The 2007–08 SASS estimates are based on a sample consisting of approximately 9,800 public schools, 2,940 private schools, and 180 BIE schools. The public school sample for the 2007–08 SASS was based on an adjusted public school universe file from the 2005–06 Common Core of Data (CCD), a database of all the nation's public school districts and public schools. The sampling frame includes regular public schools, Department of Defense-operated military base schools in the United States, and other schools such as special education, vocational, and alternative schools. SASS is designed to provide national estimates for public and private school characteristics and state estimates for school districts, public schools, principals, and teachers. In addition, the teacher survey is designed to allow comparisons between new and experienced teachers and between bilingual/English as a second language (ESL) teachers and other teachers.

The BIE sample consisted of all BIE schools that met the SASS definition of a school.

The private school sample for the 2007–08 SASS was selected from the 2005–06 Private School Universe Survey, supplemented with updates from state lists collected by the Census Bureau and lists by private school associations and religious denominations. Private school estimates are available at the national level and by private school affiliation.

In 2007–08, the weighted response rate for the Public School District Questionnaire was 87.8 percent. Weighted response rates for the Public School Principal Questionnaire, the Private School Principal Questionnaire, and the BIE-funded School Principal Questionnaire were 79.4 percent, 72.2 percent, and 79.2 percent, respectively.

Weighted response rates in 2007–08 for the Public School Questionnaire, the Private School Questionnaire, and the BIE-funded School Questionnaire were 80.4 percent, 75.9 percent, and 77.1 percent, respectively. The weighted overall response rates were 84.0 percent for public school teachers, 77.5 percent for private school teachers, and 81.8 percent for BIE-funded school teachers.

There is also a methodology report on SASS, the *Quality Profile for SASS, Rounds 1–3: 1987–1995, Aspects of the Quality of Data in the Schools and Staffing Surveys (SASS)* (NCES 2000-308). Data from the 2011–12 administration of SASS are scheduled to be released in summer 2013.

Further information on SASS may be obtained from

Kathryn Chandler
Elementary/Secondary and Libraries Studies Division
Elementary/Secondary Sample Survey Studies Program
National Center for Education Statistics
1990 K Street NW
Washington, DC 20006
kathryn.chandler@ed.gov
http://nces.ed.gov/surveys/sass

Teacher Follow-up Survey

The Teacher Follow–up Survey (TFS) is a SASS survey whose purpose is to determine how many teachers remain at the same school, move to another school, or leave the profession in the year following a SASS administration. It is administered to elementary and secondary teachers in the 50 states and the District of Columbia. The TFS uses two questionnaires, one for teachers who left teaching since the previous SASS administration and another for those who are still teaching either in the same school as last year or in a different school. The objective of the TFS is to focus on the characteristics of each group in order to answer questions about teacher mobility and attrition.

The 2008–09 TFS is different from any previous TFS administration in that it also serves as the second wave of a longitudinal study of first-year teachers. Because of this, the 2008–09 TFS consists of four questionnaires. Two are for respondents who were first-year public school teachers in the 2007–08 SASS and two are for the remainder of the sample.

Further information on the TFS may be obtained from

Freddie Cross
Elementary/Secondary and Libraries Studies Division
Elementary/Secondary Sample Survey Studies Program
National Center for Education Statistics
1990 K Street NW
Washington, DC 20006
freddie.cross@ed.gov
http://nces.ed.gov/surveys/sass

Bureau of Labor Statistics

Consumer Price Indexes

The Consumer Price Index (CPI) represents changes in prices of all goods and services purchased for consumption by urban households. Indexes are available for two population groups: a CPI for All Urban Consumers (CPI-U) and a CPI for Urban Wage Earners and Clerical Workers (CPI-W). Unless otherwise specified, data are adjusted for inflation using the CPI-U. These values are generally adjusted to a school-year basis by averaging the July through June figures. Price indexes are available for the United States, the four Census regions, size of city, cross-classifications of regions and size classes, and 26 local areas. The major uses of the CPI include as an economic indicator, as a deflator of other economic series, and as a means of adjusting income.

Also available is the Consumer Price Index research series using current methods (CPI-U-RS), which presents an estimate of the CPI-U from 1978 to the present that incorporates most of the improvements that the Bureau of Labor Statistics has made over that time span into the entire series. The historical price index series of the CPI-U does not reflect these changes, though these changes do make the present and future CPI more accurate. The limitations of the CPI-U-RS include considerable uncertainty surrounding the magnitude of the adjustments and the several improvements in the CPI that have not been incorporated into the CPI-U-RS for various reasons. Nonetheless, the CPI-U-RS can serve as a valuable proxy for researchers needing a historical estimate of inflation using current methods. This series has not been used in NCES tables.

Further information on consumer price indexes may be obtained from

Bureau of Labor Statistics
U.S. Department of Labor
2 Massachusetts Avenue NE
Washington, DC 20212
http://www.bls.gov/cpi

Employment and Unemployment Surveys

Statistics on the employment and unemployment status of the population and related data are compiled by the Bureau of Labor Statistics (BLS) using data from the Current Population Survey (CPS) (see below) and other surveys. The Current Population Survey, a monthly household survey conducted by the U.S. Census Bureau for the Bureau of Labor Statistics, provides a comprehensive body of information on the employment and unemployment experience of the nation's population, classified by age, sex, race, and various other characteristics.

Further information on unemployment surveys may be obtained from

Bureau of Labor Statistics
U.S. Department of Labor
2 Massachusetts Avenue NE
Washington, DC 20212
cpsinfo@bls.gov
http://www.bls.gov/bls/employment.htm

Census Bureau

Current Population Survey

The Current Population Survey (CPS) is a monthly survey of about 60,000 households conducted by the U.S. Census Bureau for the Bureau of Labor Statistics. The CPS is the primary source of information of labor force statistics for the U.S. noninstitutionalized population (e.g., excludes military personnel and their families living on bases and inmates of correctional institutions). In addition, supplemental questionnaires are used to provide further information about the U.S.

population. Specifically, in October, detailed questions regarding school enrollment and school characteristics are asked. In March, detailed questions regarding income are asked.

The current sample design, introduced in July 2001, includes about 72,000 households. Each month about 58,900 of the 72,000 households are eligible for interview, and of those, 7 to 10 percent are not interviewed because of temporary absence or unavailability. Information is obtained each month from those in the household who are 15 years of age and older, and demographic data are collected for children 0–14 years of age. In addition, supplemental questions regarding school enrollment are asked about eligible household members ages 3 and older in the October survey. Prior to July 2001, data were collected in the CPS from about 50,000 dwelling units. The samples are initially selected based on the decennial census files and are periodically updated to reflect new housing construction.

A major redesign of the CPS was implemented in January 1994 to improve the quality of the data collected. Survey questions were revised, new questions were added, and computer-assisted interviewing methods were used for the survey data collection. Further information about the redesign is available in *Current Population Survey, October 1995: (School Enrollment Supplement) Technical Documentation* at http://www.census.gov/prod/techdoc/cps/cpsoct95.pdf.

Caution should be used when comparing data from 1994 through 2001 with data from 1993 and earlier. Data from 1994 through 2001 reflect 1990 census-based population controls, while data from 1993 and earlier reflect 1980 or earlier census-based population controls. Also use caution when comparing data from 1994 through 2001 with data from 2002 onward, as data from 2002 reflect 2000 census-based controls. Changes in population controls generally have relatively little impact on summary measures such as means, medians, and percentage distributions. They can have a significant impact on population counts. For example, use of the 1990 census-based population control resulted in about a 1 percent increase in the civilian noninstitutional population and in the number of families and households. Thus, estimates of levels for data collected in 1994 and later years will differ from those for earlier years by more than what could be attributed to actual changes in the population. These differences could be disproportionately greater for certain subpopulation groups than for the total population.

Beginning in 2003, race/ethnicity questions expanded to include information on people of two or more races. Native Hawaiian/Pacific Islander data are collected separately from Asian data. The questions have also been worded to make it clear that self-reported data on race/ethnicity should reflect the race/ethnicity with which the responder identifies, rather than what may be written in official documentation.

The estimation procedure employed for monthly CPS data involves inflating weighted sample results to independent estimates of characteristics of the civilian noninstitutional population in the United States by age, sex, and race. These independent estimates are based on statistics from decennial censuses; statistics on births, deaths, immigration, and emigration; and statistics on the population in the armed services. Generalized standard error tables are provided in the Current Population Reports; methods for deriving standard errors can be found within the CPS technical documentation at http://www.census.gov/cps/methodology/techdocs.html. The CPS data are subject to both nonsampling and sampling errors.

Prior to 2009, standard errors were estimated using the generalized variance function. The generalized variance function is a simple model that expresses the variance as a function of the expected value of a survey estimate. Beginning with March 2009 CPS data, standard errors were estimated using replicate weight methodology. Those interested in using CPS household-level supplement replicate weights to calculate variances may refer to *Estimating Current Population Survey (CPS) Household-Level Supplement Variances Using Replicate Weights* at http://smpbff2.dsd.census.gov/pub/cps/supps/HH-level_Use_of_the_Public_Use_Replicate_Weight_File.doc.

Further information on CPS may be obtained from

Education and Social Stratification Branch
Population Division
Census Bureau
U.S. Department of Commerce
4600 Silver Hill Road
Washington, DC 20233
http://www.census.gov/cps

Dropouts

Each October, the Current Population Survey (CPS) includes supplemental questions on the enrollment status of the population ages 3 years and over as part of the monthly basic survey on labor force participation. In addition to gathering the information on school enrollment, with the limitations on accuracy as noted below under "School Enrollment," the survey data permit calculations of dropout rates. Both status and event dropout rates are tabulated from the October CPS. Event rates describe the proportion of students who leave school each year without completing a high school program. Status rates provide cumulative data on dropouts among all young adults within a specified age range. Status rates are higher than event rates because they include all dropouts ages 16 through 24, regardless of when they last attended school.

In addition to other survey limitations, dropout rates may be affected by survey coverage and exclusion of the institutionalized population. The incarcerated population has grown more rapidly and has a higher dropout rate than the general population. Dropout rates for the total population might be higher than those for the noninstitutionalized population if the prison and jail populations were included in the dropout rate calculations. On the other hand, if military personnel, who tend to be high school graduates, were included, it might offset some or all of the impact from the theoretical inclusion of the jail and prison population.

Another area of concern with tabulations involving young people in household surveys is the relatively low coverage ratio compared to older age groups. CPS undercoverage results from missed housing units and missed people within sample households. Overall CPS undercoverage for March 2008 is estimated to be about 12 percent. CPS undercoverage varies with age, sex, and race. Generally, undercoverage is larger for males than for females and larger for Blacks than for non-Blacks. For example, in 2008 the undercoverage ratio for Black 20- to 24-year-old males is 30 percent. The CPS weighting procedure partially corrects for the bias due to undercoverage. Further information on CPS methodology may be obtained from http://www.census.gov/cps.

Further information on the calculation of dropouts and dropout rates may be obtained from *Trends in High School Dropout and Completion Rates in the United States: 1972–2009* at http://nces.ed.gov/pubsearch/pubsinfo.asp?pubid=2012006 or by contacting

Chris Chapman
Early Childhood, International, and Crosscutting Studies Division
Early Childhood and Household Studies Program
National Center for Education Statistics
1990 K Street NW
Washington, DC 20006
chris.chapman@ed.gov

Educational Attainment

Reports documenting educational attainment are produced by the Census Bureau using March CPS supplement (Annual Social and Economic Supplement [ASEC]) results. The sample size for the 2012 ASEC supplement (including basic CPS) was about 99,000 households. The latest release is *Educational Attainment in the United States: 2012*; the tables may be downloaded at http://www.census.gov/hhes/socdemo/education/data/cps/2012/tables.html.

In addition to the general constraints of CPS, some data indicate that the respondents have a tendency to overestimate the educational level of members of their household. Some inaccuracy is due to a lack of the respondent's knowledge of the exact educational attainment of each household member and the hesitancy to acknowledge anything less than a high school education. Another cause of nonsampling variability is the change in the numbers in the armed services over the years.

Further information on CPS's educational attainment may be obtained from the CPS website at http://www.census.gov/cps.

Further information on CPS's educational attainment data may be obtained from

Education and Social Stratification Branch
Census Bureau
U.S. Department of Commerce
4600 Silver Hill Road
Washington, DC 20233
http://www.census.gov/hhes/socdemo/education

School Enrollment

Each October, the Current Population Survey (CPS) includes supplemental questions on the enrollment status of the population ages 3 years and over. Prior to 2001, the October supplement consisted of approximately 47,000 interviewed households. Beginning with the October 2001 supplement, the sample was expanded by 9,000 to a total of approximately 56,000 interviewed households. The main sources of nonsampling variability in the responses to the supplement are those inherent in the survey instrument. The question of current enrollment may not be answered accurately for various reasons. Some respondents may not know current grade information for every student in the household, a problem especially prevalent for households with members in college or in nursery school. Confusion over college credits or hours taken by a student may make it difficult to determine the year in which the student is enrolled. Problems may occur with the definition of nursery school (a group or class organized to provide educational experiences for children) where respondents' interpretations of "educational experiences" vary.

For the October 2011 basic CPS, the household-level nonresponse rate was 8.71 percent. The person-level nonresponse rate for the school enrollment supplement was an additional 6.9 percent. Since the basic CPS nonresponse rate is a household-level rate and the school enrollment supplement nonresponse rate is a person-level rate, these rates cannot be combined to derive an overall nonresponse rate. Nonresponding households may have fewer persons than interviewed ones, so combining these rates may lead to an overestimate of the true overall nonresponse rate for persons for the school enrollment supplement.

Further information on CPS methodology may be obtained from http://www.census.gov/cps.

Further information on the CPS School Enrollment Supplement may be obtained from

Education and Social Stratification Branch
Census Bureau
U.S. Department of Commerce
4600 Silver Hill Road
Washington, DC 20233
http://www.census.gov/hhes/school/index.html

Decennial Census, Population Estimates, and Population Projections

The Decennial Census is a universe survey mandated by the U.S. Constitution. It is a questionnaire sent to every household in the country, and it is composed of seven questions about the household and its members (name, sex, age, relationship, Hispanic origin, race, and whether the housing unit is owned or rented). The Census Bureau also produces annual estimates of the resident population by demographic characteristics (age, sex, race, and Hispanic origin) for the nation, states, and counties, as well as national and state projections for the resident population. The reference date for population estimates is July 1 of the given year. With each new issue of July 1 estimates, the Census Bureau revises estimates for each year back to the last census. Previously published estimates are superseded and archived.

Census respondents self-report race and ethnicity. In the 2000 Census, they were first asked, "Is this person Spanish/ Hispanic/Latino?" and then given the following options: No, not Spanish/Hispanic/Latino; Yes, Puerto Rican; Yes, Mexican, Mexican American, Chicano; Yes, Cuban; and Yes, other Spanish/Hispanic/Latino (with space to print the specific group). The next question was "What is this person's race?" The options were White; Black, African American, or Negro; American Indian or Alaska Native (with space to print the name of enrolled or principal tribe); Asian Indian; Japanese; Native Hawaiian; Chinese; Korean; Guamanian or Chamorro; Filipino; Vietnamese; Samoan; Other Asian; Other Pacific Islander; and Some other race. The last three options included space to print the specific race. The 2000 Census was also the first time that respondents were given the option of choosing more than one race. The Census population estimates program modified the enumerated population from the 2000 Census to produce the population estimates base for 2000 and onward. As part of the modification, the Census Bureau recoded the "Some other race" responses from the 2000 Census to one or more of the five OMB race categories used in the estimates program (for more information, see http://www.census.gov/popest/ methodology/2008-nat-meth.pdf). Prior to 2000, the Census Bureau combined the categories Asian and Native Hawaiian or Other Pacific Islander. For all years, all persons of Hispanic origin were included in the Hispanic category regardless of the race option(s) chosen. Therefore, persons of Hispanic origin may be of any race.

Further information on the Decennial Census may be obtained from http://www.census.gov.

National Population Projections

The 2012 National Population Projections, the first based on the 2010 Census, provide projections of resident population and projections of the United States resident population by age, sex, race, and Hispanic origin from 2012 through 2060. The following is a general description of the methods used to produce the 2012 National Population Projections.

The projections were produced using a cohort-component method beginning with an estimated base population for July 1, 2011. First, components of population change (mortality, fertility, and net international migration) were projected. Next, for each passing year, the population is advanced one year of age and the new age categories are updated using the projected survival rates and levels of net international migration for that year. A new birth cohort is then added to form the population under one year of age by applying projected age-specific fertility rates to the average female population aged 10 to 54 years and updating the new cohort for the effects of mortality and net international migration.

The assumptions for the components of change were based on time series analysis. Initially, demographic models were used to summarize historical trends. Further information on the methodologies used to produce the 2012 National Population Projections may be obtained from http://www.census.gov/population/projections/methodology/.

State Population Projections

These state population projections were prepared using a cohort-component method by which each component of population change—births, deaths, state-to-state migration flows, international in-migration, and international out-migration—was projected separately for each birth cohort by sex, race, and Hispanic origin. The basic framework was the same as in past Census Bureau projections.

Detailed components necessary to create the projections were obtained from vital statistics, administrative records, census data, and national projections. The cohort-component method is based on the traditional demographic accounting system:

$$P_1 = P_0 + B - D + DIM - DOM + IIM - IOM$$

where:

P_1 = population at the end of the period

P_0 = population at the beginning of the period

B = births during the period

D = deaths during the period

DIM = domestic in-migration during the period

DOM = domestic out-migration during the period

IIM = international in-migration during the period

IOM = international out-migration during the period

To generate population projections with this model, the Census Bureau created separate datasets for each of these components. In general, the assumptions concerning the future levels of fertility, mortality, and international migration are consistent with the assumptions developed for the national population projections of the Census Bureau.

Once the data for each component were developed the cohort-component method was applied to produce the projections. For each projection year, the base population for each state was disaggregated into eight race and Hispanic categories (non-Hispanic White; non-Hispanic Black; non-Hispanic American Indian, Eskimo, and Aleut; non-Hispanic Asian and Pacific Islander; Hispanic White; Hispanic Black; Hispanic American Indian, Eskimo, and Aleut; and Hispanic Asian and Pacific Islander), by sex, and single year of age (ages 0 to 85+). The next step was to survive each age-sex-race-ethnic group forward 1 year using the pertinent survival rate. The internal redistribution of the population was accomplished by applying the appropriate state-to-state migration rates to the survived population in each state. The projected out-migrants were subtracted from the state of origin and added to the state of destination (as in-migrants). Next, the appropriate number of immigrants from abroad was added to each group. The population under age 1 was created by applying the appropriate age-race-ethnic-specific birth rates to females of childbearing age (ages 15 to 49). The number of births by sex and race/ethnicity were survived forward and exposed to the appropriate migration rate to yield the population under age 1. The final results of the projection process were proportionally adjusted to be consistent with the national population projections by single years of age, sex, race, and Hispanic origin. The entire process was then repeated for each year of the projection.

More information on Census Bureau projections may be obtained from

Population Division
Census Bureau
U.S. Department of Commerce
Washington, DC 20233
http://www.census.gov

OTHER SOURCES

IHS Global Insight

IHS Global Insight provides an information system that includes databases of economic and financial information; simulation and planning models; regular publications and special studies; data retrieval and management systems; and access to experts on economic, financial, industrial, and market activities. One service is the IHS Global Insight Model of the U.S. Economy, which contains annual projections of U.S. economic and financial conditions, including forecasts for the federal government, incomes, population, prices and wages, and state and local governments, over a long-term (10- to 25-year) forecast period.

Additional information is available from

IHS Global Insight
1000 Winter Street
Suite 4300N
Waltham, MA 02451-124
http://www.ihsglobalinsight.com/

Appendix D
References

Broughman, S.P., and Swaim, N.L. (2013). *Characteristics of Private Schools in the United States: Results From the 2011–12 Private School Universe Survey* (NCES 2013-316). National Center for Education Statistics.

Chapman, C., Laird, J., Ifill, N., and KewalRamani, A. (2011). *Trends in High School Dropout and Completion Rates in the United States: 1972–2009* (NCES 2012-006). National Center for Education Statistics, Institute of Education Sciences, U.S. Department of Education. Washington, DC.

Gamkhar, S., and Oates, W. (1996). Asymmetries in the Response to Increases and Decreases in Intergovernmental Grants: Some Empirical Findings. *National Tax Journal, 49*(3): 501–512.

Greene, W. (2000). *Econometric Analysis.* New Jersey: Prentice-Hall.

Hussar, W.J. (1999). *Predicting the Need for Newly Hired Teachers in the United States to 2008–09* (NCES 99-026). National Center for Education Statistics, U.S. Department of Education. Washington, DC.

Inman, R.P. (1979). The Fiscal Performance of Local Governments: An Interpretive Review. In P. Mieszkowski and M. Straszheim (Eds.), *Current Issues in Urban Economics,* (pp. 270–321). Baltimore: Johns Hopkins Press.

Intriligator, M.D. (1978). *Econometric Models, Techniques, & Applications.* New Jersey: Prentice-Hall, Inc.

IHS Global Insight, "U.S. Monthly Model January 2013: Short-Term Projections."

Jackson, K.W., Jang, D., Sukasih, A., and Peeckson, S. (2005). *Integrated Postsecondary Education Data System Data Quality Study* (NCES 2005-175). National Center for Education Statistics, Institute of Education Sciences, U.S. Department of Education. Washington, DC.

Johnston, J., and Dinardo, J. (1996). *Econometric Methods.* New York: McGraw-Hill.

Judge, G., Hill, W., Griffiths, R., Lutkepohl, H., and Lee, T. (1985). *The Theory and Practice of Econometrics.* New York: John Wiley and Sons.

Kalton, G., Winglee, M., Krawchuk, S., and Levine, D. (2000) *Quality Profile for SASS, Rounds 1–3: 1987–1995, Aspects of the Quality of Data in the Schools and Staffing Surveys (SASS)* (NCES 2000-308). National Center for Education Statistics, Institute of Education Sciences, U.S. Department of Education. Washington, DC.

Knapp, L.G., Kelly-Reid, J.E., and Ginder, S.A. (2011a). *Employees in Postsecondary Institutions, Fall 2010, and Salaries of Full-Time Instructional Staff, 2010–11* (NCES 2012-276). National Center for Education Statistics, Institute of Education Sciences, U.S. Department of Education. Washington, DC.

Knapp, L.G., Kelly-Reid, J.E., and Ginder, S.A. (2011b). *Postsecondary Institutions and Price of Attendance in the United States: 2011–12, Degrees and Other Awards Conferred: 2010–11, and 12-Month Enrollment: 2010–11* (NCES 2012-289rev). National Center for Education Statistics, Institute of Education Sciences, U.S. Department of Education. Washington, DC.

Knapp, L.G., Kelly-Reid, J.E., and Ginder, S.A. (2012a). *2011–12 Integrated Postsecondary Education Data System (IPEDS) Methodology Report* (NCES 2012-293). National Center for Education Statistics, Institute of Education Sciences, U.S. Department of Education. Washington, DC.

Knapp, L.G., Kelly-Reid, J.E., and Ginder, S.A. (2012b). *Enrollment in Postsecondary Institutions, Fall 2011; Financial Statistics, Fiscal Year 2011; and Graduation Rates, Selected Cohorts, 2003–08* (NCES 2012-174rev). National Center for Education Statistics, Institute of Education Sciences, U.S. Department of Education. Washington, DC.

Mitias, P., and Turnbull, G. (2001). Grant Illusion, Tax Illusion, and Local Government Spending. *Public Finance Review, 29*(5): 347–368.

U.S. Department of Commerce, Census Bureau, 2012 National Population Projections, retrieved December 19, 2012, from http://www.census.gov/population/projections/data/national/2012/downloadablefiles.html.

U.S. Department of Commerce, Census Bureau, Current Population Reports, "Social and Economic Characteristics of Students," 2011.

U.S. Department of Commerce, Census Bureau, Population Estimates, retrieved December 19, 2012, from http://www.census.gov/popest/data/index.html.

U.S. Department of Commerce, Census Bureau, 2005 Interim State Population Projections, retrieved November 2, 2008, from http://www.census.gov/population/projections/data/state/projectionsagesex.html.

Appendix E
List of Abbreviations

ADA	Average daily attendance
CCD	Common Core of Data
CPI	Consumer Price Index
CPS	Current Population Survey
CV	Coefficient of Variation
D.W. statistic	Durbin-Watson statistic
FTE	Full-time-equivalent
HEGIS	Higher Education General Information Survey
IPEDS	Integrated Postsecondary Education Data System
IPEDS-C	Integrated Postsecondary Education Data System, Completions Survey
IPEDS-EF	Integrated Postsecondary Education Data System, Fall Enrollment Survey
MAPE	Mean absolute percentage error
NCES	National Center for Education Statistics
PreK	Prekindergarten
PreK–8	Prekindergarten through grade 8
PreK–12	Prekindergarten through grade 12
PSS	Private School Survey
SASS	Schools and Staffing Survey

This page intentionally left blank.

Appendix F
Glossary

A

Academic support This category of college expenditures includes expenditures for support services that are an integral part of the institution's primary missions of instruction, research, or public service. It also includes expenditures for libraries, galleries, audio/visual services, academic computing support, ancillary support, academic administration, personnel development, and course and curriculum development.

Achievement gap Occurs when one group of students outperforms another group, and the difference in average scores for the two groups is statistically significant (that is, larger than the margin of error).

Achievement levels, NAEP Specific achievement levels for each subject area and grade to provide a context for interpreting student performance. At this time they are being used on a trial basis.

> ***Basic***—denotes partial mastery of the knowledge and skills that are fundamental for *proficient* work at a given grade.
>
> ***Proficient***—represents solid academic performance. Students reaching this level have demonstrated competency over challenging subject matter.
>
> ***Advanced***—signifies superior performance.

Achievement test An examination that measures the extent to which a person has acquired certain information or mastered certain skills, usually as a result of specific instruction.

ACT The ACT (formerly the American College Testing Program) assessment program measures educational development and readiness to pursue college-level coursework in English, mathematics, natural science, and social studies. Student performance on the tests does not reflect innate ability and is influenced by a student's educational preparedness.

Administrative support staff Staff whose activities are concerned with support of teaching and administrative duties of the office of the principal or department chairpersons, including clerical staff and secretaries.

Advanced Placement (AP) A program of tertiary-level courses and examinations, taught by specially qualified teachers, that provides opportunities for secondary school students to earn undergraduate credits for first-year university courses. The schools and teachers offering AP programs must meet College Board requirements and are monitored.

Agriculture Courses designed to improve competencies in agricultural occupations. Included is the study of agricultural production, supplies, mechanization and products, agricultural science, forestry, and related services.

Alternative school A public elementary/secondary school that serves students whose needs cannot be met in a regular, special education, or vocational school; may provide nontraditional education; and may serve as an adjunct to a regular school. Although alternative schools fall outside the categories of regular, special education, and vocational education, they may provide similar services or curriculum. Some examples of alternative schools are schools for potential dropouts; residential treatment centers for substance abuse (if they provide elementary or secondary education); schools for chronic truants; and schools for students with behavioral problems.

Appropriation (federal funds) Budget authority provided through the congressional appropriation process that permits federal agencies to incur obligations and to make payments.

Appropriation (institutional revenues) An amount (other than a grant or contract) received from or made available to an institution through an act of a legislative body.

Associate's degree A degree granted for the successful completion of a sub-baccalaureate program of studies, usually requiring at least 2 years (or equivalent) of full-time college-level study. This includes degrees granted in a cooperative or work-study program.

Autocorrelation Correlation of the error terms from different observations of the same variable. Also called Serial correlation.

Auxiliary enterprises This category includes those essentially self-supporting operations which exist to furnish a service to students, faculty, or staff, and which charge a fee that is directly related to, although not necessarily equal to, the cost of the service. Examples are residence halls, food services, college stores, and intercollegiate athletics.

Average daily attendance (ADA) The aggregate attendance of a school during a reporting period (normally a school year) divided by the number of days school is in session during this period. Only days on which the pupils are under the guidance and direction of teachers should be considered days in session.

Average daily membership (ADM) The aggregate membership of a school during a reporting period (normally a school year) divided by the number of days school is in session during this period. Only days on which the pupils are under the guidance and direction of teachers should be considered as days in session. The average daily membership for groups of schools having varying lengths of terms is the average of the average daily memberships obtained for the individual schools. Membership includes all pupils who are enrolled, even if they do not actually attend.

Averaged freshman graduation rate (AFGR) A measure of the percentage of the incoming high school freshman class that graduates 4 years later. It is calculated by taking the number of graduates with a regular diploma and dividing that number by the estimated count of incoming freshman 4 years earlier, as reported through the NCES Common Core of Data (CCD). The estimated count of incoming freshman is the sum of the number of 8th-graders 5 years earlier, the number of 9th-graders 4 years earlier (when current seniors were freshman), and the number of 10th-graders 3 years earlier, divided by 3. The purpose of this averaging is to account for the high rate of grade retention in the freshman year, which adds 9th-grade repeaters from the previous year to the number of students in the incoming freshman class each year. Ungraded students are allocated to individual grades proportional to each state's enrollment in those grades. The AFGR treats students who transfer out of a school or district in the same way as it treats students from that school or district who drop out.

B

Bachelor's degree A degree granted for the successful completion of a baccalaureate program of studies, usually requiring at least 4 years (or equivalent) of full-time college-level study. This includes degrees granted in a cooperative or work-study program.

Books Nonperiodical printed publications bound in hard or soft covers, or in loose-leaf format, of at least 49 pages, exclusive of the cover pages; juvenile nonperiodical publications of any length found in hard or soft covers.

Breusch-Godfrey serial correlation LM test A statistic testing the independence of errors in least-squares regression against alternatives of first-order and higher degrees of serial correlation. The test belongs to a class of asymptotic tests known as the Lagrange multiplier (LM) tests.

Budget authority (BA) Authority provided by law to enter into obligations that will result in immediate or future outlays. It may be classified by the period of availability (1-year, multiple-year, no-year), by the timing of congressional action (current or permanent), or by the manner of determining the amount available (definite or indefinite).

Business Program of instruction that prepares individuals for a variety of activities in planning, organizing, directing, and controlling business office systems and procedures.

C

Capital outlay Funds for the acquisition of land and buildings; building construction, remodeling, and additions; the initial installation or extension of service systems and other built-in equipment; and site improvement. The category also encompasses architectural and engineering services including the development of blueprints.

Career/technical education (CTE) In high school, encompasses occupational education, which teaches skills required in specific occupations or occupational clusters, as well as nonoccupational CTE, which includes family and consumer sciences education (i.e., courses that prepare students for roles outside the paid labor market) and general labor market preparation (i.e., courses that teach general employment skills such as word processing and introductory technology skills).

Carnegie unit The number of credits a secondary student received for a course taken every day, one period per day, for a full year; a factor used to standardize all credits indicated on secondary school transcripts across studies.

Catholic school A private school over which a Roman Catholic church group exercises some control or provides some form of subsidy. Catholic schools for the most part include those operated or supported by a parish, a group of parishes, a diocese, or a Catholic religious order.

Central cities The largest cities, with 50,000 or more inhabitants, in a Metropolitan Statistical Area (MSA). Additional cities within the metropolitan area can also be classified as "central cities" if they meet certain employment, population, and employment/residence ratio requirements.

Certificate A formal award certifying the satisfactory completion of a postsecondary education program. Certificates can be awarded at any level of postsecondary education and include awards below the associate's degree level.

Charter School A school providing free public elementary and/or secondary education to eligible students under a specific charter granted by the state legislature or other appropriate authority, and designated by such authority to be a charter school.

City school See Locale codes.

Class size The membership of a class at a given date.

Classification of Instructional Programs (CIP) The CIP is a taxonomic coding scheme that contains titles and descriptions of primarily postsecondary instructional programs. It was developed to facilitate NCES' collection and reporting of postsecondary degree completions by major field of study using standard classifications that capture the majority of reportable program activity. It was originally published in 1980 and was revised in 1985, 1990, 2000, and 2010.

Classification of Secondary School Courses (CSSC) A modification of the Classification of Instructional Programs used for classifying high school courses. The CSSC contains over 2,200 course codes that help compare the thousands of high school transcripts collected from different schools.

Classroom teacher A staff member assigned the professional activities of instructing pupils in self-contained classes or courses, or in classroom situations; usually expressed in full-time equivalents.

Coefficient of variation (CV) Represents the ratio of the standard error to the estimate. For example, a CV of 30 percent indicates that the standard error of the estimate is equal to 30 percent of the estimate's value. The CV is used to compare the amount of variation relative to the magnitude of the estimate. A CV of 30 percent or greater indicates that an estimate should be interpreted with caution. For a discussion of standard errors, see Appendix A: Guide to Sources.

Cohort A group of individuals that have a statistical factor in common, for example, year of birth.

Cohort-component method A method for estimating and projecting a population that is distinguished by its ability to preserve knowledge of an age distribution of a population (which may be of a single sex, race, and Hispanic origin) over time.

College A postsecondary school that offers general or liberal arts education, usually leading to an associate's, bachelor's, master's, or doctor's degree. Junior colleges and community colleges are included under this terminology.

Combined school A school that encompasses instruction at both the elementary and the secondary levels; includes schools starting with grade 6 or below and ending with grade 9 or above.

Combined school (2007–08 Schools and Staffing Survey) A school with at least one grade lower than 7 and at least one grade higher than 8; schools with only ungraded classes are included with combined schools.

Combined Statistical Area (CSA) A combination of Core Based Statistical Areas (see below), each of which contains a core with a substantial population nucleus as well as adjacent communities having a high degree of economic and social integration with that core. A CSA is a region with social and economic ties as measured by commuting, but at lower levels than are found within each component area. CSAs represent larger regions that reflect broader social and economic interactions, such as wholesaling, commodity distribution, and weekend recreation activities.

Computer science A group of instructional programs that describes computer and information sciences, including computer programming, data processing, and information systems.

Constant dollars Dollar amounts that have been adjusted by means of price and cost indexes to eliminate inflationary factors and allow direct comparison across years.

Consumer Price Index (CPI) This price index measures the average change in the cost of a fixed market basket of goods and services purchased by consumers. Indexes vary for specific areas or regions, periods of time, major groups of consumer expenditures, and population groups. The CPI reflects spending patterns for two population groups: (1) all urban consumers and urban wage earners and (2) clerical workers. CPIs are calculated for both the calendar year and the school year using the U.S. All Items CPI for All Urban Consumers (CPI-U). The calendar year CPI is the same as the annual CPI-U. The school year CPI is calculated by adding the monthly CPI-U figures, beginning with July of the first year and ending with June of the following year, and then dividing that figure by 12.

Consumption That portion of income which is spent on the purchase of goods and services rather than being saved.

Control of institutions A classification of institutions of elementary/secondary or postsecondary education by whether the institution is operated by publicly elected or appointed officials and derives its primary support from public funds (public control) or is operated by privately elected or appointed officials and derives its major source of funds from private sources (private control).

Core Based Statistical Area (CBSA) A population nucleus and the nearby communities having a high degree of economic and social integration with that nucleus. Each CBSA includes at least one urban area of 10,000 or more people and one or more counties. In addition to a "central county" (or counties), additional "outlying counties" are included in the CBSA if they meet specified requirements of commuting to or from the central counties.

Credit The unit of value, awarded for the successful completion of certain courses, intended to indicate the quantity of course instruction in relation to the total requirements for a diploma, certificate, or degree. Credits are frequently expressed in terms such as "Carnegie units," "semester credit hours," and "quarter credit hours."

Current dollars Dollar amounts that have not been adjusted to compensate for inflation.

Current expenditures (elementary/secondary) The expenditures for operating local public schools, excluding capital outlay and interest on school debt. These expenditures include such items as salaries for school personnel, benefits, student transportation, school books and materials, and energy costs. Beginning in 1980–81, expenditures for state administration are excluded.

> **Instruction expenditures** Includes expenditures for activities related to the interaction between teacher and students. Includes salaries and benefits for teachers and instructional aides, textbooks, supplies, and purchased services such as instruction via television. Also included are tuition expenditures to other local education agencies.

Administration expenditures Includes expenditures for school administration (i.e., the office of the principal, full-time department chairpersons, and graduation expenses), general administration (the superintendent and board of education and their immediate staff), and other support services expenditures.

Transportation Includes expenditures for vehicle operation, monitoring, and vehicle servicing and maintenance.

Food services Includes all expenditures associated with providing food to students and staff in a school or school district. The services include preparing and serving regular and incidental meals or snacks in connection with school activities, as well as the delivery of food to schools.

Enterprise operations Includes expenditures for activities that are financed, at least in part, by user charges, similar to a private business. These include operations funded by sales of products or services, together with amounts for direct program support made by state education agencies for local school districts.

Current expenditures per pupil in average daily attendance Current expenditures for the regular school term divided by the average daily attendance of full-time pupils (or full-time equivalency of pupils) during the term. See also Current expenditures and Average daily attendance.

Current-fund expenditures (postsecondary education) Money spent to meet current operating costs, including salaries, wages, utilities, student services, public services, research libraries, scholarships and fellowships, auxiliary enterprises, hospitals, and independent operations; excludes loans, capital expenditures, and investments.

Current-fund revenues (postsecondary education) Money received during the current fiscal year from revenue which can be used to pay obligations currently due, and surpluses reappropriated for the current fiscal year.

D

Deaf-blindness See Disabilities, children with.

Deafness See Disabilities, children with.

Default rate The percentage of loans that are in delinquency and have not been repaid according to the terms of the loan. According to the federal government, a federal student loan is in default if there has been no payment on the loan in 270 days. The Department of Education calculates a *2-year cohort* default rate, which is the percentage of students who entered repayment in a given fiscal year (from October 1 to September 30) and then defaulted within the following two fiscal years.

Degree An award conferred by a college, university, or other postsecondary education institution as official recognition for the successful completion of a program of studies.

Refers specifically to associate's or higher degrees conferred by degree-granting institutions. See also Associate's degree, Bachelor's degree, Master's degree, and Doctor's degree.

Degree/certificate-seeking student A student enrolled in courses for credit and recognized by the institution as seeking a degree, certificate, or other formal award. High school students also enrolled in postsecondary courses for credit are not considered degree/certificate-seeking. See also Degree and Certificate.

Degree-granting institutions Postsecondary institutions that are eligible for Title IV federal financial aid programs and grant an associate's or higher degree. For an institution to be eligible to participate in Title IV financial aid programs it must offer a program of at least 300 clock hours in length, have accreditation recognized by the U.S. Department of Education, have been in business for at least 2 years, and have signed a participation agreement with the Department.

Degrees of freedom The number of free or linearly independent sample observations used in the calculation of a statistic. In a time series regression with t time periods and k independent variables including a constant term, there would be t minus k degrees of freedom.

Dependency status A designation of whether postsecondary students are financially dependent on their parents or financially independent of their parents. Undergraduates are assumed to be dependent unless they meet one of the following criteria: are age 24 or older, are married or have legal dependents other than a spouse, are veterans, are orphans or wards of the court, or provide documentation that they self-supporting.

Dependent variable A mathematical variable whose value is determined by that of one or more other variables in a function. In regression analysis, when a random variable, y, is expressed as a function of variables $x1, x2, ... xk$, plus a stochastic term, then y is known as the "dependent variable."

Disabilities, children with Those children evaluated as having any of the following impairments and needing special education and related services because of these impairments. (These definitions apply specifically to data from the U.S. Office of Special Education and Rehabilitative Services presented in this publication.)

Deaf-blindness Having concomitant hearing and visual impairments which cause such severe communication and other developmental and educational problems that the student cannot be accommodated in special education programs solely for deaf or blind students.

Deafness Having a hearing impairment which is so severe that the student is impaired in processing linguistic information through hearing (with or without amplification) and which adversely affects educational performance.

Hearing impairment Having a hearing impairment, whether permanent or fluctuating, which adversely affects the student's educational performance, but which is not included under the definition of "deaf" in this section.

Intellectual disability Having significantly subaverage general intellectual functioning, existing concurrently with defects in adaptive behavior and manifested during the developmental period, which adversely affects the child's educational performance.

Multiple disabilities Having concomitant impairments (such as intellectually disabled-blind, intellectually disabled-orthopedically impaired, etc.), the combination of which causes such severe educational problems that the student cannot be accommodated in special education programs solely for one of the impairments. Term does not include deaf-blind students.

Orthopedic impairment Having a severe orthopedic impairment which adversely affects a student's educational performance. The term includes impairment resulting from congenital anomaly, disease, or other causes.

Other health impairment Having limited strength, vitality, or alertness due to chronic or acute health problems, such as a heart condition, tuberculosis, rheumatic fever, nephritis, asthma, sickle cell anemia, hemophilia, epilepsy, lead poisoning, leukemia, or diabetes which adversely affect the student's educational performance.

Serious emotional disturbance Exhibiting one or more of the following characteristics over a long period of time, to a marked degree, and adversely affecting educational performance: an inability to learn which cannot be explained by intellectual, sensory, or health factors; an inability to build or maintain satisfactory interpersonal relationships with peers and teachers; inappropriate types of behavior or feelings under normal circumstances; a general pervasive mood of unhappiness or depression; or a tendency to develop physical symptoms or fears associated with personal or school problems. This term does not include children who are socially maladjusted, unless they also display one or more of the listed characteristics.

Specific learning disability Having a disorder in one or more of the basic psychological processes involved in understanding or in using spoken or written language, which may manifest itself in an imperfect ability to listen, think, speak, read, write, spell, or do mathematical calculations. The term includes such conditions as perceptual disabilities, brain injury, minimal brain dysfunction, dyslexia, and developmental aphasia. The term does not include children who have learning problems which are primarily the result of visual, hearing, or environmental, cultural, or economic disadvantage.

Speech/language impairment Having a communication disorder, such as stuttering, impaired articulation, language impairment, or voice impairment, which adversely affects the student's educational performance.

Visual impairment Having a visual impairment which, even with correction, adversely affects the student's educational performance. The term includes partially seeing and blind children.

Discipline divisions Degree programs that include breakouts to the 6-digit level of the Classification of Instructional Programs (CIP). See also Fields of study.

Disposable personal income Current income received by people less their contributions for social insurance, personal tax, and nontax payments. It is the income available to people for spending and saving. Nontax payments include passport fees, fines and penalties, donations, and tuitions and fees paid to schools and hospitals operated mainly by the government. See also Personal income.

Doctor's degree The highest award a student can earn for graduate study. Includes such degrees as the Doctor of Education (Ed.D.); the Doctor of Juridical Science (S.J.D.); the Doctor of Public Health (Dr.P.H.); and the Doctor of Philosophy (Ph.D.) in any field, such as agronomy, food technology, education, engineering, public administration, ophthalmology, or radiology. The doctor's degree classification encompasses three main subcategories—research/scholarship degrees, professional practice degrees, and other degrees—which are described below.

Doctor's degree—research/scholarship A Ph.D. or other doctor's degree that requires advanced work beyond the master's level, including the preparation and defense of a dissertation based on original research, or the planning and execution of an original project demonstrating substantial artistic or scholarly achievement. Examples of this type of degree may include the following and others, as designated by the awarding institution: the Ed.D. (in education), D.M.A. (in musical arts), D.B.A. (in business administration), D.Sc. (in science), D.A. (in arts), or D.M (in medicine).

Doctor's degree—professional practice A doctor's degree that is conferred upon completion of a program providing the knowledge and skills for the recognition, credential, or license required for professional practice. The degree is awarded after a period of study such that the total time to the degree, including both preprofessional and professional preparation, equals at least 6 full-time-equivalent academic years. Some doctor's degrees of this type were formerly classified as first-professional degrees. Examples of this type of degree may include the following and others, as designated by the awarding institution: the D.C. or D.C.M. (in chiropractic); D.D.S. or D.M.D. (in dentistry); L.L.B. or J.D. (in law); M.D. (in medicine); O.D. (in optometry); D.O. (in osteopathic medicine); Pharm.D. (in pharmacy); D.P.M., Pod.D., or D.P. (in podiatry); or D.V.M. (in veterinary medicine).

Doctor's degree—other A doctor's degree that does not meet the definition of either a doctor's degree—research/scholarship or a doctor's degree—professional practice.

Double exponential smoothing A method that takes a single smoothed average component of demand and smoothes it a second time to allow for estimation of a trend effect.

Dropout The term is used to describe both the event of leaving school before completing high school and the status of an individual who is not in school and who is not a high school completer. High school completers include both graduates of school programs as well as those completing high school through equivalency programs such as the General Educational Development (GED) program. Transferring from a public school to a private school, for example, is not regarded as a dropout event. A person who drops out of school may later return and graduate but is called a "dropout" at the time he or she leaves school. Measures to describe these behaviors include the event dropout rate (or the closely related school persistence rate), the status dropout rate, and the high school completion rate.

Durbin-Watson statistic A statistic testing the independence of errors in least squares regression against the alternative of first-order serial correlation. The statistic is a simple linear transformation of the first-order serial correlation of residuals and, although its distribution is unknown, it is tested by bounding statistics that follow R. L. Anderson's distribution.

E

Early childhood school Early childhood program schools serve students in prekindergarten, kindergarten, transitional (or readiness) kindergarten, and/or transitional first (or prefirst) grade.

Econometrics The quantitative examination of economic trends and relationships using statistical techniques, and the development, examination, and refinement of those techniques.

Education specialist/professional diploma A certificate of advanced graduate studies that advance educators in their instructional and leadership skills beyond a master's degree level of competence.

Educational and general expenditures The sum of current funds expenditures on instruction, research, public service, academic support, student services, institutional support, operation and maintenance of plant, and awards from restricted and unrestricted funds.

Educational attainment The highest grade of regular school attended and completed.

Educational attainment (Current Population Survey) This measure uses March CPS data to estimate the percentage of civilian, noninstitutionalized people who have achieved certain levels of educational attainment. Estimates of educational attainment do not differentiate between those who graduated from public schools, those who graduated from private schools, and those who earned a GED; these estimates also include individuals who earned their credential or completed their highest level of education outside of the United States.

1972–1991 During this period, an individual's educational attainment was considered to be his or her last fully completed year of school. Individuals who completed 12 years of schooling were deemed to be high school graduates, as were those who began but did not complete the first year of college. Respondents who completed 16 or more years of schooling were counted as college graduates.

1992–present Beginning in 1992, CPS asked respondents to report their highest level of school completed or their highest degree received. This change means that some data collected before 1992 are not strictly comparable with data collected from 1992 onward and that care must be taken when making comparisons across years. The revised survey question emphasizes credentials received rather than the last grade level attended or completed. The new categories include the following:

- High school graduate, high school diploma, or the equivalent (e.g., GED)
- Some college but no degree
- Associate's degree in college, occupational/vocational program
- Associate's degree in college, academic program (e.g., A.A., A.S., A.A.S.)
- Bachelor's degree (e.g., B.A., A.B., B.S.)
- Master's degree (e.g., M.A., M.S., M.Eng., M.Ed., M.S.W., M.B.A.)
- Professional school degree (e.g., M.D., D.D.S., D.V.M., LL.B., J.D.)
- Doctor's degree (e.g., Ph.D., Ed.D.)

Elementary education/programs Learning experiences concerned with the knowledge, skills, appreciations, attitudes, and behavioral characteristics which are considered to be needed by all pupils in terms of their awareness of life within our culture and the world of work, and which normally may be achieved during the elementary school years (usually kindergarten through grade 8 or kindergarten through grade 6), as defined by applicable state laws and regulations.

Elementary school A school classified as elementary by state and local practice and composed of any span of grades not above grade 8.

Elementary/secondary school Includes only schools that are part of state and local school systems, and also most nonprofit private elementary/secondary schools, both religiously affiliated and nonsectarian. Includes regular, alternative, vocational, and special education schools. U.S. totals exclude federal schools for American Indians, and federal schools on military posts and other federal installations.

Employees in degree-granting institutions Persons employed by degree-granting institutions, who are classified into the following occupational categories in this publication:

Executive/administrative/managerial staff Employees whose assignments require management of the institution or of a customarily recognized department or subdivision thereof. These employees perform work that is directly related to management policies or general business operations and that requires them to exercise discretion and independent judgment.

Faculty (instruction/research/public service) Employees whose principal activities are for the purpose of providing instruction or teaching, research, or public service. These employees may hold such titles as professor, associate professor, assistant professor, instructor, or lecturer. Graduate assistants are not included in this category.

Graduate assistants Graduate-level students who are employed on a part-time basis for the primary purpose of assisting in classroom or laboratory instruction or in the conduct of research.

Nonprofessional staff Employees whose primary activities can be classified as one of the following: technical and paraprofessional work (which generally requires less formal training and experience than required for professional status); clerical and secretarial work; skilled crafts work; or service/maintenance work.

Other professional staff Employees who perform academic support, student service, and institutional support and who need either a degree at the bachelor's or higher level or experience of such kind and amount as to provide a comparable background.

Professional staff Employees who are classified as executive/administrative/managerial staff, faculty, graduate assistants, or other professional staff.

Employment Includes civilian, noninstitutional people who: (1) worked during any part of the survey week as paid employees; worked in their own business, profession, or farm; or worked 15 hours or more as unpaid workers in a family-owned enterprise; or (2) were not working but had jobs or businesses from which they were temporarily absent due to illness, bad weather, vacation, labor-management dispute, or personal reasons whether or not they were seeking another job.

Employment (Current Population Survey) According to the October Current Population Survey (CPS), employed persons are persons age 16 or older who, during the reference week, (1) did any work at all (at least 1 hour) as paid employees or (2) were not working but had jobs or businesses from which they were temporarily absent because of vacation, illness, bad weather, child care problems, maternity or paternity leave, labor-management dispute, job training, or other family or personal reasons, whether or not they were paid for the time off or were seeking other jobs.

Employment status A classification of individuals as employed (either full or part time), unemployed (looking for work or on layoff), or not in the labor force (due to being retired, having unpaid employment, or some other reason).

Endowment A trust fund set aside to provide a perpetual source of revenue from the proceeds of the endowment investments. Endowment funds are often created by donations from benefactors of an institution, who may designate the use of the endowment revenue. Normally, institutions or their representatives manage the investments, but they are not permitted to spend the endowment fund itself, only the proceeds from the investments. Typical uses of endowments would be an endowed chair for a particular department or for a scholarship fund. Endowment totals tabulated in this book also include funds functioning as endowments, such as funds left over from the previous year and placed with the endowment investments by the institution. These funds may be withdrawn by the institution and spent as current funds at any time. Endowments are evaluated by two different measures, book value and market value. Book value is the purchase price of the endowment investment. Market value is the current worth of the endowment investment. Thus, the book value of a stock held in an endowment fund would be the purchase price of the stock. The market value of the stock would be its selling price as of a given day.

Engineering Instructional programs that describe the mathematical and natural science knowledge gained by study, experience, and practice and applied with judgment to develop ways to utilize the materials and forces of nature economically. Include programs that prepare individuals to support and assist engineers and similar professionals.

English A group of instructional programs that describes the English language arts, including composition, creative writing, and the study of literature.

English language learner (ELL) An individual who, due to any of the reasons listed below, has sufficient difficulty speaking, reading, writing, or understanding the English language to be denied the opportunity to learn successfully in classrooms where the language of instruction is English or to participate fully in the larger U.S. society. Such an individual (1) was not born in the United States or has a native language other than English; (2) comes from environments where a language other than English is dominant; or (3) is an American Indian or Alaska Native and comes from environments where a language other than English has had a significant impact on the individual's level of English language proficiency.

Enrollment The total number of students registered in a given school unit at a given time, generally in the fall of a year.

Estimate A numerical value obtained from a statistical sample and assigned to a population parameter. The particular value yielded by an estimator in a given set of circumstances or the rule by which such particular values are calculated.

Estimating equation An equation involving observed quantities and an unknown that serves to estimate the latter.

Estimation Estimation is concerned with inference about the numerical value of unknown population values from incomplete data, such as a sample. If a single figure is calculated for each unknown parameter, the process is called point estimation. If an interval is calculated within which the parameter is likely, in some sense, to lie, the process is called interval estimation.

Executive/administrative/managerial staff See Employees in degree-granting institutions.

Expenditures, Total For elementary/secondary schools, these include all charges for current outlays plus capital outlays and interest on school debt. For degree-granting institutions, these include current outlays plus capital outlays. For government, these include charges net of recoveries and other correcting transactions other than for retirement of debt, investment in securities, extension of credit, or as agency transactions. Government expenditures include only external transactions, such as the provision of perquisites or other payments in kind. Aggregates for groups of governments exclude intergovernmental transactions among the governments.

Expenditures per pupil Charges incurred for a particular period of time divided by a student unit of measure, such as average daily attendance or fall enrollment.

Exponential smoothing A method used in time series analysis to smooth or to predict a series. There are various forms, but all are based on the supposition that more remote history has less importance than more recent history.

Extracurricular activities Activities that are not part of the required curriculum and that take place outside of the regular course of study. They include both school-sponsored (e.g., varsity athletics, drama, and debate clubs) and community-sponsored (e.g., hobby clubs and youth organizations like the Junior Chamber of Commerce or Boy Scouts) activities.

F

Faculty (instruction/research/public service) See Employees in degree-granting institutions.

Family A group of two or more people (one of whom is the householder) related by birth, marriage, or adoption and residing together. All such people (including related subfamily members) are considered as members of one family.

Family income Includes all monetary income from all sources (including jobs, businesses, interest, rent, and social security payments) over a 12-month period. The income of nonrelatives living in the household is excluded, but the income of all family members age 15 or older (age 14 or older in years prior to 1989), including those temporarily living outside of the household, is included. In the October CPS, family income is determined from a single question asked of the household respondent.

Federal funds Amounts collected and used by the federal government for the general purposes of the government. There are four types of federal fund accounts: the general fund, special funds, public enterprise funds, and intragovernmental funds. The major federal fund is the general fund, which is derived from general taxes and borrowing. Federal funds also include certain earmarked collections, such as those generated by and used to finance a continuing cycle of business-type operations.

Federal sources (postsecondary degree-granting institutions) Includes federal appropriations, grants, and contracts, and federally funded research and development centers (FFRDCs). Federally subsidized student loans are not included.

Fields of study The primary field of concentration in postsecondary certificates and degrees. In the Integrated Postsecondary Education Data System (IPEDS), refers to degree programs that are broken out only to the 2-digit level of the Classification of Instructional Programs (CIP). See also Discipline divisions.

Financial aid Grants, loans, assistantships, scholarships, fellowships, tuition waivers, tuition discounts, veteran's benefits, employer aid (tuition reimbursement), and other monies (other than from relatives or friends) provided to students to help them meet expenses. Except where designated, includes Title IV subsidized and unsubsidized loans made directly to students.

First-order serial correlation When errors in one time period are correlated directly with errors in the ensuing time period.

First-professional degree NCES no longer uses this classification. Most degrees formerly classified as first-professional (such as M.D., D.D.S., Pharm.D., D.V.M., and J.D.) are now classified as doctor's degrees—professional practice. However, master's of divinity degrees are now classified as master's degrees.

First-time student (undergraduate) A student who has no prior postsecondary experience (except as noted below) attending any institution for the first time at the undergraduate level. Includes students enrolled in the fall term who attended college for the first time in the prior summer term, and students who entered with advanced standing (college credits earned before graduation from high school).

Fiscal year A period of 12 months for which accounting records are compiled. Institutions and states may designate their own accounting period, though most states use a July 1 through June 30 accounting year. The yearly accounting period for the federal government begins on October 1 and ends on the following September 30. The fiscal year is designated by the calendar year in which it ends; e.g., fiscal year 2006 begins on October 1, 2005, and ends on September 30, 2006. (From fiscal year 1844 to fiscal year 1976, the federal fiscal year began on July 1 and ended on the following June 30.)

Forecast An estimate of the future based on rational study and analysis of available pertinent data, as opposed to subjective prediction.

Forecasting Assessing the magnitude that a quantity will assume at some future point in time, as distinct from "estimation," which attempts to assess the magnitude of an already existent quantity.

Foreign languages A group of instructional programs that describes the structure and use of language that is common or indigenous to people of a given community or nation, geographical area, or cultural traditions. Programs cover such features as sound, literature, syntax, phonology, semantics, sentences, prose, and verse, as well as the development of skills and attitudes used in communicating and evaluating thoughts and feelings through oral and written language.

For-profit institution A private institution in which the individual(s) or agency in control receives compensation other than wages, rent, or other expenses for the assumption of risk.

Free or reduced-price lunch See National School Lunch Program.

Full-time enrollment The number of students enrolled in postsecondary education courses with total credit load equal to at least 75 percent of the normal full-time course load. At the undergraduate level, full-time enrollment typically includes students who have a credit load of 12 or more semester or quarter credits. At the postbaccalaureate level, full-time enrollment includes students who typically have a credit load of 9 or more semester or quarter credits, as well as other students who are considered full time by their institutions.

Full-time-equivalent (FTE) enrollment For postsecondary institutions, enrollment of full-time students, plus the full-time equivalent of part-time students. The full-time equivalent of the part-time students is estimated using different factors depending on the type and control of institution and level of student.

FTE staff Full-time staff, plus the full-time equivalent of the part-time staff.

FTE teacher See Instructional staff.

Full-time instructional faculty Those members of the instruction/research staff who are employed full time as defined by the institution, including faculty with released time for research and faculty on sabbatical leave. Full-time counts exclude faculty who are employed to teach less than two semesters, three quarters, two trimesters, or two 4-month sessions; replacements for faculty on sabbatical leave or those on leave without pay; faculty for preclinical and clinical medicine; faculty who are donating their services; faculty who are members of military organizations and paid on a different pay scale from civilian employees; those academic officers whose primary duties are administrative; and graduate students who assist in the instruction of courses.

Full-time worker In educational institutions, an employee whose position requires being on the job on school days throughout the school year at least the number of hours the schools are in session. For higher education, a member of an educational institution's staff who is employed full time, as defined by the institution.

Function A mathematical correspondence that assigns exactly one element of one set to each element of the same or another set. A variable that depends on and varies with another.

Functional form A mathematical statement of the relationship among the variables in a model.

G

General administration support services Includes salary, benefits, supplies, and contractual fees for boards of education staff and executive administration. Excludes state administration.

General Educational Development (GED) program Academic instruction to prepare people to take the high school equivalency examination. See also GED recipient.

GED certificate This award is received following successful completion of the General Educational Development (GED) test. The GED program—sponsored by the GED Testing Service (a joint venture of the American Council on Education and Pearson)—enables individuals to demonstrate that they have acquired a level of learning comparable to that of high school graduates. See also High school equivalency certificate.

GED recipient A person who has obtained certification of high school equivalency by meeting state requirements and passing an approved exam, which is intended to provide an appraisal of the person's achievement or performance in the broad subject matter areas usually required for high school graduation.

General program A program of studies designed to prepare students for the common activities of a citizen, family member, and worker. A general program of studies may include instruction in both academic and vocational areas.

Geographic region One of the four regions of the United States used by the U.S. Census Bureau, as follows:

Northeast	Midwest
Connecticut (CT)	Illinois (IL)
Maine (ME)	Indiana (IN)
Massachusetts (MA)	Iowa (IA)
New Hampshire (NH)	Kansas (KS)
New Jersey (NJ)	Michigan (MI)
New York (NY)	Minnesota (MN)
Pennsylvania (PA)	Missouri (MO)
Rhode Island (RI)	Nebraska (NE)
Vermont (VT)	North Dakota (ND)
	Ohio (OH)
	South Dakota (SD)
	Wisconsin (WI)

South
Alabama (AL)
Arkansas (AR)
Delaware (DE)
District of Columbia (DC)
Florida (FL)
Georgia (GA)
Kentucky (KY)
Louisiana (LA)
Maryland (MD)
Mississippi (MS)
North Carolina (NC)
Oklahoma (OK)
South Carolina (SC)
Tennessee (TN)
Texas (TX)
Virginia (VA)
West Virginia (WV)

West
Alaska (AK)
Arizona (AZ)
California (CA)
Colorado (CO)
Hawaii (HI)
Idaho (ID)
Montana (MT)
Nevada (NV)
New Mexico (NM)
Oregon (OR)
Utah (UT)
Washington (WA)
Wyoming (WY)

Government appropriation An amount (other than a grant or contract) received from or made available to an institution through an act of a legislative body.

Government grant or contract Revenues received by a postsecondary institution from a government agency for a specific research project or other program. Examples are research projects, training programs, and student financial assistance.

Graduate An individual who has received formal recognition for the successful completion of a prescribed program of studies.

Graduate assistants See Employees in degree-granting institutions.

Graduate enrollment The number of students who are working towards a master's or doctor's degree and students who are in postbaccalaureate classes but not in degree programs.

Graduate Record Examination (GRE) Multiple-choice examinations administered by the Educational Testing Service and taken by college students who are intending to attend certain graduate schools. There are two types of testing available: (1) the general exam which measures critical thinking, analytical writing, verbal reasoning, and quantitative reasoning skills, and (2) the subject test which is offered in eight specific subjects and gauges undergraduate achievement in a specific field. The subject tests are intended for those who have majored in or have extensive background in that specific area.

Graduation Formal recognition given to an individual for the successful completion of a prescribed program of studies.

Gross domestic product (GDP) The total national output of goods and services valued at market prices. GDP can be viewed in terms of expenditure categories which include purchases of goods and services by consumers and government, gross private domestic investment, and net exports of goods and services. The goods and services included are largely those bought for final use (excluding illegal transactions) in the market economy. A number of inclusions, however, represent imputed values, the most important of which is rental value of owner-occupied housing.

Group quarters Living arrangements where people live or stay in a group situation that is owned or managed by an entity or organization providing housing and/or services for the residents. Group quarters include such places as college residence halls, residential treatment centers, skilled nursing facilities, group homes, military barracks, correctional facilities, and workers' dormitories.

Noninstitutionalized group quarters Include college and university housing, military quarters, facilities for workers and religious groups, and temporary shelters for the homeless.

Institutionalized group quarters Include adult and juvenile correctional facilities, nursing facilities, and other health care facilities.

H

Handicapped See Disabilities, children with.

Head Start A local public or private nonprofit or for-profit entity authorized by the Department of Health and Human Services' Administration for Children and Families to operate a Head Start program to serve children age 3 to compulsory school age, pursuant to section 641(b) and (d) of the Head Start Act.

Hearing impairment See Disabilities, children with.

High school A secondary school offering the final years of high school work necessary for graduation, usually includes grades 10, 11, 12 (in a 6-3-3 plan) or grades 9, 10, 11, and 12 (in a 6-2-4 plan).

High school (2007–08 Schools and Staffing Survey) A school with no grade lower than 7 and at least one grade higher than 8.

High school completer An individual who has been awarded a high school diploma or an equivalent credential, including a General Educational Development (GED) certificate.

High school diploma A formal document regulated by the state certifying the successful completion of a prescribed secondary school program of studies. In some states or communities, high school diplomas are differentiated by type, such as an academic diploma, a general diploma, or a vocational diploma.

High school equivalency certificate A formal document certifying that an individual has met the state requirements for high school graduation equivalency by obtaining satisfactory scores on an approved examination and meeting other performance requirements (if any) set by a state education agency or other appropriate body. One particular version of this certificate is the General Educational Development (GED) test. The GED test is a comprehensive test used primarily to appraise the educational development of students who have not completed their formal high school education and who may earn a high school equivalency certificate by achieving satisfactory scores. GEDs are awarded by the states or other agencies, and the test is developed and distributed by the GED Testing Service (a joint venture of the American Council on Education and Pearson).

High school program A program of studies designed to prepare students for employment and postsecondary education. Three types of programs are often distinguished— academic, vocational, and general. An academic program is designed to prepare students for continued study at a college or university. A vocational program is designed to prepare students for employment in one or more semiskilled, skilled, or technical occupations. A general program is designed to provide students with the understanding and competence to function effectively in a free society and usually represents a mixture of academic and vocational components.

Higher education Study beyond secondary school at an institution that offers programs terminating in an associate's, bachelor's, or higher degree.

Higher education institutions (basic classification and Carnegie classification) See Postsecondary institutions (basic classification by level) and Postsecondary institutions (Carnegie classification of degree-granting institutions)

Higher Education Price Index A price index which measures average changes in the prices of goods and services purchased by colleges and universities through current-fund education and general expenditures (excluding expenditures for sponsored research and auxiliary enterprises).

Hispanic serving institutions Pursuant to 302 (d) of Public Law 102-325 (20 U.S.C. 1059c), most recently amended December 20, 1993, in 2(a)(7) of Public Law 103-208, where Hispanic serving institutions are defined as those with full-time-equivalent undergraduate enrollment of Hispanic students at 25 percent or more.

Historically black colleges and universities Accredited institutions of higher education established prior to 1964 with the principal mission of educating black Americans. Federal regulations (20 USC 1061 (2)) allow for certain exceptions of the founding date.

Hours worked per week According to the October CPS, the number of hours a respondent worked in all jobs in the week prior to the survey interview.

Household All the people who occupy a housing unit. A house, an apartment, a mobile home, a group of rooms, or a single room is regarded as a housing unit when it is occupied or intended for occupancy as separate living quarters, that is, when the occupants do not live and eat with any other people in the structure, and there is direct access from the outside or through a common hall.

Housing unit A house, an apartment, a mobile home, a group of rooms, or a single room that is occupied as separate living quarters.

I

Income tax Taxes levied on net income, that is, on gross income less certain deductions permitted by law. These taxes can be levied on individuals or on corporations or unincorporated businesses where the income is taxed distinctly from individual income.

Independent operations A group of self-supporting activities under control of a college or university. For purposes of financial surveys conducted by the National Center for Education Statistics, this category is composed principally of federally funded research and development centers (FFRDC).

Independent variable In regression analysis, a random variable, y, is expressed as a function of variables $x1$, $x2$, ... xk, plus a stochastic term; the x's are known as "independent variables."

Individuals with Disabilities Education Act (IDEA) IDEA is a federal law requiring services to children with disabilities throughout the nation. IDEA governs how states and public agencies provide early intervention, special education, and related services to eligible infants, toddlers, children, and youth with disabilities. Infants and toddlers with disabilities (birth–age 2) and their families receive early intervention services under IDEA, Part C. Children and youth (ages 3–21) receive special education and related services under IDEA, Part B.

Inflation A rise in the general level of prices of goods and services in an economy over a period of time, which generally corresponds to a decline in the real value of money or a loss of purchasing power. See also Constant dollars and Purchasing Power Parity indexes.

Institutional support The category of higher education expenditures that includes day-to-day operational support for colleges, excluding expenditures for physical plant operations. Examples of institutional support include general administrative services, executive direction and planning, legal and fiscal operations, and community relations.

Instruction (colleges and universities) That functional category including expenditures of the colleges, schools, departments, and other instructional divisions of higher education institutions and expenditures for departmental research and public service which are not separately budgeted; includes expenditures for both credit and noncredit activities. Excludes expenditures for academic administration where the primary function is administration (e.g., academic deans).

Instruction (elementary and secondary) Instruction encompasses all activities dealing directly with the interaction between teachers and students. Teaching may be provided for students in a school classroom, in another location such as a home or hospital, and in other learning situations such as those involving co-curricular activities. Instruction may be provided through some other approved medium, such as the Internet, television, radio, telephone, and correspondence.

Instructional staff Full-time-equivalent number of positions, not the number of different individuals occupying the positions during the school year. In local schools, includes all public elementary and secondary (junior and senior high) day-school positions that are in the nature of teaching or in the improvement of the teaching-learning situation; includes consultants or supervisors of instruction, principals, teachers, guidance personnel, librarians, psychological personnel, and other instructional staff, and excludes administrative staff, attendance personnel, clerical personnel, and junior college staff.

Instructional support services Includes salary, benefits, supplies, and contractual fees for staff providing instructional improvement, educational media (library and audiovisual), and other instructional support services.

Intellectual disability See Disabilities, children with.

Interest on debt Includes expenditures for long-term debt service interest payments (i.e., those longer than 1 year).

International baccalaureate (IB) A recognized international program of primary, middle, and secondary studies leading to the International Baccalaureate (IB) Diploma. This diploma (or certificate) is recognized in Europe and elsewhere as qualifying holders for direct access to university studies. Schools offering the IB program are approved by the International Baccalaureate Organization (IBO) and their regional office and may use IBO instructional materials, local school materials, or a combination.

International finance data Include data on public and private expenditures for educational institutions. Educational institutions directly provide instructional programs (i.e., teaching) to individuals in an organized group setting or through distance education. Business enterprises or other institutions that provide short-term courses of training or instruction to individuals on a "one-to-one" basis are not included. Where noted, international finance data may also include publicly subsidized spending on education-related purchases, such as school books, living costs, and transportation.

Public expenditures Corresponds to the nonrepayable current and capital expenditures of all levels of the government directly related to education. Expenditures that are not directly related to education (e.g., cultures, sports, youth activities) are, in principle, not included. Expenditures on education by other ministries or equivalent institutions (e.g., Health and Agriculture) are included. Public subsidies for students' living expenses are excluded to ensure international comparability of the data.

Private expenditures Refers to expenditures funded by private sources (i.e., households and other private entities). "Households" means students and their families. "Other private entities" includes private business firms and nonprofit organizations, including religious organizations, charitable organizations, and business and labor associations. Private expenditures are composed of school fees, the cost of materials (such as textbooks and teaching equipment), transportation costs (if organized by the school), the cost of meals (if provided by the school), boarding fees, and expenditures by employers on initial vocational training.

Current expenditures Includes final consumption expenditures (e.g., compensation of employees, consumption of intermediate goods and services, consumption of fixed capital, and military expenditures); property income paid; subsidies; and other current transfers paid.

Capital expenditures Includes spending to acquire and improve fixed capital assets, land, intangible assets, government stocks, and nonmilitary, nonfinancial assets, as well as spending to finance net capital transfers.

International Standard Classification of Education (ISCED) Used to compare educational systems in different countries. ISCED is the standard used by many countries to report education statistics to the United Nations Educational, Scientific, and Cultural Organization (UNESCO) and the Organization for Economic Cooperation and Development (OECD). ISCED divides educational systems into the following seven categories, based on six levels of education.

ISCED Level 0 Education preceding the first level (early childhood education) usually begins at age 3, 4, or 5 (sometimes earlier) and lasts from 1 to 3 years, when it is provided. In the United States, this level includes nursery school and kindergarten.

ISCED Level 1 Education at the first level (primary or elementary education) usually begins at age 5, 6, or 7 and continues for about 4 to 6 years. For the United States, the first level starts with 1st grade and ends with 6th grade.

ISCED Level 2 Education at the second level (lower secondary education) typically begins at about age 11 or 12 and continues for about 2 to 6 years. For the United States, the second level starts with 7th grade and typically ends with 9th grade. Education at the lower secondary level continues the basic programs of the first level, although teaching is typically more subject focused, often using more specialized teachers who conduct classes in their field of specialization. The main criterion for distinguishing lower secondary education from primary education is whether programs begin to be organized in a more subject-oriented pattern, using more specialized teachers conducting classes in their field of specialization. If there is no clear breakpoint for this organizational change, lower secondary education is considered to begin at the end of 6 years of primary education. In countries with no clear division between lower secondary and upper secondary education, and where lower secondary education lasts for more than 3 years, only the first 3 years following primary education are counted as lower secondary education.

ISCED Level 3 Education at the third level (upper secondary education) typically begins at age 15 or 16 and lasts for approximately 3 years. In the United States, the third level starts with 10th grade and ends with 12th grade. Upper secondary education is the final stage of secondary education in most OECD countries. Instruction is often organized along subject-matter lines, in contrast to the lower secondary level, and teachers typically must have a higher level, or more subject-specific, qualification. There are substantial differences in the typical duration of programs both across and between countries, ranging from 2 to 5 years of schooling. The main criteria for classifications are (1) national boundaries between lower and upper secondary education and (2) admission into educational programs, which usually requires the completion of lower secondary education or a combination of basic education and life experience that demonstrates the ability to handle the subject matter in upper secondary schools.

ISCED Level 4 Education at the fourth level (postsecondary nontertiary education) straddles the boundary between secondary and postsecondary education. This program of study, which is primarily vocational in nature, is generally taken after the completion of secondary school and typically lasts from 6 months to 2 years. Although the content of these programs may not be significantly more advanced than upper secondary programs, these programs serve to broaden the knowledge of participants who have already gained an upper secondary qualification.

ISCED Level 5 Education at the fifth level (first stage of tertiary education) includes programs with more advanced content than those offered at the two previous levels. Entry into programs at the fifth level normally requires successful completion of either of the two previous levels.

ISCED Level 5A Tertiary-type A programs provide an education that is largely theoretical and is intended to provide sufficient qualifications for gaining entry into advanced research programs and professions with high skill requirements. Entry into these programs normally requires the successful completion of an upper secondary education; admission is competitive in most cases. The minimum cumulative theoretical duration at this level is 3 years of full-time enrollment. In the United States, tertiary-type A programs include first university programs that last approximately 4 years and lead to the award of a bachelor's degree and second university programs that lead to a master's degree.

ISCED Level 5B Tertiary-type B programs are typically shorter than tertiary-type A programs and focus on practical, technical, or occupational skills for direct entry into the labor market, although they may cover some theoretical foundations in the respective programs. They have a minimum duration of 2 years of full-time enrollment at the tertiary level. In the United States, such programs are often provided at community colleges and lead to an associate's degree.

ISCED Level 6 Education at the sixth level (advanced research qualification) is provided in graduate and professional schools that generally require a university degree or diploma as a minimum condition for admission. Programs at this level lead to the award of an advanced, postgraduate degree, such as a Ph.D. The theoretical duration of these programs is 3 years of full-time enrollment in most countries (for a cumulative total of at least 7 years at levels five and six), although the length of the actual enrollment is often longer. Programs at this level are devoted to advanced study and original research.

Interpolation See Linear interpolation.

J

Junior high school A separately organized and administered secondary school intermediate between the elementary and senior high schools, usually includes grades 7, 8, and 9 (in a 6-3-3 plan) or grades 7 and 8 (in a 6-2-4 plan).

L

Labor force People employed (either full time or part time) as civilians, unemployed but looking for work, or in the armed services during the survey week. The "civilian labor force" comprises all civilians classified as employed or unemployed. See also Unemployed.

Lag An event occurring at time $t + k$ $(k > 0)$ is said to lag behind an event occurring at time t, the extent of the lag being k. An event occurring k time periods before another may be regarded as having a negative lag.

Land-grant colleges The First Morrill Act of 1862 facilitated the establishment of colleges through grants of land or funds in lieu of land. The Second Morrill Act in 1890 provided for money grants and for the establishment of land-grant colleges and universities for blacks in those states with dual systems of higher education.

Lead time When forecasting a statistic, the number of time periods since the last time period of actual data for that statistic used in producing the forecast.

Level of school A classification of elementary/secondary schools by instructional level. Includes elementary schools, secondary schools, and combined elementary and secondary schools. See also Elementary school, Secondary school, and Combined elementary and secondary school.

Limited-English proficient Refers to an individual who was not born in the United States and whose native language is a language other than English, or who comes from an environment where a language other than English has had a significant impact on the individual's level of English language proficiency. It may also refer to an individual who is migratory, whose native language is a language other than English, and who comes from an environment where a language other than English is dominant; and whose difficulties in speaking, reading, writing, or understanding the English language may be sufficient to deny the individual the ability to meet the state's proficient level of achievement on state assessments as specified under the No Child Left Behind Act, the ability to successfully achieve in classrooms where the language of instruction is English, or the opportunity to participate fully in society. See also English language learner.

Linear interpolation A method that allows the prediction of an unknown value if any two particular values on the same scale are known and the rate of change is assumed constant.

Local education agency (LEA) See School district.

Locale codes A classification system to describe a type of location. The "Metro-Centric" locale codes, developed in the 1980s, classified all schools and school districts based on their county's proximity to a Metropolitan Statistical Area (MSA) and their specific location's population size and density. In 2006, the "Urban-Centric" locale codes were introduced. These locale codes are based on an address's proximity to an urbanized area. For more information see http://nces.ed.gov/ccd/rural_locales.asp.

Pre-2006 Metro-Centric Locale Codes

Large City: A central city of a consolidated metropolitan statistical area (CMSA) or MSA, with the city having a population greater than or equal to 250,000.

Mid-size City: A central city of a CMSA or MSA, with the city having a population less than 250,000.

Urban Fringe of a Large City: Any territory within a CMSA or MSA of a Large City and defined as urban by the Census Bureau.

Urban Fringe of a Mid-size City: Any territory within a CMSA or MSA of a Mid-size City and defined as urban by the Census Bureau.

Large Town: An incorporated place or Census-designated place with a population greater than or equal to 25,000 and located outside a CMSA or MSA.

Small Town: An incorporated place or Census-designated place with a population less than 25,000 and greater than or equal to 2,500 and located outside a CMSA or MSA.

Rural, Outside MSA: Any territory designated as rural by the Census Bureau that is outside a CMSA or MSA of a Large or Mid-size City.

Rural, Inside MSA: Any territory designated as rural by the Census Bureau that is within a CMSA or MSA of a Large or Mid-size City.

2006 Urban-Centric Locale Codes

City, Large: Territory inside an urbanized area and inside a principal city with population of 250,000 or more.

City, Midsize: Territory inside an urbanized area and inside a principal city with population less than 250,000 and greater than or equal to 100,000.

City, Small: Territory inside an urbanized area and inside a principal city with population less than 100,000.

Suburb, Large: Territory outside a principal city and inside an urbanized area with population of 250,000 or more.

Suburb, Midsize: Territory outside a principal city and inside an urbanized area with population less than 250,000 and greater than or equal to 100,000.

Suburb, Small: Territory outside a principal city and inside an urbanized area with population less than 100,000.

Town, Fringe: Territory inside an urban cluster that is less than or equal to 10 miles from an urbanized area.

Town, Distant: Territory inside an urban cluster that is more than 10 miles and less than or equal to 35 miles from an urbanized area.

Town, Remote: Territory inside an urban cluster that is more than 35 miles from an urbanized area.

Rural, Fringe: Census-defined rural territory that is less than or equal to 5 miles from an urbanized area, as well as rural territory that is less than or equal to 2.5 miles from an urban cluster.

Rural, Distant: Census-defined rural territory that is more than 5 miles but less than or equal to 25 miles from an urbanized area, as well as rural territory that is more than 2.5 miles but less than or equal to 10 miles from an urban cluster.

Rural, Remote: Census-defined rural territory that is more than 25 miles from an urbanized area and is also more than 10 miles from an urban cluster.

M

Magnet school or program A special school or program designed to reduce, prevent, or eliminate racial isolation and/or to provide an academic or social focus on a particular theme.

Mandatory transfer A transfer of current funds that must be made in order to fulfill a binding legal obligation of the institution. Included under mandatory transfers are debt service provisions relating to academic and administrative buildings, including (1) amounts set aside for debt retirement and interest and (2) required provisions for renewal and replacement of buildings to the extent these are not financed from other funds.

Master's degree A degree awarded for successful completion of a program generally requiring 1 or 2 years of full-time college-level study beyond the bachelor's degree. One type of master's degree, including the Master of Arts degree, or M.A., and the Master of Science degree, or M.S., is awarded in the liberal arts and sciences for advanced scholarship in a subject field or discipline and demonstrated ability to perform scholarly research. A second type of master's degree is awarded for the completion of a professionally oriented program, for example, an M.Ed. in education, an M.B.A. in business administration, an M.F.A. in fine arts, an M.M. in music, an M.S.W. in social work, and an M.P.A. in public administration. Some master's degrees—such as divinity degrees (M.Div. or M.H.L./Rav), which were formerly classified as "first-professional"—may require more than 2 years of full-time study beyond the bachelor's degree.

Mathematics A group of instructional programs that describes the science of numbers and their operations, interrelations, combinations, generalizations, and abstractions and of space configurations and their structure, measurement, transformations, and generalizations.

Mean absolute percentage error (MAPE) The average value of the absolute value of errors expressed in percentage terms.

Mean test score The score obtained by dividing the sum of the scores of all individuals in a group by the number of individuals in that group for which scores are available.

Median earnings The amount which divides the income distribution into two equal groups, half having income above that amount and half having income below that amount. Earnings include all wage and salary income. Unlike mean earnings, median earnings either do not change or change very little in response to extreme observations.

Middle school A school with no grade lower than 5 and no higher than 8.

Migration Geographic mobility involving a change of usual residence between clearly defined geographic units, that is, between counties, states, or regions.

Minimum-competency testing Measuring the acquisition of competence or skills to or beyond a certain specified standard.

Model A system of postulates, data, and inferences presented as a mathematical description of a phenomenon, such as an actual system or process. The actual phenomenon is represented by the model in order to explain, predict, and control it.

Montessori school A school that provides instruction using Montessori teaching methods.

Multiple disabilities See Disabilities, children with.

N

National Assessment of Educational Progress (NAEP) See Appendix A: Guide to Sources.

National School Lunch Program Established by President Truman in 1946, the program is a federally assisted meal program operated in public and private nonprofit schools and residential child care centers. To be eligible for free lunch, a student must be from a household with an income at or below 130 percent of the federal poverty guideline; to be eligible for reduced-price lunch, a student must be from a household with an income between 130 percent and 185 percent of the federal poverty guideline.

Newly qualified teacher People who: (1) first became eligible for a teaching license during the period of the study referenced or who were teaching at the time of survey, but were not certified or eligible for a teaching license; and (2) had never held full-time, regular teaching positions (as opposed to substitute) prior to completing the requirements for the degree which brought them into the survey.

Non-degree-granting institutions Postsecondary institutions that participate in Title IV federal financial aid programs but do not offer accredited 4-year or 2-year degree programs. Includes some institutions transitioning to higher level program offerings, though still classified at a lower level.

Nonprofessional staff See Employees in degree-granting institutions.

Nonprofit institution A private institution in which the individual(s) or agency in control receives no compensation other than wages, rent, or other expenses for the assumption of risk. Nonprofit institutions may be either independent nonprofit (i.e., having no religious affiliation) or religiously affiliated.

Nonresident alien A person who is not a citizen of the United States and who is in this country on a temporary basis and does not have the right to remain indefinitely.

Nonsectarian school Nonsectarian schools do not have a religious orientation or purpose and are categorized as regular, special program emphasis, or special education schools. See also Regular school, Special program emphasis school, and Special education school.

Nonsupervisory instructional staff People such as curriculum specialists, counselors, librarians, remedial specialists, and others possessing education certification, but not responsible for day-to-day teaching of the same group of pupils.

Nursery school An instructional program for groups of children during the year or years preceding kindergarten, which provides educational experiences under the direction of teachers. See also Prekindergarten and Preschool.

O

Obligations Amounts of orders placed, contracts awarded, services received, or similar legally binding commitments made by federal agencies during a given period that will require outlays during the same or some future period.

Occupational home economics Courses of instruction emphasizing the acquisition of competencies needed for getting and holding a job or preparing for advancement in an occupational area using home economics knowledge and skills.

Occupied housing unit Separate living quarters with occupants currently inhabiting the unit. See also Housing unit.

Off-budget federal entities Organizational entities, federally owned in whole or in part, whose transactions belong in the budget under current budget accounting concepts, but that have been excluded from the budget totals under provisions of law. An example of an off-budget federal entity is the Federal Financing Bank, which provides student loans under the Direct Loan Program.

On-budget funding Federal funding for education programs that is tied to appropriations. On-budget funding does not include the Direct Loan Program, under which student loans are provided by the Federal Financing Bank, an off-budget federal entity. See also Off-budget federal entities.

Operation and maintenance services Includes salary, benefits, supplies, and contractual fees for supervision of operations and maintenance, operating buildings (heating, lighting, ventilating, repair, and replacement), care and upkeep of grounds and equipment, vehicle operations and maintenance (other than student transportation), security, and other operations and maintenance services.

Ordinary least squares (OLS) The estimator that minimizes the sum of squared residuals.

Organization for Economic Cooperation and Development (OECD) An intergovernmental organization of industrialized countries that serves as a forum for member countries to cooperate in research and policy development on social and economic topics of common interest. In addition to member countries, partner countries contribute to the OECD's work in a sustained and comprehensive manner.

Orthopedic impairment See Disabilities, children with.

Other foreign languages and literatures Any instructional program in foreign languages and literatures not listed in the table, including language groups and individual languages, such as the non-Semitic African languages, Native American languages, the Celtic languages, Pacific language groups, the Ural-Altaic languages, Basque, and others.

Other health impairment See Disabilities, children with.

Other professional staff See Employees in degree-granting institutions.

Other religious school Other religious schools have a religious orientation or purpose, but are not Roman Catholic. Other religious schools are categorized according to religious association membership as Conservative Christian, other affiliated, or unaffiliated.

Other support services Includes salary, benefits, supplies, and contractual fees for business support services, central support services, and other support services not otherwise classified.

Other support services staff All staff not reported in other categories. This group includes media personnel, social workers, bus drivers, security, cafeteria workers, and other staff.

Outlays The value of checks issued, interest accrued on the public debt, or other payments made, net of refunds and reimbursements.

P

Parameter A quantity that describes a statistical population.

Part-time enrollment The number of students enrolled in postsecondary education courses with a total credit load less than 75 percent of the normal full-time credit load. At the undergraduate level, part-time enrollment typically includes students who have a credit load of less than 12 semester or quarter credits. At the postbaccalaureate level, part-time enrollment typically includes students who have a credit load of less than 9 semester or quarter credits.

Pass-through transaction A payment that a postsecondary institution applies directly to a student's account. The payment "passes through" the institution for the student's benefit. Most private institutions treat Pell grants as pass-through transactions. At these institutions, any Pell grant funds that are applied to a student's tuition are reported as tuition revenues. In contrast, the vast majority of public institutions report Pell grants both as federal revenues and as allowances that reduce tuition revenues.

Personal income Current income received by people from all sources, minus their personal contributions for social insurance. Classified as "people" are individuals (including owners of unincorporated firms), nonprofit institutions serving individuals, private trust funds, and private noninsured welfare funds. Personal income includes transfers (payments not resulting from current production) from government and business such as social security benefits and military pensions, but excludes transfers among people.

Physical plant assets Includes the values of land, buildings, and equipment owned, rented, or utilized by colleges. Does not include those plant values which are a part of endowment or other capital fund investments in real estate; excludes construction in progress.

Postbaccalaureate enrollment The number of students working towards advanced degrees and of students enrolled in graduate-level classes but not enrolled in degree programs. See also Graduate enrollment.

Postsecondary education The provision of formal instructional programs with a curriculum designed primarily for students who have completed the requirements for a high school diploma or equivalent. This includes programs of an academic, vocational, and continuing professional education purpose, and excludes avocational and adult basic education programs.

Postsecondary institutions (basic classification by level)

4-year institution An institution offering at least a 4-year program of college-level studies wholly or principally creditable toward a baccalaureate degree.

2-year institution An institution offering at least a 2-year program of college-level studies which terminates in an associate degree or is principally creditable toward a baccalaureate degree. Data prior to 1996 include some institutions that have a less-than-2-year program, but were designated as institutions of higher education in the Higher Education General Information Survey.

Less-than-2-year institution An institution that offers programs of less than 2 years' duration below the baccalaureate level. Includes occupational and vocational schools with programs that do not exceed 1,800 contact hours.

Postsecondary institutions (Carnegie classification of degree-granting institutions)

Doctorate-granting Characterized by a significant level and breadth of activity in commitment to doctoral-level education as measured by the number of doctorate recipients and the diversity in doctoral-level program offerings. These institutions are assigned to one of the three subcategories listed below based on level of research activity (for more information on the research activity index used to assign institutions to the subcategories, see http://classifications.carnegiefoundation.org/methodology/basic.php):

Research university, very high Characterized by a very high level of research activity.

Research university, high Characterized by a high level of research activity.

Doctoral/research university Awarding at least 20 doctor's degrees per year, but not having a high level of research activity.

Master's Characterized by diverse postbaccalaureate programs but not engaged in significant doctoral-level education.

Baccalaureate Characterized by primary emphasis on general undergraduate, baccalaureate-level education. Not significantly engaged in postbaccalaureate education.

Special focus Baccalaureate or postbaccalaureate institution emphasizing one area (plus closely related specialties), such as business or engineering. The programmatic emphasis is measured by the percentage of degrees granted in the program area.

Associate's Institutions conferring at least 90 percent of their degrees and awards for work below the bachelor's level. In NCES tables, excludes all institutions offering any 4-year programs leading to a bachelor's degree.

Tribal Colleges and universities that are members of the American Indian Higher Education Consortium, as identified in IPEDS Institutional Characteristics.

Poverty The U.S. Census Bureau uses a set of money income thresholds that vary by family size and composition. A family, along with each individual in it, is considered poor if the family's total income is less than that family's threshold. The poverty thresholds do not vary geographically and are adjusted annually for inflation using the Consumer Price Index. The official poverty definition counts money income before taxes and does not include capital gains and noncash benefits (such as public housing, Medicaid, and food stamps).

Prekindergarten Preprimary education for children typically ages 3–4 who have not yet entered kindergarten. It may offer a program of general education or special education and may be part of a collaborative effort with Head Start.

Preschool An instructional program enrolling children generally younger than 5 years of age and organized to provide children with educational experiences under professionally qualified teachers during the year or years immediately preceding kindergarten (or prior to entry into elementary school when there is no kindergarten). See also Nursery school and Prekindergarten.

Primary school A school with at least one grade lower than 5 and no grade higher than 8.

Private institution An institution that is controlled by an individual or agency other than a state, a subdivision of a state, or the federal government, which is usually supported primarily by other than public funds, and the operation of whose program rests with other than publicly elected or appointed officials.

Private nonprofit institution An institution in which the individual(s) or agency in control receives no compensation other than wages, rent, or other expenses for the assumption of risk. These include both independent nonprofit institutions and those affiliated with a religious organization.

Private for-profit institution An institution in which the individual(s) or agency in control receives compensation other than wages, rent, or other expenses for the assumption of risk (e.g., proprietary schools).

Private school Private elementary/secondary schools surveyed by the Private School Universe Survey (PSS) are assigned to one of three major categories (Catholic, other religious, or nonsectarian) and, within each major category, one of three subcategories based on the school's religious affiliation provided by respondents.

Catholic Schools categorized according to governance, provided by Catholic school respondents, into parochial, diocesan, and private schools.

Other religious Schools that have a religious orientation or purpose but are not Roman Catholic. Other religious schools are categorized according to religious association membership, provided by respondents, into Conservative Christian, other affiliated, and unaffiliated schools. Conservative Christian schools are those "Other religious" schools with membership in at least one of four associations: Accelerated Christian Education, American Association of Christian Schools, Association of Christian Schools International, and Oral Roberts University Education Fellowship. Affiliated schools are those "Other religious" schools not classified as Conservative Christian with membership in at least 1 of 11 associations— Association of Christian Teachers and Schools, Christian Schools International, Evangelical Lutheran Education Association, Friends Council on Education, General Conference of the Seventh-Day Adventist Church, Islamic School League of America, National Association of Episcopal Schools, National Christian School Association, National Society for Hebrew Day Schools, Solomon Schechter Day Schools, and Southern Baptist Association of Christian Schools—or indicating membership in "other religious school associations." Unaffiliated schools are those "Other religious" schools that have a religious orientation or purpose but are not classified as Conservative Christian or affiliated.

Nonsectarian Schools that do not have a religious orientation or purpose and are categorized according to program emphasis, provided by respondents, into regular, special emphasis, and special education schools. Regular schools are those that have a regular elementary/secondary or early childhood program emphasis. Special emphasis schools are those that have a Montessori, vocational/technical, alternative, or special program emphasis. Special education schools are those that have a special education program emphasis.

Professional staff See Employees in degree-granting institutions.

Program for International Student Assessment (PISA) A system of international assessments organized by the OECD that focuses on 15-year-olds' capabilities in reading literacy, mathematics literacy, and science literacy. PISA also includes measures of general, or cross-curricular, competencies such as learning strategies. The measures emphasize functional skills that students have acquired as they near the end of mandatory schooling. PISA was administered for the first time in 2000, when 43 countries participated. Forty-one countries participated in the 2003 administration of PISA; 57 jurisdictions (30 OECD members and 27 nonmembers) participated in 2006; and 65 jurisdictions (34 OECD members and 31 nonmembers) participated in 2009.

Projection In relation to a time series, an estimate of future values based on a current trend.

Property tax The sum of money collected from a tax levied against the value of property.

Proprietary (for profit) institution A private institution in which the individual(s) or agency in control receives compensation other than wages, rent, or other expenses for the assumption of risk.

Public school or institution A school or institution controlled and operated by publicly elected or appointed officials and deriving its primary support from public funds.

Pupil/teacher ratio The enrollment of pupils at a given period of time, divided by the full-time-equivalent number of classroom teachers serving these pupils during the same period.

Purchasing Power Parity (PPP) indexes PPP exchange rates, or indexes, are the currency exchange rates that equalize the purchasing power of different currencies, meaning that when a given sum of money is converted into different currencies at the PPP exchange rates, it will buy the same basket of goods and services in all countries. PPP indexes are the rates of currency conversion that eliminate the difference in price levels among countries. Thus, when expenditures on gross domestic product (GDP) for different countries are converted into a common currency by means of PPP indexes, they are expressed at the same set of international prices, so that comparisons among countries reflect only differences in the volume of goods and services purchased.

R

R^2 The coefficient of determination; the square of the correlation coefficient between the dependent variable and its ordinary least squares (OLS) estimate.

Racial/ethnic group Classification indicating general racial or ethnic heritage. Race/ethnicity data are based on the *Hispanic* ethnic category and the race categories listed below (five single-race categories, plus the *Two or more races* category). Race categories exclude persons of Hispanic ethnicity unless otherwise noted.

White A person having origins in any of the original peoples of Europe, the Middle East, or North Africa.

Black or African American A person having origins in any of the black racial groups of Africa. Used interchangeably with the shortened term *Black*.

Hispanic or Latino A person of Cuban, Mexican, Puerto Rican, South or Central American, or other Spanish culture or origin, regardless of race. Used interchangeably with the shortened term *Hispanic*.

Asian A person having origins in any of the original peoples of the Far East, Southeast Asia, or the Indian subcontinent, including, for example, Cambodia, China, India, Japan, Korea, Malaysia, Pakistan, the Philippine Islands, Thailand, and Vietnam. Prior to 2010–11, the Common Core of Data (CCD) combined Asian and Pacific Islander categories.

Native Hawaiian or Other Pacific Islander A person having origins in any of the original peoples of Hawaii, Guam, Samoa, or other Pacific Islands. Prior to 2010–11, the Common Core of Data (CCD) combined Asian and Pacific Islander categories. Used interchangeably with the shortened term *Pacific Islander.*

American Indian or Alaska Native A person having origins in any of the original peoples of North and South America (including Central America), and who maintains tribal affiliation or community attachment.

Two or more races A person identifying himself or herself as of two or more of the following race groups: White, Black, Asian, Native Hawaiian or Other Pacific Islander, or American Indian or Alaska Native. Some, but not all, reporting districts use this category. "Two or more races" was introduced in the 2000 Census and became a regular category for data collection in the Current Population Survey (CPS) in 2003. The category is sometimes excluded from a historical series of data with constant categories. It is sometimes included within the category "Other."

Region See Geographic region.

Regression analysis A statistical technique for investigating and modeling the relationship between variables.

Regular school A public elementary/secondary or charter school providing instruction and education services that does not focus primarily on special education, vocational/technical education, or alternative education.

Related children Related children in a family include own children and all other children in the household who are related to the householder by birth, marriage, or adoption.

Remedial education Instruction for a student lacking those reading, writing, or math skills necessary to perform college-level work at the level required by the attended institution.

Resident population Includes civilian population and armed forces personnel residing within the United States; excludes armed forces personnel residing overseas.

Revenue All funds received from external sources, net of refunds, and correcting transactions. Noncash transactions, such as receipt of services, commodities, or other receipts in kind are excluded, as are funds received from the issuance of debt, liquidation of investments, and nonroutine sale of property.

Revenue receipts Additions to assets that do not incur an obligation that must be met at some future date and do not represent exchanges of property for money. Assets must be available for expenditures.

Rho A measure of the correlation coefficient between errors in time period t and time period t minus 1.

Rural school See Locale codes.

S

Salary The total amount regularly paid or stipulated to be paid to an individual, before deductions, for personal services rendered while on the payroll of a business or organization.

Sales and services Revenues derived from the sales of goods or services that are incidental to the conduct of instruction, research, or public service. Examples include film rentals, scientific and literary publications, testing services, university presses, and dairy products.

Sales tax Tax imposed upon the sale and consumption of goods and services. It can be imposed either as a general tax on the retail price of all goods and services sold or as a tax on the sale of selected goods and services.

SAT An examination administered by the Educational Testing Service and used to predict the facility with which an individual will progress in learning college-level academic subjects. It was formerly called the Scholastic Assessment Test.

Scholarships and fellowships This category of college expenditures applies only to money given in the form of outright grants and trainee stipends to individuals enrolled in formal coursework, either for credit or not. Aid to students in the form of tuition or fee remissions is included. College work-study funds are excluded and are reported under the program in which the student is working.

School A division of the school system consisting of students in one or more grades or other identifiable groups and organized to give instruction of a defined type. One school may share a building with another school or one school may be housed in several buildings. Excludes schools that have closed or are planned for the future.

School administration support services Includes salary, benefits, supplies, and contractual fees for the office of the principal, full-time department chairpersons, and graduation expenses.

School climate The social system and culture of the school, including the organizational structure of the school and values and expectations within it.

School district An education agency at the local level that exists primarily to operate public schools or to contract for public school services. Synonyms are "local basic administrative unit" and "local education agency."

Science The body of related courses concerned with knowledge of the physical and biological world and with the processes of discovering and validating this knowledge.

Secondary enrollment The total number of students registered in a school beginning with the next grade following an elementary or middle school (usually 7, 8, or 9) and ending with or below grade 12 at a given time.

Secondary instructional level The general level of instruction provided for pupils in secondary schools (generally covering grades 7 through 12 or 9 through 12) and any instruction of a comparable nature and difficulty provided for adults and youth beyond the age of compulsory school attendance.

Secondary school A school comprising any span of grades beginning with the next grade following an elementary or middle school (usually 7, 8, or 9) and ending with or below grade 12. Both junior high schools and senior high schools are included.

Senior high school A secondary school offering the final years of high school work necessary for graduation.

Serial correlation Correlation of the error terms from different observations of the same variable. Also called Autocorrelation.

Serial volumes Publications issued in successive parts, usually at regular intervals, and as a rule, intended to be continued indefinitely. Serials include periodicals, newspapers, annuals, memoirs, proceedings, and transactions of societies.

Serious emotional disturbance See Disabilities, children with.

Social studies A group of instructional programs that describes the substantive portions of behavior, past and present activities, interactions, and organizations of people associated together for religious, benevolent, cultural, scientific, political, patriotic, or other purposes.

Socioeconomic status (SES) The SES index is a composite of often equally weighted, standardized components, such as father's education, mother's education, family income, father's occupation, and household items. The terms high, middle, and low SES refer to ranges of the weighted SES composite index distribution.

Special education Direct instructional activities or special learning experiences designed primarily for students identified as having exceptionalities in one or more aspects of the cognitive process or as being underachievers in relation to general level or model of their overall abilities. Such services usually are directed at students with the following conditions: (1) physically handicapped; (2) emotionally disabled; (3) culturally different, including compensatory education; (4) intellectually disabled; and (5) students with learning disabilities. Programs for the mentally gifted and talented are also included in some special education programs. See also Disabilities, children with.

Special education school A public elementary/secondary school that focuses primarily on special education for children with disabilities and that adapts curriculum, materials, or instruction for students served. See also Disabilities, children with.

Special program emphasis school A science/mathematics school, a performing arts high school, a foreign language immersion school, and a talented/gifted school are examples of schools that offer a special program emphasis.

Specific learning disability See Disabilities, children with.

Speech/language impairment See Disabilities, children with.

Standard error of estimate An expression for the standard deviation of the observed values about a regression line. An estimate of the variation likely to be encountered in making predictions from the regression equation.

Standardized test A test composed of a systematic sampling of behavior, administered and scored according to specific instructions, capable of being interpreted in terms of adequate norms, and for which there are data on reliability and validity.

Standardized test performance The weighted distributions of composite scores from standardized tests used to group students according to performance.

Status dropout rate The percentage of individuals within a given age range who are not enrolled in school and lack a high school credential, irrespective of when they dropped out.

Status dropout rate (Current Population Survey) The percentage of civilian, noninstitutionalized young people ages 16–24 who are not in school and have not earned a high school credential (either a diploma or equivalency credential such as a General Educational Development [GED] certificate). The numerator of the status dropout rate for a given year is the number of individuals ages 16–24 who, as of October of that year, have not completed a high school credential and are not currently enrolled in school. The denominator is the total number of individuals ages 16–24 in the United States in October of that year. Status dropout rates count as dropouts individuals who never attended school and immigrants who did not complete the equivalent of a high school education in their home country.

Status dropout rate (American Community Survey) Similar to the status dropout rate (Current Population Survey), except that institutionalized persons, incarcerated persons, and active duty military personnel living in barracks in the United States may be included in this calculation.

STEM fields Science, Technology, Engineering, and Mathematics (STEM) fields of study that are considered to be of particular relevance to advanced societies. For the purposes of *The Condition of Education 2012*, STEM fields include agriculture and natural resources, biological and biomedical sciences, computer and information sciences and support services, engineering and engineering technologies, mathematics and statistics, physical sciences, and science technologies.

Student An individual for whom instruction is provided in an educational program under the jurisdiction of a school, school system, or other education institution. No distinction is made between the terms "student" and "pupil," though "student" may refer to one receiving instruction at any level while "pupil" refers only to one attending school at the elementary or secondary level. A student may receive instruction in a school facility or in another location, such as at home or in a hospital. Instruction may be provided by direct student-teacher interaction or by some other approved medium such as television, radio, telephone, and correspondence.

Student membership Student membership is an annual headcount of students enrolled in school on October 1 or the school day closest to that date. The Common Core of Data (CCD) allows a student to be reported for only a single school or agency. For example, a vocational school (identified as a "shared time" school) may provide classes for students from a number of districts and show no membership.

Student support services Includes salary, benefits, supplies, and contractual fees for staff providing attendance and social work, guidance, health, psychological services, speech pathology, audiology, and other support to students.

Study abroad population U.S. citizens and permanent residents, enrolled for a degree at an accredited higher education institution in the United States, who received academic credit for study abroad from their home institutions upon their return. Students studying abroad without receiving academic credit are not included, nor are U.S. students enrolled for a degree overseas.

Subject-matter club Organizations that are formed around a shared interest in a particular area of study and whose primary activities promote that interest. Examples of such organizations are math, science, business, and history clubs.

Supervisory staff Principals, assistant principals, and supervisors of instruction; does not include superintendents or assistant superintendents.

T

Tax base The collective value of objects, assets, and income components against which a tax is levied.

Tax expenditures Losses of tax revenue attributable to provisions of the federal income tax laws that allow a special exclusion, exemption, or deduction from gross income or provide a special credit, preferential rate of tax, or a deferral of tax liability affecting individual or corporate income tax liabilities.

Teacher see Instructional staff.

Technical education A program of vocational instruction that ordinarily includes the study of the sciences and mathematics underlying a technology, as well as the methods, skills, and materials commonly used and the services performed in the technology. Technical education prepares individuals for positions—such as draftsman or lab technician—in the occupational area between the skilled craftsman and the professional person.

Three-year moving average An arithmetic average of the year indicated, the year immediately preceding, and the year immediately following. Use of a 3-year moving average increases the sample size, thereby reducing the size of sampling errors and producing more stable estimates.

Time series A set of ordered observations on a quantitative characteristic of an individual or collective phenomenon taken at different points in time. Usually the observations are successive and equally spaced in time.

Time series analysis The branch of quantitative forecasting in which data for one variable are examined for patterns of trend, seasonality, and cycle.

Title I school A school designated under appropriate state and federal regulations as a high-poverty school that is eligible for participation in programs authorized by Title I of the Reauthorization of the Elementary and Secondary Education Act, P.L. 107-110.

Title IV Refers to a section of the Higher Education Act of 1965 that covers the administration of the federal student financial aid program.

Title IV eligible institution A postsecondary institution that meets the criteria for participating in federal student financial aid programs. An eligible institution must be any of the following: (1) an institution of higher education (with public or private, nonprofit control), (2) a proprietary institution (with private for-profit control), and (3) a postsecondary vocational institution (with public or private, nonprofit control). In addition, it must have acceptable legal authorization, acceptable accreditation and admission standards, eligible academic program(s), administrative capability, and financial responsibility.

Total expenditure per pupil in average daily attendance Includes all expenditures allocable to per pupil costs divided by average daily attendance. These allocable expenditures include current expenditures for regular school programs, interest on school debt, and capital outlay. Beginning in 1980–81, expenditures for state administration are excluded and expenditures for other programs (summer schools and designated subsidies for community colleges and private schools) are included.

Town school See Locale codes.

Trade and industrial occupations The branch of vocational education which is concerned with preparing people for initial employment or with updating or retraining workers in a wide range of trade and industrial occupations. Such occupations are skilled or semiskilled and are concerned with layout designing, producing, processing, assembling, testing, maintaining, servicing, or repairing any product or commodity.

Traditional public school Publicly funded schools other than public charter schools. See also Public school or institution and Charter school.

Transcript An official list of all courses taken by a student at a school or college showing the final grade received for each course, with definitions of the various grades given at the institution.

Trust funds Amounts collected and used by the federal government for carrying out specific purposes and programs according to terms of a trust agreement or statute, such as the social security and unemployment trust funds. Trust fund receipts that are not anticipated to be used in the immediate future are generally invested in interest-bearing government securities and earn interest for the trust fund.

Tuition and fees A payment or charge for instruction or compensation for services, privileges, or the use of equipment, books, or other goods. Tuition may be charged per term, per course, or per credit.

Type of school A classification of public elementary and secondary schools that includes the following categories: regular schools, special education schools, vocational schools, and alternative schools. See also Regular school, Special education school, Vocational school, and Alternative school.

U

Unadjusted dollars See Current dollars.

Unclassified students Students who are not candidates for a degree or other formal award, although they are taking higher education courses for credit in regular classes with other students.

Undergraduate students Students registered at an institution of postsecondary education who are working in a baccalaureate degree program or other formal program below the baccalaureate, such as an associate's degree, vocational, or technical program.

Unemployed Civilians who had no employment but were available for work and: (1) had engaged in any specific job seeking activity within the past 4 weeks; (2) were waiting to be called back to a job from which they had been laid off; or (3) were waiting to report to a new wage or salary job within 30 days.

Ungraded student (elementary/secondary) A student who has been assigned to a school or program that does not have standard grade designations.

Urban fringe school See Locale codes.

U.S. Service Academies These institutions of higher education are controlled by the U.S. Department of Defense and the U.S. Department of Transportation. The five institutions counted in the NCES surveys of degree-granting institutions include: the U.S. Air Force Academy, U.S. Coast Guard Academy, U.S. Merchant Marine Academy, U.S. Military Academy, and the U.S. Naval Academy.

V

Variable A quantity that may assume any one of a set of values.

Visual and performing arts A group of instructional programs that generally describes the historic development, aesthetic qualities, and creative processes of the visual and performing arts.

Visual impairment See Disabilities, children with.

Vocational education Organized educational programs, services, and activities which are directly related to the preparation of individuals for paid or unpaid employment, or for additional preparation for a career, requiring other than a baccalaureate or advanced degree.

Vocational school A public school that focuses primarily on providing formal preparation for semiskilled, skilled, technical, or professional occupations for high school–age students who have opted to develop or expand their employment opportunities, often in lieu of preparing for college entry.

Y

Years out In forecasting by year, the number of years since the last year of actual data for that statistic used in producing the forecast.